LAMENT

LAMENT

Reclaiming Practices in Pulpit, Pew, and Public Square

Edited by
Sally A. Brown
and
Patrick D. Miller

WESTMINSTER
JOHN KNOX PRESS
LOUISVILLE · KENTUCKY

Scripture quotations from the New Revised Standard Version of the Bible are copyright © 1989 by the Division of Christian Education of the National Council of the Churches of Christ in the U.S.A. and are used by permission.

Scripture quotations from the Revised Standard Version of the Bible are copyright © 1946, 1952, 1971, and 1973 by the Division of Christian Education of the National Council of the Churches of Christ in the U.S.A. and are used by permission.

"Lament Psalm Twelve" is from *Psalms of Lament* by Ann Weems. Copyright © Ann Barr Weems. Used by permission of Westminster John Knox Press.

Quotations from *The Old Testament Pseudepigrapha* are by permission of the editor, J. H. Charlesworth.

The poem "Bassamat al-farah" (The Smile of Joy) by Charles L. Bartow is copyright © 2002 *Theology Today*. Originally published in *Theology Today* 58 (2002): 567. Reprinted with permission.

The poems "Sonnet on Grief," "Cancer Vigil," "When I Grew Up," "The Dogwood Stays," "Sonnet in Remembrance of Pan American Flight 103," and "Heading West on the Jericho Turnpike" are copyright © by Charles L. Bartow and are used by permission of Charles L. Bartow.

Quotations from *The Bacchae and Other Plays* by Euripides, translated by Philip Vellacott (Penguin, 1954) are copyright © by Philip Vellacott, 1954, 1972. Reproduced by permission of Penguin Books Ltd.

Book design by Sharon Adams
Cover design by Eric Walljasper, Minneapolis, MN

First edition
Published by Westminster John Knox Press
Louisville, Kentucky

This book is printed on acid-free paper that meets the American National Standards Institute Z39.48 Standard. ♾

PRINTED IN THE UNITED STATES OF AMERICA

05 06 07 08 09 10 11 12 13 14 — 10 9 8 7 6 5 4 3 2 1

Library of Congress Cataloging-in-Publication Data

Lament : reclaiming practices in pulpit, pew, and public square / Sally A. Brown and
    Patrick D. Miller, editors.
        p. cm.
    Includes bibliographical references.
    ISBN 0-664-22750-3 (alk. paper)
    1. Suffering—Religious aspects—Christianity.   2. Laments—United States.
    3. Mourning customs—United States.   I. Brown, Sally A. (Sally Ann)   II. Miller, Patrick D.

BT732.7.L34 2004
277.3'083—dc22   2004056127

We honor four members of the Princeton Theological Seminary community
who drew out of us lament's anguish and hope:

James E. Loder, 1931–2001
G. Robert Jacks, 1934–2002
Donald H. Juel, 1942–2003
Dana Charry, MD, 1946–2003

Contents

Contributors

Charles L. Bartow is Carl and Helen Egner Professor of Speech Communication in Ministry.

C. Clifton Black is Otto A. Piper Professor of Biblical Theology.

Brian K. Blount is Richard J. Dearborn Professor of New Testament Interpretation.

Sally A. Brown is Elizabeth M. Engle Assistant Professor of Preaching and Worship.

Donald Capps is William Harte Felmeth Professor of Pastoral Theology.

Ellen T. Charry is Margaret W. Harmon Associate Professor of Systematic Theology.

Nancy J. Duff is Stephen Colwell Associate Professor of Christian Ethics.

Robert C. Dykstra is Associate Professor of Pastoral Theology.

Richard K. Fenn is Maxwell M. Upson Professor of Christianity and Society.

Nancy Lammers Gross is Associate Professor of Speech Communication in Ministry.

William Stacy Johnson is Arthur M. Adams Associate Professor of Systematic Theology.

Patrick D. Miller is Charles T. Haley Professor of Old Testament Theology.

Peter J. Paris is Elmer G. Homrighausen Professor of Christian Social Ethics, and Liaison with the Princeton University Afro-American Studies Program.

Luis N. Rivera-Pagán is Henry Winters Luce Professor of Ecumenics and Mission.

All are members of the faculty at Princeton Theological Seminary.

Acknowledgments

We are grateful for the enthusiastic support and wise counsel of our editor at Westminster John Knox Press, Stephanie Egnotovich, and for the diligence of research assistants Joshua McPaul and Ericka Parkinson.

Introduction

Sally A. Brown and Patrick D. Miller

A COMMUNITY LAMENTS

Cries and prayers of lament erupt from the human heart and voice in the grip of painful experience. So it was for the Princeton Seminary community during the months when many of the essays in this volume were being prepared. While motivated by scholarly interest, to be sure, these essays emerged as well out of the struggle to pray and bear Christian witness in the face of profound distress and loss. Over a span of two and a half years, untimely death claimed several active Princeton Seminary faculty members or their spouses. Through those months, the seminary community cried out again and again in prayer individually, in small gatherings, and in community-wide worship. We often found in the psalms of lament the most fitting voice for our prayer.

The community's deeply personal losses occurred within a larger horizon, that of the "post–9-11" reality that has recalibrated the agenda of theological reflection and education at the dawn of the twenty-first century. Since that Tuesday, September 11, 2001, when jets became missiles and claimed thousands of lives in New York City, the Pentagon, and the Pennsylvania countryside, those of us engaged in theological education and the leadership of the church have been made freshly aware that our faith and work must take into account the deep sense of vulnerability to violence that many feel. While loss and pain have always marked human experience, the threat of violence, ranging from domestic abuse to gang conflict, from acts of terrorism to the sophisticated preemptive attacks of a superpower, has redefined the context of Christian prayer, theological reflection, and witness all over the world.

Finding language adequate to our global situation is part of the challenge of theological education and ministry today. Many believers and pastors within the biblical traditions (Jewish, Christian, and Muslim) were alarmed by the triumphalist tone of official announcements in response to the events of September 11. Almost immediately after the attacks, public officials took to the airwaves with an aggressive political rhetoric, declaring "war on terror" in language that was an amalgam of nationalistic, religious, and militaristic vocabulary and imagery. Pleas from some quarters for our leaders to pause and inquire carefully into those characteristically American economic values and political behaviors that might have contributed to the fury of the attackers were brushed aside.

Seeking an alternative mode of prayer and reflection appropriate to these troubling days, many pastors turned to the oft-neglected literature of lament in the Scriptures. In the lament psalms they found a pattern for prayer and proclamation more adequate to the ambiguous nature of our global and national situation than cries for righteous aggression.

LAMENT REDISCOVERED

In fact, the rediscovery of lament as a pattern for Christian prayer, public worship, and the care of souls had already been under way for some time prior to the fall of 2001. By the late 1990s, studies such as Daniel Migliore and Kathleen Billman's *Rachel's Cry: Prayer of Lament and the Rebirth of Hope* were reintroducing the church to the much-neglected lament prayers of the Bible as resources for worship and Christian ministries of care.[1] These projects relied, in turn, on the fruits of nearly a decade of fresh work on lament in biblical studies. Although the lament genre had been a recognized part of the biblical and psalmic types of speech, at least since the work of Hermann Gunkel early in the twentieth century, it was especially the translation into English of some of the books and essays of the German scholar Claus Westermann and the subsequent investigations of Walter Brueggemann and others, building upon the German form-critical study of these psalms, that brought the topic to the fore.

Distinguishing features of the biblical lament psalms and other prayers of lament came into more public view and began to influence pastoral and theological thinking. Among the distinctive features of the lament genre are the following:

- The prayers of Scripture take shape in a form that is consistent enough to impress itself upon the community of faith as a mode of praying that merits imitation in our own prayers.

- That form or structure may itself be the vehicle for carrying the one praying beyond the present predicament into a new mode of trust and confidence.[2]
- Central to such praying is a large element of lament and complaint: lament in the sense of bemoaning the troubles that one has undergone and that evoke the present prayer; complaint in the sense of arguing with and complaining to God about one's situation and protesting its continuation.
- Identifying lament and complaint as central elements of biblical prayer has uncovered the possibility, if not the inevitability, of both rage about one's condition and anger against God as legitimate dimensions of prayer.
- Nearly all of the lament prayers move to some expression of confidence or assurance of being heard. The complaint without trust is not the lament. The complaint is itself an act of trust (see Psalm 22:3–4).
- Such psalms are not merely complaints or laments about one's condition. They have at their center petitions for God's help.
- Inasmuch as the fundamental aim of the laments is to seek God's deliverance from troubles, the various elements of the prayer, including the laments about one's condition and the complaints against God, are to be understood as acts of persuasion, motivations laid out to persuade God to act in behalf of the innocent, the victim, and the sufferer, that is, to persuade God to be God.
- The lament prayer is not an act of mourning; it is an act of protest.

This last point bears elaboration. What is customarily understood by the lament psalm is not the only mode of lament in the biblical literature. Some sense of the distinction as well as awareness of overlap can illuminate our thinking about the place and practice of lament in the church today. While the impact of the lament genre on thinking about contemporary modes of worship and prayer has focused on the individual lament, which is the most common psalm genre and the standard mode of prayer in Scripture, a few psalms are regarded as communal laments (for example, Psalms 44, 74, 79, 80, and 83). Their place in the ongoing discussion is less clear, in part because of uncertainties about their original function. They share features with the individual lament, such as address to God, complaint, a situation of terrible crisis. They seem to belong to settings of community disaster, such as the destruction of Jerusalem, but they may have functioned much earlier and more regularly. While one might expect to find in the laments of the community a strong penitential element, that is not as evident as is the protest to the deity and the challenge to the Lord's faithfulness.

Alongside these individual and communal laments is another genre, the funeral dirge, an act of mourning often in proximity to the burial of the dead. One interpreter has described the difference as follows:

> While both genres deal with the general topic of suffering and loss, the lament prayer (modeled in many psalms) is essentially a *plea* [that is, a prayer] addressed to the deity for intervention for help (thus it is characterized by

second-person speech). The dirge, on the other hand, *forewarns against* or *commemorates* the fact of a death and/or destruction (and usually employs third-person speech).[3]

The lament prayer is oriented as a plea for help in the terrible moment of suffering and loss, while the dirge, also an act of lamenting, mourns the loss. The lament is often a cry of protest at circumstances of suffering, oppression, and injustice. The dirge, however, can also function in that respect, raising "the voice of public justice" as the "usual 'complaint' about death in the dirge moves to 'accusation' against the perpetrator," the one responsible for the death and destruction.[4]

The distinctions are important as the church thinks about its practices, the contexts in which they take place, and the appropriate move or act at any particular moment. Yet one must recognize that the distinctions are often blurred in Scripture. The book of Lamentations joins individual and communal lament prayer with funeral dirge in a single whole. Psalm 137, probably as close to a funeral dirge or lament as it is to anything, includes a vow and a petition, albeit one that often horrifies the reader of the psalm. It is not surprising that this text rose to the fore in services of worship in the aftermath of September 11, 2001. Its mix of mourning, rage, imprecation, and petition reflected the anguished mix in the souls and hearts of many persons as they mourned that terrible destruction and cried out to God.

Increasing awareness of the centrality of all the above to the understanding of biblical prayer has had a large impact upon the church's thinking about how and when and what we pray. Many of the usual assumptions about prayer—for example, that it is passive and not aggressive, that it is simply a prayer for God's will no matter what, that one is not supposed to complain about one's condition much less about God, and that anger at God is a form of distrust and disobedience—have been called into radical question by this continuing look at the prayers of Scripture. What follows in these pages is an effort to continue thinking about the implications of what we have learned about lament for the way we worship and pray, the way we do pastoral care, what we believe about God, how we think theologically, and how we respond to a world increasingly marked by the ravages of calculated political and religious violence.

RECOVERING LAMENT IN PULPIT, PEW, AND PUBLIC SQUARE

Readers will recognize in the essays to follow differently nuanced understandings of lament, with some contributors stressing the threefold rhetoric of grief, protest, and hope in biblical lament and others grounding their work in a broader, more "public" understanding of lament. Yet, from many angles of vision and in different voices, all of the contributors to this volume urge upon the church a deeper embrace of lament as a paradigm for Christian practice in a world where the faces and forms of human suffering are legion.

The essays are grouped into three parts. Part I, "Reclaiming Lament in Christian Prayer and Proclamation," begins with Nancy J. Duff's essay, in which she argues in a broad sense for the recovery of lament in Christian worship. Duff makes her case with specific reference to two concrete experiences that are all too common for many who gather for worship Sunday by Sunday, the loss of a loved one and sexual abuse. By reclaiming lament in the church, argues Duff, we make a space for these experiences to be taken seriously and integrated into the public and private faith of the church. Next, Patrick Miller invites us to learn the cadences of lament prayer by attending to three voices from which lament arises: the human voice, the voice of Christ, and the voice of the world. At one and the same time a voice of pain, prayer, and hope, our laments are joined always by the lament of Christ. In turn, our own prayers of lament are lifted in solidarity with the world's lament, an intercession for all human sufferers.

Without doubt, lament in the Bible is first of all a form of prayer. This being said, are there other legitimate ways to appropriate biblical lament in Christian worship and witness? The canonical status of these texts, that is, specifically their status *as Scripture,* suggests that these texts function for today's church as a resource for theological reflection, worship, ministry, and public witness. Proceeding from that conviction, Sally A. Brown argues that the rhetorical structure of biblical lament can function as an interpretive guide for sermons dealing with suffering and crisis. By taking seriously the tropes that comprise lament, preacher and congregation can come to terms, theologically, with the feelings and impulses that suffering engenders in us and in others. Nancy Lammers Gross develops yet another way that a lament psalm may shape preaching in her creative sermon joining Psalm 22, one of the best known psalms of lament, with Psalm 23, inviting us to a new perspective on each of these psalms in light of the other. In an important sense, the very possibility of lament is rooted in the conviction that there is a trustworthy shepherd who hears.

Part II, "Loss and Lament, Human and Divine," explores lament as both a human and a divine response to pain and loss. Clifton Black suggests that lament, no less pervasive in the New Testament than the Old, is the "signature theme" of Christian experience. Tellingly, the Risen One appears even in apocalyptic visions as none other than the Crucified, the bearer of unmistakable wounds. God shares creation's travail and bears its marks. Robert Dykstra turns our attention to the moment of Jesus' death, focusing not on the cross but on the rending of the temple curtain. This "unveiling," Dykstra argues, signifies divine lament, an act of radical self-exposure, and suggests that lament, both human and divine, is an act of commitment to utter vulnerability. Inquiring from a different perspective into the vulnerability of lament, Donald Capps's essay explores death-related humor as a near cousin of lament, a coping mechanism for handling the deep anxieties that our vulnerability produces in us. We return to the subject of the death of Jesus as William Stacy Johnson pursues a penetrating examination of what has been known as the cry of dereliction, the outcry of Jesus from the cross. In contrast with Black's view of the cry, Johnson contends on exegetical, theological, and ethical grounds that Jesus is not abandoned by God on the cross; rather, in

Jesus' cry we hear God's cry too, and the cries of all who suffer and have suffered throughout human history. As God did not abandon Jesus, so God does not abandon us, nor can we abandon one another.

In the final chapter in this section we are reminded how suddenly health and all its attendant securities can be stripped from us. In a profoundly personal theological meditation, Ellen Charry reflects upon a series of letters that her late husband, Dr. Dana Charry, wrote to family and friends beginning in December, 2002 when his advanced lung cancer was discovered, and continuing into July 2003, days before his death. What was at stake for Dana, Charry suggests, is at stake for all of us: When every security and comfort is stripped from us, can we lament and yet trust God?

In Part III, "Reclaiming the Public Voice of Lament," four authors invite us to rediscover lament as a social practice, a public response to shared grief, to the ravages of war, and to national crisis. Peter Paris, well known for his studies of the spiritual practices of African peoples, both in African settings and in the diaspora cultures of North America, explores practices of lament in African, African American, and African Canadian faith communities. Social practices in these contexts respond to grief and suffering in ways that legitimate and ritually express sorrow and rage, empowering mourners and sufferers to confront their situations actively rather than suffer in isolated, passive silence. In the next essay, Luis Rivera-Pagán guides us through a subtle exploration of the epic war poems of ancient Greece, focusing particularly on the laments of women in these poems. Rivera-Pagán urges us to attend to the contemporary echo of these laments in the cries of women the world over, who, like their foremothers of ancient times, are often the most vulnerable victims of war. Lament is a fitting rhetoric not only for war's victims, argues Richard Fenn, but for those who are tempted to invoke religion to justify their own impulses toward vengeful destruction. Fenn suggests that learning to lament as a people will require that we question political and religious dogmas that divide the world into "God's chosen" (us) and "all others." Finally, Brian Blount's thought-provoking sermon "Breaking Point" issues both a challenge and a warning: if we truly wish to recover lament, it will cost us. Lament's grief and protest are empty unless joined to sacrificial action that confronts the conditions that produce suffering in the first place.

It is fitting to bring this collection to a close with Charles L. Bartow's evocation through poetry of lament's "soulful fury." In a skillful interweaving of careful theological reflection with his own poems and those of others, Bartow takes us into the depths of lament's anguish, yet does so in the confidence that the last word is a living Word of hope, the One "who is for us light in the darkness."

RECLAIMING LAMENT: AN ONGOING TASK

The times we live in continue to be fraught with deep tension. The church itself is split by debates over the relationship of faith to the empowerment of women and over the stance of faith communities on homosexual orientation as an alternative expression of human sexuality. On the global scale, religious and political conflicts foster polarizing rhetoric and threaten to erupt in violence. Nations and warring ethnic groups within the boundaries of nation-states carry poisonous legacies scarred either by humiliation or hubris, while galling disparities of economic and educational opportunity in different parts of the world become ever more pronounced. Add to this the ongoing competition for scarce resources, especially fuel and water, and the race for nuclear development among so-called "second tier" nations, and the result around the globe is a combustible ether of discontent, wounded pride, distrust, and desperation. It is little wonder that daily newscasts are filled with stories of suffering and loss.

Lament indispensably shapes prayer, proclamation, ministry, and witness for such times. Perhaps it is only in learning both to express and to hear lament that we can become sensitized to the often bitter and tragic ironies of our situation as both perpetrators and victims of violence and suffering. Contributors to this volume, whatever their particular theoretical and theological commitments, share a concern to help the church genuinely mourn the world's enmity and pain, give a voice to the voiceless, and witness against injustice. Such witness, on the one hand, must include concrete self-critical practices that allow churches and their host cultures to uncover and address complicity in the world's evils and, on the other, must lift up a sustaining, hopeful vision for the future of this world that God loves utterly, even unto death.

It is our shared conviction that lament, particularly biblical lament, provides the church with a rhetoric for prayer and reflection that befits these volatile times, a rhetoric that mourns loss, examines complicity in evil, cries for divine help, and sings and prays with hope. For indeed, what ultimately shapes biblical lament is not the need of the creature to cry its woe, but the faithfulness of the God who hears and acts.

NOTES

1. Kathleen Billman and Daniel Migliore, *Rachel's Cry: Prayer of Lament and the Rebirth of Hope* (Cleveland: United Church Press, 1999). Years earlier, Donald Capps had discussed the role of lament psalms in grief counseling in *Biblical Approaches to Pastoral Counseling* (Philadelphia: Westminster Press, 1981). A number of articles published in the mid-1990s called for the recovery of lament psalms in liturgy.
2. See in this regard the essay by Walter Brueggemann, "The Formfulness of Grief," in Brueggemann, *The Psalms and the Life of Faith*, ed. Patrick D. Miller (Minneapolis: Fortress, 1995), 84–97.
3. Nancy C. Lee, *The Singers of Lamentations: Cities under Siege, from Ur to Jerusalem to Sarajevo*, Biblical Interpretation Series 60 (Leiden: Brill, 2002), 33.
4. Ibid., 35.

PART I
RECLAIMING LAMENT IN CHRISTIAN PRAYER AND PROCLAMATION

Chapter 1

Recovering Lamentation as a Practice in the Church

Nancy J. Duff

For most of us today, the words *lament* and *lamentation* have a curiously anachronistic ring about them. While most Christians have at least heard of the biblical book of Lamentations (even if we haven't actually read it) and some of us are familiar with psalms of lament (though we don't hear them frequently read in our services of worship), the majority of Christians would be hard pressed to identify lamentation as an important aspect of their lives of faith and worship. We may on occasion say that we "lament" that something has happened, but in this case the word refers to regret. Biblical literary forms of lament, however, move well beyond regret to provide an avenue for expressing intense feelings of grief, such as sorrow and anger. Whether that grief arises from illness or tragedy or an act of injustice toward the worshipper, psalms of lament indicate that the Hebrew worshipper was free to express complaints, anxiety, rage, and deep sorrow before God and other members of the community. What was quite natural for the Hebrew worshipper, however, seems foreign to most of us now.

Our lack of familiarity with lamentation does not, of course, result from any lack of experience with situations that give rise to grief. It is part of the human condition to grieve. Our sense of loss can be overwhelming, and our grief can last as long as life itself. Whether grief results from the death of a loved one, an encounter with serious illness, or an injustice done to us at the hands of another, we can feel abandoned by God, so that with the psalmist we demand to know, "How long, O LORD? Will you forget me forever?" (Ps. 13:1). When our anger at the perpetrator of violence against us wells up within us, we may wish to exact vengeance, hoping that "his children [will] be orphans and his wife a widow" (Ps. 109:9). Although we may share such sentiments with the psalmist, we usually express them only in the secrecy of our innermost thoughts or, if we are lucky, with a close friend who will tolerate our giving voice to them. Our hearts may cry out with all the anguish and rage expressed in biblical lamentation, but our contemporary liturgies provide very few ritualistic means for expressing our grief, despair, and anger in the presence of others and in the context of faith in God. More often than not, we are taught that true faith in God mitigates such intense feelings and expressions of sorrow and rage.

Clinton McCann claims that in the book of Psalms lament psalms far out-number psalms of praise, and yet in the responsive readings found in a commonly used Presbyterian hymnal, psalms of praise outnumber psalms of lament sixteen to six.[1] McCann agrees with Walter Brueggemann that the minimal attention given to psalms of lament in the church's liturgical practices results from the commonly held notion that faith should not "acknowledge and embrace negativity."[2] Proclaiming hope and praising God when one knows full well the reality of the darkness can be an eschatological challenge to the status quo, but if one is not careful, it can become confused with a self-deceptive refusal to acknowledge things for how they really are. One must never lose sight of the difference between genuine hope, on the one hand, and a veil of pretense, on the other.

In this essay I argue that the practice of lament needs to be recovered in the church and that psalms of lament can be used to encourage the Christian church today to allow room for true lamentation in our corporate and individual lives of prayer and worship. Eventually such a recovery would move us to examine our funeral services and services of remembrance in light of the psalms of lament, as well as to explore liturgies that have been created for survivors of abuse, for community tragedies, and for other specific situations of grief, vulnerability, and need. I do not, however, analyze present liturgies or formulate new ones. Rather, I seek to lay the foundation for such analysis and formulation, showing how psalms of lament can encourage us to change the way the church and its members respond to various expressions of the feelings that accompany grief.

Three aspects of psalms of lament will be addressed. Psalms of lament (1) challenge our inability to acknowledge the intense emotions that grief entails, (2) free us to make a bold expression of grief before God and in the presence of others, and (3) allow us to rely on God and the community to carry forth hope on our behalf when we ourselves have no hope in us.

The psalms identify various situations that give rise to lamentation, such as illness, false accusations, and defeat at the hands of others. The fact that descriptions of some of these situations may actually be metaphorical expands rather than limits the situations for which lamentation becomes an appropriate expression. According to Patrick Miller, the "open and metaphorical" character of the psalms indicate that "the laments become appropriate for persons who cry out to God in all kinds of situations in which they may encounter various kinds of opposition."[3] In our world there are endless events that cause us to grieve. Loss of a job, a broken marriage, the end of a lifelong friendship, the death of someone we love, or an act of injustice and violence against us at the hands of another can generate the need to express our frustration, anger, and despair. As I explore the three aspects of lament identified above, I will refer to two of these situations: the death of one we love and the experience of one who is a survivor of physical battering or sexual abuse. I do this because the psalms invite us to name situations of grief honestly and such honesty requires specificity. The reader, however, is invited to consider other situations of grief for which lamentation is appropriate, even as we focus on these two.

COMING TO TERMS WITH OUR INABILITY TO FACE GRIEF HONESTLY

An old song gives the advice to smile even if our hearts are aching.[4] The song carries an appropriate message when understood in the context of someone feeling blue. Sometimes our mood—even if we have reason to feel down—can be changed dramatically when someone cajoles us into smiling. Sometimes we have simply fallen into the comfortable habit of feeling sad, and we need someone to shake us gently out of it by making us smile. The song, of course, is rather lighthearted and was never intended to address someone in the throes of serious distress and sorrow. Only the most insensitive persons would tell someone who has experienced a great loss through death or who is the victim of violence to "hide every trace of sadness" and smile. Yet we seem in various ways, consciously or not, to do exactly that. A poem by Ella Wheeler Wilcox, though not necessarily addressed to those who grieve, poignantly describes our attitude toward one who would venture to express sorrow too openly or too persistently:

> Laugh and the world laughs with you.
> Weep and you weep alone.
> This sad, old earth must borrow its mirth
> But has troubles enough of its own.[5]

Unfortunately, weeping alone is often the plight of those who grieve.

Society and the church discourage us from expressing intense feelings of sorrow or anger when we experience a significant loss in our lives. When there is a death in the family, for instance, people are allowed very little time off from work, and when they return they are not expected to talk too much about their loss. No one wears visible signs of mourning as was once the custom, and the expectation is that one will move quickly back into the everyday routines of life. For Christians, continued expressions of grief after a death are considered a sign of weak faith: "Isn't the person in a better place?" The notion that one cannot bear the grief is rejected: "God doesn't give us more than we can bear." We do not in fact intend to be cruel when making such remarks. It is not callousness toward the pain of grief that makes us want people to recover from it quickly. Often it is simply an inability to know what to say or do, as well as a genuine desire to ease the pain of the one who grieves, that leads us to resort to questions and claims that in reality dismiss rather than ease someone's anguish.

Refraining from an outward expression of grief that results from death of a loved one has not always been the norm. In the nineteenth century, for instance, there were four stages of mourning for widows (deep mourning, second mourning, ordinary mourning, and half mourning), each dictating what the widow should wear. The first stage, deep mourning, lasted for two years.

> A widow wore the deepest possible mourning for the first two years of her widowhood. A black dress of parmetta or bombazine was completely covered by crepe, and all her accessories were black. . . . Over her bonnet hung a veil of transparent crepe—to emphasize her isolation from the world.[6]

The second mourning lasted nine months, during which time the crepe could be lessened. Ordinary mourning (the third stage) lasted another three months, when black silk could be worn without the crepe and some black jewelry could be worn. Finally, during half mourning (the fourth stage) the widow could exchange black for gray, mauve, or lavender. In addition to rules regarding dress, there were clearly defined rules of behavior that applied to the widow. A woman was expected to stay close to home and to avoid participation in frivolous activities. Hence, as Susan Lyons points out, when Scarlett O'Hara in *Gone with the Wind* dares to dance in her "widow's weeds," the other guests are scandalized.[7]

Victorian mourning practices allowed for a public display of grief that is unheard of today. The problem, of course, is that the rigors of that public display could become a greater burden than the grief itself. We rightly protest these excessive rules for mourning and perhaps applaud someone who, like the fictional Scarlett O'Hara, would dare to defy them. Nevertheless, something is to be said for the Victorian willingness to accept death openly and demonstrate signs of mourning publicly. By contrast, in the twentieth and twenty-first centuries, grief has become an almost entirely private matter. As Susan Lyons points out, only the funeral itself provides a public acknowledgment of grief; after the funeral the bereaved are expected to get on with their lives as quickly as possible.[8]

Our uneasiness in the face of one who has lost someone to death and our wish for the sufferer to move beyond the grief are even more pronounced when we encounter the recent victim of a violent crime such as rape. We hope that the person will not mention the trauma and will instead adjust, recover, and leave the event behind as quickly as possible. Surely, we reason, that would be best for everyone involved. Why dwell on such a terrible event? Furthermore, our initial feeling of sympathy can shift into impatience as time goes on. We may hear the question from coworkers or friends, or may even ask it ourselves, "Hasn't she gotten over that yet?" When the victim is a Christian, the expectation of forgiveness is raised early on: "Have you been able to forgive him?" For those who are the victim of sexual violence, silence has almost always been the norm. The crime becomes a source of shame for the victim, as if she or he is the guilty one. No mourning clothes, no rules for appropriate action, no avenue for expressing rage over the enormous sense of loss and violation of the self are available to the victim. When survivors of sexual abuse tell someone what has happened to them, they are often faced with denial on the part of the one in whom they have confided: "Are you sure you haven't misunderstood what happened?" Such denial also comes in the form of the immediate counsel toward forgiveness of the perpetrator, because it is "the Christian thing to do." Sometimes the listener even comes to the defense of the perpetrator: "He's married and he's only 19. Do you really want to ruin his life by sending him to jail?"

Whenever we expect and encourage someone who has experienced the death of a loved one or been the victim of a violent crime to "move on with life," we deceive ourselves and others into believing that people can move through the various stages of grief and recovery until they have in fact overcome their grief altogether and can leave behind forever the event which precipitated it. In fact, one never completely "gets over" grief or completely leaves behind the event that caused it. The persistent intensity of grief certainly eases over time as we learn to incorporate our loss and trauma into our lives and make it part of our identity, but we never "get over it." A woman whose husband has died is no longer a wife, but a widow; a child (even an adult son or daughter) whose only surviving parent dies takes on the identity of orphan; one who has experienced sexual violence can eventually move from the identity of "victim" to "survivor," but being a survivor remains a permanent part of who he is; a parent who has lost a child will forever stumble over the question "How many children do you have?"

As William F. May observes, the event of loss and trauma becomes the marker that forever defines a person's life in terms of "before" and "after." One now talks about the time before and after the stroke, the accident, the attack, or the death.[9] Lives are forever changed by the death of someone we love or by violence done to us by another person, and the grief that results is not a process we enter and leave but an experience we incorporate into who we are. Those who counsel someone who is grieving can help him learn to live with the experience, can help her through the passage of time that makes the emotions less intense, but the counselor or the friend cannot erase the grief from the person's life.

Against our tendency to deny the intensity of grief, there is a biblical tradition of lament, which allows the individual to express anguish and anger directly to God and before the community of believers. The Bible recognizes the overwhelming reality of grief that cannot be consoled. In light of the grief brought on by death, or the anguish and pain that result from sexual assault, or the seemingly endless events of tragedy and injustice that people experience in life, the church needs to turn to the biblical concept of lament to provide a space where people can express their sorrow before God and one another.

A BOLD EXPRESSION OF OUR GRIEF

In contrast to our contemporary experience of avoiding open expression of lament, psalms of lament invite us to bring our sorrow and the rage that may accompany it before God and one another. As Dietrich Bonhoeffer points out, the psalms know it all: "serious illness, deep isolation from God and humanity, threats, persecution, imprisonment, and whatever conceivable peril there is on earth."[10] Furthermore, the psalms "do not deny it, they do not deceive themselves with pious words about it, they allow it to stand as a severe ordeal of faith, indeed at times they no longer see beyond the sufferings (Ps. 88), but they complain about it all to God."[11] Although psalms of lament often claim unshaken trust in God, they can also be characterized by a sense that God is no longer present: "O LORD, why do you cast me off? Why do you hide your face from me?" (Ps. 88:14). Impatience with suffering is expressed freely: "I am weary with my moaning; every night I flood my bed with tears" (Ps. 6: 6). Psalms of lament can freely show anger toward enemies and ask God to punish them: "Make them bear their guilt, O God; let them fall by their own counsels; because of their many transgressions cast them out" (Ps. 5:10). In the imprecatory psalms the anger leads to a desire for vengeance against enemies: "Happy shall they be who pay you back what you have done to us" (Ps. 137:8). Christians, however, tend to be uneasy with such expressions of God-forsakenness, anger, impatience, and revenge. Forgiveness and reconciliation are expected to occur with as little reference as possible to the events that made them necessary.

The psalmist, however, knows better. Psalms of lament, as James Mays has pointed out, identify in the liturgy of prayer the worshipper's suffering and vulnerability and provide us with "a vocabulary of need [and] a rhetoric of affliction."[12] The individual in the psalm, according to Mays, "is a paradigm of the one who in trouble cries out to God for deliverance."[13] Hence, the identification of the one who wrote the psalm is not as important as the one who now reads it:

> The identity in the psalm is given to and assumed by the one who prays the prayer. The language of the prayer is disclosive. It brings to light who one must be and who one is in crying out to the Lord from the depths of existence.[14]

Even when the contemporary reader finds no identification with the words of a particular psalm of lament, Dietrich Bonhoeffer suggests that one read the psalm as a prayer anyway, for in such a case one reads it on behalf of another whose experience is represented in the psalm. "Even if a verse or a psalm is not my own prayer," Bonhoeffer says, "it is nevertheless the prayer of another member of the community."[15]

Given that psalms of lament can either represent the situation of the one who reads them or be read on behalf of another, an intimate connection with members of the congregation is made in these psalms. Perhaps every Sunday liturgy should include a prayer of lament in the same way that many of us are accustomed to reading a prayer of confession. Just as we are called to confess our sin before God, we can be called to lament. These prayers could come directly from Scripture or be composed by the liturgist, making reference to contemporary situations. Leanne Simmons rightly suggests that a prayer of confession of sin should include not only a confession of sins we have committed but also an acknowledgment that we have been damaged by the sins of others.[16] Perhaps her suggestion could be further enhanced if such acknowledgment came in its own particular place and form. Though some of the elements of lament may already be included in the pastoral prayer, having a separate reading of lament could accustom the congregation to the notion that just as we confess our sin, profess our faith, and bring forth praise, we also bring our sorrows, anger, frustration, and anguish before God.

According to Walter Brueggemann, repeating the psalms of lament is a bold act of faith on two accounts. First, it insists that we must look at the world and our lives the way they really are. We can't approach devastating events in our lives by pretending that things are not as bad as they appear, when in fact things may be just as bad as, if not worse than, appearance reveals. Second, it is a bold act of faith because "it insists that all such experiences of disorder are a proper subject of discourse with God."[17] There is nothing about the reality of the world or of the self that cannot be brought before God.

Brueggemann suggests that psalms of lament can "evoke reality" for someone who is caught up in self-deception. This can apply to the one who has heard the story of a victim, but also to the victim herself. Referring to situations of domestic violence, Marie Fortune says that such an invocation of reality is necessary for everyone involved.

> The common response to evidence of violence in the family is minimization and denial. This response is the individual's emotional distancing, used as a means of coping with a reality that is distasteful, disquieting, and generally overwhelming. The response is common for victim and abuser alike as well as for all manner of helpers, friends, family members, and ministers. The things that victims of abuse will hesitantly describe . . . are often unbelievable. However this does not mean that they are untrue. In an effort to make the situation more manageable and tolerable, there is the temptation to minimize and deny the particulars. This temptation, while ever present, should be resisted.[18]

The church can play a critical role in helping the victim of abuse to resist the temptation to minimize what has happened. If psalms of lament were well known by Christian worshippers, if they were frequently read in worship, individuals would be familiar with the practice of naming the feelings that accompany grief before entering into a situation of grief. While this is not meant to undercut the initial denial that almost every victim of violence or every terminal patient uses for self-protection, it does establish a pattern and a goal of learning how to face the truth about the things that happen to us and to express our feelings about what has happened with courage and honesty.

Reading and understanding psalms of lament provide an avenue for creating space and freedom to express the powerful emotions that accompany grief. The victim of domestic violence who has discovered that the husband she loves is now the one who beats her, or the victim of date rape who has been betrayed by the person she trusted, or the victim of clergy sexual abuse who respected his spiritual advisor only to be violated by him may be surprised to find that the psalmist knows about such betrayals where one's closest companion or confidant becomes one's worst enemy:

> It is not an enemy who taunts me—
>   then I could bear it;
> it is not an adversary who deals insolently with me—
>   then I could hide from him.
> But it is you, my equal,
>   my companion, my familiar friend.
> We used to hold sweet converse together;
>   within God's house we walked in fellowship.
>   (Psalm 55:12–14 RSV)

The companion has now violated the covenant. The psalmist now understands that while originally the companion's "speech was smoother than butter" (v. 21), there was all along war in the companion's heart.

Reading and understanding psalms of lament can inform individuals that they are not the first to feel abandoned by God. The widow who feels unbearable isolation as she locks her door and faces another evening alone, the man who in desperation wonders how he will ever find another job, the teenager whose despair focuses more and more often on the possibility of death may be surprised to find that the psalmist knows of situations of such dire pain that one feels cut off not only from friends, but also from God.

> For my soul is full of troubles,
>   and my life draws near to Sheol.
> I am counted among those who go down to the Pit;
>   I am like those who have no help,
> like those forsaken among the dead,
>   like the slain that lie in the grave,
> like those whom you remember no more,
>   for they are cut off from your hand.
>   (Ps. 88:3–5)

The sufferer is "shut in" and "cannot escape" (v. 8). His "eye grows dim through sorrow" (v. 9), and God seems to be the one who has thrown the sufferer into "regions dark and deep" (v. 6). Can we actually bring such thoughts to God in prayer? Are not such tormented feelings of being abandoned by God a sign that our faith has failed us? Do we dare speak such words to our brothers and sisters in the faith? We find the answer to those questions in Jesus' own prayer. Drawing on a psalm of lament, he cried out in anguish, "My God, my God, why have you forsaken me?" (Ps. 22:1).

The Psalms, according to Bonhoeffer, are the only place where the word of God becomes our own prayer. According to Bonhoeffer, we are drawn into the prayer of the Psalms, even the psalms of lament, on our own behalf and on behalf of the neighbor because these psalms are first understood by Christians as the prayers of Christ.

> The psalms that will not cross our lips as prayers, those that make us falter and offend us, make us suspect that here someone else is praying, not we— that the one who is here affirming his innocence, who is calling for God's judgment, who has come to such infinite depths of suffering, is none other than Jesus Christ himself.[19]

Why would we possibly believe that our anguish, our despair, and our feeling that God has abandoned us must never be expressed to others, when Jesus himself cried out in lamentation before God?

PRAYERS OF LAMENT AND HOPE

Just as we hear words of lamentation from Jesus on the cross, so we hear them at the beginning of the Gospel story, at the story of Jesus' birth. In the story of the slaughter of the innocents, Matthew draws upon an Old Testament figure whose voice comes as close as any could to recognizing the utter lack of consolation that a mother feels in light of losing her children: "A voice was heard in Ramah, wailing and loud lamentation, Rachel weeping for her children; she refused to be consoled, because they are no more" (Matt. 2:18).[20] When the biblical understanding of lament, as we have examined it in the book of Psalms, allows us to name the worst instances of grief and despair, can we dare move from such lamentation and speak of hope? If the answer is yes, it can only be spoken carefully, respectfully, and in honest recognition of grief, which, like Rachel's, refuses consolation. Christopher Morse points out that in the biblical account Rachel refuses "all false comfort and facile explanation."[21] Not only does she refuse to be consoled; the Gospels honor her refusal as "faithful testimony."[22] Does this mean that the Gospel acknowledges that there are situations for which there is no hope? According to Morse, one can answer that question with a clear no, but only if one is equally clear that hope in a hopeless situation comes only from God.

> As biblically viewed, there are situations in which only God may speak of hope. There is a hope that only God can give. Who can give hope to a slave or exile and make that captive "see freedom in the air" when there is none on the ground? Who can give hope when innocent children become the victims of the evils of nature and history? For anyone to speak cheaply and glibly about hope in the midst of such evil is certainly to utter blasphemy. Rachel refuses all consolation. This the biblical testimonies recognize and respect. Rachel "refuses to be comforted."[23]

Morse points out that God alone gives a word of hope when Rachel's cry is repeated by others in the book of Jeremiah. As the conquered Israelites march past Rachael's grave into exile, Jeremiah recalls as Matthew does, "A voice is heard in Ramah, lamentation and bitter weeping. Rachel is weeping for her children; she refuses to be comforted for her children, because they are no more" (Jer. 31:15). In this situation of despair Jeremiah hears the word of the Lord, "Keep your voice from weeping, and your eyes from tears; . . . there is hope for your future" (Jer. 31:16–17). According to Morse, this coincidence of inconsolable grief and hope for the future gives a clue for why the biblical testimony speaks of Rachel in the context of Jesus' birth:

> In the darkness surrounding Rachel, just as much as in the light surrounding the natal star, the birthplace of the Christ is revealed. At the Nativity a manger somehow adjoins her tomb. Of this her disbelief of all consolation not of God becomes the faithful witness. Her voice, so Jeremiah tells us, is the one God hears.[24]

According to Morse, for the biblical account to testify that only God can proclaim hope for the future in the context of inconsolable grief means that the church refuses any offer of false hope, as well as any cynical claim that there is no hope. In a similar manner, in the story of the valley of dry bones God asks Ezekiel, "Can these bones live?" Ezekiel, who knows the bleakness and destitution of the situation, who knows that no life or hope can spring from these bones on their own accord, rightly answers, "Lord GOD, thou knowest." God alone gives hope when the situation and we ourselves have none.

In his book on God and suffering Stanley Hauerwas insists that Christians have no "solution" to the problem of evil and suffering. Rather, they have "a community of care that has made it possible for them to absorb the destructive terror of evil that constantly threatens to destroy all human relations."[25] A large part of that care consists in listening to the story of the one who suffers. Hauerwas concludes his book with a quotation from Nicholas Wolterstorff, who wrote *Lament for a Son* after his son died in a climbing accident. Wolterstorff, too, insists on the lack of any appropriate answer to the anguished questions of those who grieve and for the need for others to listen.

> Death is awful, demonic. If you think your task as comforter is to tell me that really, all things considered, it's not so bad, you do not sit with me in my grief but place yourself off in the distance away from me. Over there, you are of no help. What I need to hear from you is that you recognize how painful it is. I need to hear from you that you are with me in my desperation. To comfort me, you have to come close. Come sit beside me on my mourning bench.[26]

When lamentation makes space for the sufferer to give voice to anguish, anger, and despair, by definition it provides the space for others to listen to the words of lamentation and even to pray those words with and on behalf of the other. This essay on lament, therefore, has a great deal to do with listening. Rather than seeking ways to ensure that the one who grieves will do so quickly and quietly, the biblical tradition of lamentation invites worshippers to give voice to their anguish, even if what they say seemingly sounds "unchristian," and it calls others to listen with no judgment or censure. Patrick Miller points to the paradox of despair and faith when the psalms of lamentation become our own prayers: "The human being who speaks in and through and with this psalm is a lamenter, a fact that signifies a dual reality: he or she is in the depths but also is one who prays."[27] Psalms of lament allow us to speak from the darkest regions of the heart, where our despair threatens to overwhelm us. In so speaking we do not exhibit a lack of faith, but stand in a biblical tradition that recognizes that no part of life, including the most hideous and painful parts, is to be withheld from God, who loves us, who in Jesus Christ speaks the psalms of lament alongside us, and who proclaims hope, when there can—at least for the time being—be no hope in us. The church would do well to recover this biblical practice of lamentation.

NOTES

1. J. Clinton McCann, *A Theological Introduction to the Book of Psalms: The Psalms as Torah* (Nashville: Abingdon Press, 1993), 85.
2. McCann, *A Theological Introduction to the Book of Psalms,* 85. The quotation from Brueggemann is found in Walter Brueggemann, *The Message of the Psalms* (Minneapolis: Augsburg Press, 1984), 52.
3. Patrick D. Miller, *Interpreting the Psalms* (Philadelphia: Fortress Press, 1986), 51.
4. "Smile," Charlie Chaplin, Geoffrey Parsons, and James Phillips. The lyrics can be found in a CD by Rod Stewart, *As Time Goes By: The Great American Songbook, Volume II.*
5. Ella Wheeler Wilcox, "Solitude," in *One Hundred and One Famous Poems,* revised edition, ed. Roy J. Cook (Chicago: Reilly & Lee Co., 1958), 72.
6. Susan Lyons, "The After Life: Mourning Rituals of the Civil War Era." http://southernhomefront.tripod.com/mourning/mourning1.html (Temporary website posting).
7. Ibid.
8. Ibid.
9. William F. May, *The Patient's Ordeal* (Bloomington: Indiana University Press, 1994), 5–6.
10. Dietrich Bonhoeffer, *Prayerbook of the Bible,* in *Dietrich Bonhoeffer Works,* vol. 5 (Minneapolis: Fortress Press, 1996), 169.
11. Bonhoeffer, *Prayerbook,* 169. I disagree when Bonhoeffer says that "no single human being can pray the psalms of lamentation out of his or her own experience," but that "spread out before us here is the anguish of the entire Christian community throughout all time, as Jesus Christ alone has wholly experienced it" (169). To suggest that Christ's sufferings are worse than ours stands on the brink of docetism. An individual person can and often does know exactly from personal experience the lamentations found in the Psalms.
12. James Mays, *Psalms,* Interpretation (Louisville, KY: John Knox Press, 1994), 22.
13. Mays, *Psalms,* 23.
14. Mays, *Psalms,* 23.

15. Bonhoeffer, *Life Together,* in *Dietrich Bonhoeffer Works,* vol. 5, 55.
16. Leanne Simmons made this comment in a lecture given in the course "Feminist and Womanist Theologies" taught at Princeton Theological Seminary, Fall 2002. See her dissertation, "Taking Back the Body: Eating Disorders, Feminist Theological Ethics, and Christic Gynodicy," in the Speer Library, Princeton Theological Seminary.
17. Brueggemann, *The Message of the Psalms,* 52.
18. Marie Fortune, *Violence in the Family: A Worship Curriculum for Clergy and Other Helpers* (Cleveland: Pilgrim Press, 1991), 193.
19. Bonhoeffer, *Prayerbook,* 54.
20. Matt. 2:18, Jer. 31:15. For insightful reflection on Rachel's refusal to be consoled, see Christopher L. Morse, *Not Every Spirit: A Dogmatics of Christian Disbelief* (Valley Forge, PA: Trinity Press), 9–12.
21. Morse, *Not Every Spirit,* 10.
22. Morse, *Not Every Spirit,* 10.
23. Morse, *Not Every Spirit,* 10, emphasis in the original.
24. Morse, *Not Every Spirit,* 10–11.
25. Stanley Hauerwas, *Naming the Silences: God, Medicine, and the Problem of Suffering* (Grand Rapids: Wm. B. Eerdmans Publishing Co., 1990), 53. This book has been republished more recently under the title *God, Medicine, and Suffering.*
26. Hauerwas, *Naming the Silences,* 151. The quotation is from Nicholas Wolterstorff, *Lament for a Son* (Grand Rapids: Wm. B. Eerdmans Publishing Co., 1987), 34.
27. Miller, *Interpreting the Psalms,* 139.

Chapter 2

Heaven's Prisoners: The Lament as Christian Prayer

Patrick D. Miller

The thesis of this chapter is that the Christian community learns about the place and practice of lament from attending to the voices that lament. There are three different but related voices from which we hear the sounds of lament: the human voice, the voice of Christ, and the voice of the world. There is, in my judgment, an actual and a theological order to those voices, and recovering the language and practice of lament means being attentive to the order in which the lament is heard on the lips of these three speakers: the human being, the Christ of God, and the world of trouble and woe.

THE VOICE OF THE HUMAN

The laments, as such, are *the voice of the human.* They are irrepressible. They are not genre specific. They are not bound to class or race or language or religious affiliation. They serve to define our humanness.

I hear that from several directions. I read it in the newpapers. I hear it on the newscasts; I read about it in all kinds of books. But I hear it first from Scripture. And I hear it there under the conviction that the Scriptures are where one learns most truly about the human story. I hear the lament as the human voice at the very beginning of Scripture, and I hear it all through Scripture. The first time that God appears on the human scene in response to human address is at the very beginning, in response to the inarticulate but voiced cries of the blood of "the brother" Abel, crying out from the ground after his murder by Cain. And Cain, like his father Adam the tiller of the soil, is the continuing line of Adam, the human one. Abel is but his brother. So at the very beginning of the human story and of the biblical story—and they really are one and the same story—the voice of the suffering one, the brother, who cries out for help, is what brings God on the scene, what initiates a divine response.

It is instructive that the first time the voice of lament is heard in Scripture, it is the voice of one who is *already murdered, already dead*. That warns us against assuming that the only laments that matter are those where there is still possibility of help, that once the suffering has destroyed the human creature it is too late, nothing can be done, God cannot and will not help. But we are told at the beginning that the Lord has a special set of antennae, that the ears of God are tuned to a particular frequency, and can hear it even when it comes from deep in the pit—despite what some of the psalmists may assume. The redemptive and just work of God does not operate in some instances and not in others. "The LORD works vindication for *all* who are oppressed" (Ps. 103:6). Cries for God's justice and mercy are not silenced forever, even in death.

What is true at the beginning of the human story and of God's story with humanity is true all the way through. The sounds of these human cries run through Scripture from beginning to end. They come up to God from the victims of injustice at Sodom, and once again they bring God on the scene (Gen. 18:21; 19:13).[1] The cries of those who suffer are heard by God at the exodus, and so a people in slavery are freed to become the Lord's own people (Exod. 2:23–25; 3:7–9). But these human cries never stop. They are who we are, and it is only in that eschatological transformation that the Bible speaks of as a new heaven and a new earth that the pain and tears of suffering are wiped away and death is no more. Until then, human beings will cry out and God will hear. This is indeed the primary mode of *conversation* between God and the human creature. It begins not in ritual, not in Israel, not in any particularity, but in our being human. The story of God and the human creature is rooted in and shaped by the experience of pain and suffering and what God does about it, in the human voice that cries out and the God whose ears cannot miss those cries. We tend to think of the laments primarily in relation to the Psalms and Job and Lamentations. That is where they are especially lodged. But theologically the cry to God and the response of God are a fundamental theme of the whole of Scripture.[2] The human cry to God for help is not one element in the biblical story; it is one of its *foundation stones*, foundational for both our anthropology and our theology.

The lament, therefore, is not exceptional. It is the rule. It is at one and the same time the voice of pain and the voice of prayer. It is the voice of pain, the possibility of language when suffering is so great that it is hard even to speak.

The importance of being able to give speech to pain has been suggested to me by two quite different pieces of literature. One of these is Elaine Scarry's book *The Body in Pain*.[3] She deals there with the reality of physical pain and the vulnerability of the human body, as indicated especially in the experiences of torture and war, but also in other types of physical pain. One of her fundamental claims is that it is difficult to give language to pain, that pain is language shattering, that the certainty of a person in pain about the reality of that pain is matched only by the doubt of other persons about its reality. She speaks of the need to find language to express that pain. At one point she says: "To witness the moment when pain causes a reversion to the pre-language of cries and groans is to witness the destruction of language; but conversely, to be present when a person moves up out of that pre-language and projects the facts of sentience into speech is almost to have been permitted to be present at the birth of language itself."[4] That birth of language in pain, that giving voice and language to the experience of suffering, is precisely what happens in the form and words of the lament.

The other piece of literature, an essay by Lawrence Cunningham, refers to a scene in Iris Murdoch's *The Good Apprentice* (1986) in which a young man tries to help his tortured stepbrother overcome deep despair over the death of a friend for which he was the cause. In attempting to help the brother out of a black mood of depression and self-recrimination, he says:

> Try to sort of pray, say "deliver me from evil," say you're sorry, ask for help, find some light, something the blackness can't blacken. There must be things you have, things you can get to, some poetry, something from the Bible, Christ, if he still means anything to you. Let the pain go on but let something else touch it like a ray coming through from outside, from *that* place outside.[5]

Here also the novelist is speaking of that need to find voice and form in the face of suffering, to seek help, to cry out, utter petition, say something on the way to finding new possibilities, help from outside.

If the lament is the voice of *pain*, it is also the voice of *prayer*. To recover the voice of lament is to recover the voice of prayer as it has defined the human reality before God. The lament is utterly human and profoundly theological. It arises out of the reality of human existence; it assumes there is something beyond that reality that can transform human existence without destroying it. The laments of Scripture make clear what is present in every human cry for help, the assumption that God is there, God can be present, and God can help. As such, the voice of lament, the cry for help we call lament, is always our prayer. It is our humanness, the sign of our being here as man and woman, as sentient beings, who feel and hurt, who remember and despair, who cry and try to speak. We cannot avoid these prayers. They are who we are. Recovering the language and practice of lament is no more and no less than recovering our human voice and learning the language of prayer.

Several things are involved in recovering the practice of lament as our universal human prayer:

1. The term *lament*, which is a modern invention, is in some ways an unfortunate one for the Psalms. The Bible knows lament and speaks specifically about lament, but it is the dirge for the dead that is in mind there, another important mode of protest and mourning.[6] The lament encountered in the Psalms and elsewhere is a prayer for help, and to pray that way is not simply to lament our condition and complain to God. That is always on the way and part of the petition for God's help in our trouble. I am not really sure we need to recover the language of complaint, to learn again how to complain. That has never been a large problem for me. But we may need to learn again how to ask for God's help in the midst of trouble and woe.

2. As cries for help, and thus as prayers, the laments belong to us in our aloneness and become the voice of that *isolation*. This is not the voice of solitude. That is a different matter altogether. The laments are especially prayers of terrible loneliness and shame before others—whether the shame is that of guilt, anger, sorrow, or something else. These are not community prayers. There are, of course, communal laments in Scripture—not many but a few.[7] But these are a different matter altogether. There are some interesting exceptions—for example, the companions of Jephthah's daughter who bewail her virginity with her—but such communal lament over an individual is not the rule, insofar as one can tell from the text of Scripture.[8]

3. As far as one can tell from Scripture, the lament, that is, the prayer for help, does not seem to be a feature of worship.[9] That may suggest that such prayers of individuals for help in the form of lament do not belong as features of Christian worship. They are prayers to be heard by God, not by others. They arise out of human pain in all sorts of situations, not out of liturgical movement. In most cases the community is not there. Indeed the community is often part of the problem, either in the oppression that members cause or in the shame they create in the one who prays in trouble (see above). The prayer for help is spontaneous, unplanned, wrenched from the experience of pain, but it is not formless. Its aim is to secure help. Its resolution is in words and deeds that transform the situation.

Since that claim is somewhat against the grain of much contemporary thinking, including the voices of others in this volume, let me elaborate briefly with an illustrative example, the story of Hannah in 1 Samuel 1.[10] In that context, we meet her as a barren wife whose husband, Elkanah, has another wife, Penninah, who has several children. Hannah's situation is one of terrible shame. She lives in a world in which a woman's status is very much defined by her role as mother, as someone able to bear children, especially a male heir. The text is explicit about the source of the problem. Twice it says: "The LORD had closed her womb." Her shame is augmented by the treatment of her "rival wife." The story that is told in this chapter recounts how this family would regularly go up to Shiloh for participation in an annual festival. But for Hannah there is nothing festive about the occasion. Her barrenness, already sharply evident alongside her rival, whose children are very visible, is accentuated by Penninah's regular mocking and taunting Hannah because she has no children. We are told that when the family sits down to eat at this feast, Hannah is too depressed to eat and simply cries. Finally she leaves the table and goes to the sanctuary to weep and pray to God. She is deeply distressed. Several aspects of what happens then are worth observing:

a. Hannah's prayer is in the sanctuary and so in a worship setting. But there is no indication that worship is taking place when she prays. The priest Eli is sitting outside the sanctuary and does not even realize the woman is praying. He thinks she is drunk. This is hardly an occasion of worship.

b. The priest's role in this context is not one of liturgical leadership or worship. His location and his response place him in relation to the distressed one and her lament as a pastor and in terms of pastoral care to one who is sorely troubled. While lament and worship may not come together in this instance, lament and ministry clearly do.

c. The priest-pastor is not directly involved at all in the lament. He hears by overhearing. He is brought into the situation in awareness of the private and terrible distress of the woman.

d. The priest-pastor misunderstands what is going on. When, however, he finds out that Hannah is praying in her deep trouble, he knows what is the proper pastoral response: declaration of the good news that the Lord has heard her prayer and she may go in peace.[11]

4. At the heart of the prayer for help as we find it in Scripture is a distinctive conjoining of *question* and *trust*, of protest and acceptance, of fear and confidence. This is the particularity and peculiarity of the biblical laments. We do not have to learn how to complain. We may need to learn how to protest and trust at the same time. In Psalm 22, the one who laments this prayer remembers what her mothers and fathers before her did in this manner:

> In you our ancestors *trusted*;
> they *trusted*, and you delivered them.
> To you they *cried*, and were saved;
> in you they *trusted*, and were not put to shame.
> (vv. 4–5)

There is a stark equation: three times "trusted" and the fourth and parallel term "cried out." The crying out for help in complaint, anger, questioning, and supplication is all an act of trust. How does one spell "trust"? You spell it out in the words of the lament. The passage from Psalm 22 reminds us that to pray in this manner to the God who made us and loves us and never leaves us, who is absent and far away and has left us alone, is one of the primary manifestations of our obedience to the First Commandment, whose fundamental issue, as Luther reminds us, is where we place our ultimate trust.

Recovering the language of lament means finding the possibility of this combination. The prayers of lament are prayers of *persuasion*, full of reasons to try to persuade God to help, so they do not assume God's deliverance; they are also prayers of *trust*, so they do assume God's deliverance. Nowhere is that tension more deeply felt than in the first sentence of Psalm 22, indeed its best-known verse: "My God, my God, why have you forsaken me?" The question about and to God is at its clearest, articulated in its most unambiguous form, in this sentence that gives voice to the real experience of utter God-forsakenness. But it is preceded by the words "My God, my God," an address that assumes a deep personal and continuing relationship. Nowhere else in all the laments can I find this personal address to God repeated as it is here, an emphatic claim of trust that stands in an unbearable but real conflict and tension with the questions that follow. Such tension between question and complaint to God, on the one hand, and expressions of trust and confidence, on the other, belongs not simply to the form of the lament but to the very nature of human existence under God. That is, we live in the tension between fearfulness in the face of the contingency of life, and trust in the ground of our being, that God's providential blessing and saving help in time of trouble can be counted on, even in the terror when there is no sign of them. This is perhaps the most radical form of the dialectic of faith.

So to recover the language of lament is to learn to pray as if there is no God around anywhere who can or will do anything about our situation—except possibly to make it worse—and it is to pray as if God is always listening and can be trusted to help. These are not two different prayers; they are together. Sometimes the question dominates, as in Job; sometimes the confidence dominates, as in many of the psalmic laments. Sometimes God's abandonment is real; sometimes it is what is felt and seems most real. But the story of Job makes it clear that the questions are just as true to the conversation with God as are the statements of confidence. We cannot ever forget the judgment of the Lord: it is Job, Job with his protests—not his friends, not the theologians with their answers—who "has spoken rightly of me" (Job 42:7).

THE VOICE OF CHRIST

So the laments are the voice of human existence before God, even for those who do not know God and in their crying out claim in suffering what they do not claim in blessing—that God is there and matters to our life. The church, however, has regularly placed the psalms, including the laments, on the lips of Christ. So there is *another voice* that prays these prayers—though it is not really another voice. And that is the first crucial meaning of our hearing these prayers now from the mouth of Jesus. The human lament on the lips of Jesus is one of the primary *incarnational* clues in all of Scripture. When the New Testament hears the laments in Jesus' voice, this is not simply a prophetic and messianic move. Something even more fundamental is going on. For what this means is that all the cries for help that have come forth and still come forth from human lips, all the laments that we have uttered and will utter, are taken up in the laments of Christ.

In the Gospel accounts of Jesus' passion, Psalm 22 and other laments are cited or alluded to in detail as a way of claiming a direct relationship between their words and what happened to Jesus. We hear these psalms now not only as giving voice to the human reality, but also as the words and deeds of the God who in Jesus Christ has become one with our humanity and in so doing has shaped forever the way in which we understand both who we are and what God is about. The incarnation is a declaration of God's oneness with us and our condition. The cry of Jesus is a declaration that this really is one of us, who, as Psalm 103 tells us, "knows our frame" (v. 14 RSV) because he has borne our sorrows and suffered with us. To understand the incarnation and death of Jesus through the prism of the lament psalms is to know that both the incarnation and Jesus' death are his identification with all those innocent/righteous/faithful sufferers who have experienced the pain of human existence, the terrible absence and silence of God, and human torment, oppression, mockery, and reproach. In Jesus' death, the crucified God takes up all that suffering and becomes one with it. It is now in the very heart and being of God. The death of Jesus is the confirmation of the claim of Scripture that God knows our suffering. God knows it as one who has experienced it and as one whose child has gone through it. That is, whoever experiences what Psalm 22 or Psalm 69 speaks about knows now that is a reality known also to God. This is what we mean by a theology of the cross. Luther called it the *revelatio sub contrario specie,* "the revelation [of God] under the appearance of the opposite," or as one Lutheran scholar has aptly translated his words, "finding God in the last place we would reasonably look."[12]

But the lament opens to us not only the meaning of the *person* of Christ. The lament is also critical for understanding *the work of God* in Jesus Christ, for it is our chief clue that Christ died not simply as one *of* us but also as one *for* us, both *with* us and *in our behalf.* As we hear our human voice of lament on the lips of the dying Jesus, it now becomes crystal clear: Jesus died for our *suffering* as much as for our *sins*. In the Gospels, the interpretive clue from the Old Testament for the meaning of the death of Jesus is not a rehearsal or a recall of Genesis 3 but the lament psalms. In seeking to understand the meaning of the death of Christ, we have listened primarily to those voices of Scripture that speak of it as atonement for our sins, as the justification of the unrighteous. There are texts that indeed tell us about that. But the reading of the death of Jesus in relation to the prayers of lament tells us that the power of the resurrection is not over sin alone but also over death and all its many manifestations within human life. To recover the place of lament is finally not simply a matter of our own prayers but of learning at the deepest level the meaning of God's vindication of the suffering of Christ in the resurrection. It is as much our hope in the face of *pain* as it is in the face of *sin*.

There is then a further word to be said about the lament as the prayer of Christ. If our human prayers now become the prayers of Christ and enter into the heart of God, is there any sense in which Christ's prayers now become our prayers? Do they teach us to pray? When the disciples asked Jesus to teach them to pray, he did so. I would suggest that his teaching did not stop with the Lord's

Prayer. One of the things we learn so clearly from Paul and Luther and Bonhoeffer is that the teaching of Jesus was not confined to his life, that he taught us also from the cross. I would suggest, therefore, that his words from the cross continue to teach us how to pray.

The words we know best are the complaint at the beginning of Psalm 22: "My God, my God, why have you forsaken me?" I have already indicated how important these words are for understanding the lament as human voice and as the voice of Christ. Our tendency, however, is to stop with this cry of dereliction—and trust—and not pay that much attention to the other words Jesus utters in his suffering. I am not going to focus on all of them, but I do want to call attention to the other *prayers* that come from Jesus' lips in that unspeakable agony—unspeakable except in prayer. In Matthew and Mark, we hear only that Jesus cried out before he died. In John and Luke, however, we hear other prayers of lament from his dying lips. So the Gospel of John reports Jesus praying the words of Psalm 69, "I thirst," a testimony to the long hours of suffering, the mocking of the bystanders, and the exacerbation of his suffering in the offer of sour wine or vinegar to alleviate the excruciating thirst. In Luke we hear that Jesus' final crying out with a loud voice (what Psalm 22 calls "the words of my roaring"[13]) was once more in the words of a psalmic lament, this time from Psalm 31: "Father, into your hands I commend my spirit" (Luke 23:46). Whereas the cry from Psalm 22 is the roar of protest and questioning, and the complaint of thirst is the testimony to the long hours of horrendous suffering, the *final* cry of Jesus is where the psalm of lament ends up, the protest placed now and always within and under trust in God.

Luke tells us, however, that there is one other prayer from the cross. It is Jesus' words to his Father as the nails are hammered into his hands and feet: "Father, forgive them; for they do not know what they are doing" (Luke 23:34). In the Luke–Acts story of Jesus and the early church, there is no doubt that in this prayer the community of faith learns how to pray. For we hear words just like these in one of the earliest postresurrection prayers. They are the final words of the dying Stephen as he is stoned by the crowds who became enraged by his sermon: "Lord, do not hold this sin against them" (Acts 7:60). The prayer for others from the cross has become now the prayer of the disciple, especially before the terror of death at the hands of others.

As the lament becomes the voice of Christ, therefore, three things happen that now shape our own prayer:

1. In his own praying, Jesus exemplifies the depths of despair and forsakenness and also the profoundest and simplest trust that hands over one's life and story, one's suffering and hopelessness, into the hands of God—and that in the only way possible: in prayer. Christ's praying on the cross puts its stamp upon the mode of prayer we learn from the Psalter: the raging and despairing anger and questions thrown at God *and* the simplest and utter confidence and trust in God's care. This word from the cross is not a new word. It is confirmation that if our Lord can

pray that way, so can we. It is indeed the only way we can pray. For we cannot let go of the questions, and we cannot let go of the trust.

2. But to hear these prayers now in the voice of Christ radically transforms our suffering and changes its face. The face of suffering for us is now the face of Christ. It is no less real for us than it was for him. But he has walked that way before us and walked that way for us. So we do not ever walk that way alone. We know how terrible it was for him, so we know we cannot avoid that terror when it strikes us. But we know also that it was not the last word for him. So our human suffering is terrible and our cries still roar, but neither the suffering nor the cries are the last word.

3. And if I see now the face of suffering not simply in a mirror but in the face of Christ, it is now not my own suffering that I see. It is the suffering of the other. So finally Christ teaches us a new mode of crying out, a crying out in behalf of others.

THE VOICE OF THE WORLD

Listening to the voice of Christ is what teaches us to listen to the voice of the world. Our own cries for help cannot simply disappear. They are our human voice. But listening to the prayers of Christ helps us begin to hear more loudly and more clearly the laments of the world. The imitation of Christ attunes our ears to hear the anger and despair, the loneliness and terror of others, more loudly now than our own. Christian faith learns from Christ to be able to say to the world: *Your* suffering matters even more than my own. It is in this way, I would argue, that the lament comes fully and strongly into Christian worship, not in our prayers of loneliness and despair, which cannot be controlled and scheduled and do not belong to the gathering of the community in praise and thanksgiving. That community does indeed cry out for help, but its prayer takes a different form. The prayer of the community gathered in the presence of God and around the Table commemorating the suffering of Christ in our behalf, that prayer is not the lament of Scripture. Or to put it more precisely, the prayer of the community is now the lament that has become intercession.

This does not mean that we pray differently, that the rage and despair, the questions and trust are not still at the heart of our prayers. Quite the contrary. Two small experiences have made me aware that while the face of the sufferer may be different, our language and form are still the language and form of lament. One was in the context of studying about prayer with a group of theological students, where I asked the students to write an imprecatory prayer, a curse prayer against their enemies. As you might imagine, the response to that assignment—and I am not sure it was a very helpful assignment—was quite varied. Some refused to do what I asked; some said they tried and could not. Several students, however, wrote powerful prayers of rage and despair and anger at God, prayers that called for God's wrath and judgment against those who could only be called the wicked and the enemies. They were truly reminiscent of that particular brand of lament encountered in the imprecatory or curse psalms. In every instance, however, these prayers were prayers of *solidarity with a neighbor*, either one well known or one representative of suffering. The raging prayer of curse was still there, but it had now become a prayer in behalf of the suffering of others.

The other experience happened on Youth Sunday at our church. Several young people participated in the service, including one who was especially at ease, articulate, and able to communicate with some flare and poise. She spoke for just a few minutes, very impressively, and then led the congregation in prayer. As she came to the point when she lifted up before God the suffering of the children of Afghanistan and Palestine and the Sudan who do not have homes, she broke down. She finished her prayer, but with tears and with difficulty. Only a few days later I heard an older person praying a similar prayer, who finally was simply unable to continue because of the tears of sadness and despair before the terrible plight of these people. I realized then that in both instances I had heard what I so rarely hear in our worship—certainly not in my own prayers in the leadership of worship—a genuine anguish in praying to God for God's presence and God's deliverance in the face of the trouble of the world. The rivers of weeping flowed on as these two women literally "cried out" their laments for the world.

Finally, I would like to come back to Abel's "prayer," the blood of the dead Abel crying out to God from the ground on which Cain had murderously spilled it. If the laments are cries for help, they are also cries for justice. So are our prayers for the dead, for those nameless children whose lives are cut short, for those young men who die by the thousands on fields of battle, for those women whose lives are cut short by abusive husbands or who are stoned to death because a man has raped them. For all these and many more, we listen in the silence for their cries for justice that go up to God, and we join them in their laments. Our dirges and our laments give voice to their silent cries for justice.

But I believe we do that in hope. I have been helped in this regard by Jürgen Moltmann, who has written these words:

> I think of the life of those who were unable to live and were not allowed to live: the beloved child dying at birth; the little boy run over when he was four; the sixteen-year-old friend torn to pieces by a bomb as he stood beside you, a bomb that left you unscathed; and all the many people who have been raped and murdered and exterminated. . . .
>
> The idea that for these people their death is the finish would surely plunge the whole world into absolute absurdity; for if their lives had no meaning, have ours? The modern notion about a "natural death" may be appropriate enough for members of the affluent society, with their life insurances, who can afford a death in old age. But in the countries of the Third World most people die a premature, violent, and by no means affirmed death, like so many people of my generation who died in the Second World War. . . .
>
> I believe that God will [also] complete the work that he has begun with a human life. If God is God, even violent death cannot stop him from doing

so. So I believe that God's history with our lives will go on after our deaths, until that completion has been reached in which a soul finds rest.

Those whom we call the dead are not lost. But they are not yet finally saved either. Together with us who are still alive, they are hidden, sheltered, in the same hope, and are hence together with us on the way to God's future. They "watch" with us, and we "watch" with them. That is the community of hope shared by the dead with the living, and by the living with the dead.[14]

I have heard something similar in even more poetic form from a less traditional theological source. One of our best detective story writers today is James Lee Burke, whose locale is the Louisiana bayous and whose regular protagonist is a detective named Dave Robicheaux. In the particular novel I have in mind, the title of which comes from the conclusion to the passage quoted here, Robicheaux's wife has been killed because of his involvement with some criminals. He has an adopted child named Alafair, and at this particular point he tells about watching a movie with her and says these words:

> In the glow of the movie screen I looked at Alafair's upraised and innocent face and wondered about the victims of greed and violence and political insanity all over the world. I have never believed that their suffering is accidental or a necessary part of the human condition. I believe it is the direct consequence of corporate avarice, the self-serving manipulations of politicians who wage wars but never serve in them themselves, and, perhaps worse, the indifference of those of us who know better.
>
> . . . [O]ne image from a photograph I had seen as a child seemed to encapsulate the dark reverie I had fallen into. It had been taken by a Nazi photographer at Bergen-Belsen, and it showed a Jewish mother carrying her baby down a concrete ramp toward the gas chamber while she led a little boy with her other hand and a girl of about nine walked behind her. The lighting in the picture was bad, the faces of the family shadowy and indistinct, but for some reason the little girl's white sock, which had worked down over her heel, stood out in the gloom as though it had been struck by a shaft of gray light. The image of her sock pulled down over her heel in that cold corridor had always stayed with me. I feel the same way when I relive Annie's death, or remember Alafair's story about her Indian village, or review that tired old film strip from Vietnam. I commit myself once again to that black box that I cannot think myself out of.
>
> Instead, I sometimes recall a passage from the Book of Psalms. I have no theological insight, my religious ethos is a battered one; but those lines seem to suggest an answer that my reason cannot, namely that the innocent who suffer for the rest of us become anointed and loved by God in a special way; the votive candle of their lives has made them heaven's prisoners.[15]

NOTES

1. The contemporary church has listened to this story too much in relation to issues of sexuality and failed to perceive it for what it really is, a story of the compassion and righteousness of God in the face of suffering and injustice.

2. See Patrick D. Miller, *They Cried to the Lord: The Form and Theology of Biblical Prayer* (Minneapolis: Fortress Press, 1994), esp. chap. 3.
3. Scarry, *The Body in Pain: The Making and Unmaking of the World* (New York: Oxford University Press, 1985).
4. Ibid., 6.
5. L. Cunningham, "Old Prayers Made New," *Theology Today* 44 (1987): 362.
6. See, e.g., Nancy Lee, *The Singers of Lamentations: Cities under Siege from Ur to Jerusalem to Sarajevo*, Biblical Intepretation Series (Leiden: Brill, 2002); F. W. Dobbs-Allsopp, *Weep, O Daughter of Zion: A Study of the City-Lament Genre in the Hebrew Bible*, Analecta Biblica (Rome: Editrice Pontificio Istituto Biblico, 1993); and Dobbs-Allsopp, *Lamentations*, Interpretation (Louisville, KY: Westminster John Knox, 2002).
7. See in this regard, in addition to works cited in the preceding note, Walter C. Bouzard, *We Have Heard with Our Ears, O God: Sources of the Communal Laments in the Psalms*, SBL Dissertation Series (Atlanta: Scholars Press, 1996).
8. In this regard, see the proposal of Erhard Gerstenberger that lament took place in a kind of small group setting and was aimed at the rehabilitation of the one in trouble into the full community (*Der bittende Mensch* [Neukirchen—Vluyn: Neukirchener Verlag, 1980]). For brief discussion of his proposal, see P. D. Miller, *Interpreting the Psalms* (Philadelphia: Fortress Press, 1986), 6–7.
9. This is not a fully settled matter. But the biblical data point in that direction, especially if one considers not only the lament psalms but also the many prayers for help of the same genre as psalmic laments in the narrative texts of the Old Testament.
10. For more extended discussion of this text and the issues dealt with here, see P. D. Miller, "Prayer and Worship," *Calvin Theological Journal* 36 (2001): 54–57. Reprinted in Miller, *The Way of the Lord: Essays in Old Testament Theology*, Forschungen zum Alten Testament 39 (Tübingen: Mohr Siebeck, 2004), 203–13.
11. Many translations interpret Eli's response as a blessing wish, "May the God of Israel grant your petition." It is just as likely, if not more likely, that he says: "The Lord has granted your petition." The Hebrew can be read both ways. Reluctance to translate thus may reflect the translators' hesitancy to claim such certitude on the part of the priest-pastor. That fails, however, to understand the typical response to human prayers, which is "Don't be afraid, I will help you." See Miller, *They Cried to the Lord*, chap. 4.
12. Timothy Wengert, "'Peace, Peace Cross, Cross': Reflections on How Martin Luther Relates the Theology of the Cross to Suffering," *Theology Today* (2002): 205.
13. The word *groaning* at the end of verse 2 in the NRSV is better translated as *roaring*.
14. Jürgen Moltmann, "Is There Life after Death?" in *The End of the World and the Ends of God: Science and Theology on Eschatology* (Harrisburg, PA: Trinity Press, 2000), 252–53.
15. James Lee Burke, *Heaven's Prisoners* (New York: H. Holt, 1988), 199–200.

Chapter 3

When Lament Shapes the Sermon

Sally A. Brown

"Human beings are born to trouble just as sparks fly upward." So said sages of old (Job 5:7). One could say that nearly the entire biblical witness has emerged in that space bounded by two fundamental realities of human existence: God and trouble. In the biblical tradition, wrestling with trouble in the presence of God has produced, among other genres, a rhetorically and theologically distinctive mode of prayer and theological reflection, the prayer of lament.[1]

Kathleen Billman and Daniel Migliore define lament as "that unsettling biblical tradition of prayer that includes expressions of complaint, anger, grief, despair and protest to God."[2] Evoked by a great range of experiences of affliction, individual or community-wide, biblical laments are most fundamentally prayers for divine help.[3] Lament prayers, individual and corporate, comprise over one-third of the Psalter and are generously represented elsewhere in the canon as well.[4] Psalms of lament are on the lips of the dying Jesus (Psalm 22:1) and provide an interpretive framework for the manner of his death (compare Mark 15:24, 31, 36 and Ps. 22:18; 22:7–8; and see Ps. 69:21).[5]

The prominence of such prayers in the Bible alerts us that faith truly grounded in the biblical tradition does not dodge suffering and evil by invoking a rhetoric of shallow triumphalism calculated to anaesthetize pain, drown doubt, and rationalize injustice.[6] Biblical lament addresses God in the full anguish of suffering; yet it does not end there. It presses on, interrogating the causes of suffering and crying out for God's help.

Yet lament psalms are seldom said or sung in regular Sunday worship. When they find their way into the weekly cycle of readings, the most extreme expressions of anger are often excised.[7] Compounding this eclipse of biblical lament in liturgy is the fact that many preachers bypass these psalms in their preaching.[8] In the last two decades, a chorus of voices has urged the church to reclaim the psalms of lament in Christian worship, pastoral care, and personal devotion, arguing that congregations unfamiliar with biblical lament will lack the rhetorical, psychological, or theological resources for honest engagement with God in the face of trouble.[9] I want to suggest in the pages to follow that biblical lament needs to shape not only the prayer and caregiving of today's church, but its preaching.

RECLAIMING LAMENT IN THE PULPIT

Mary Catherine Hilkert has argued that lament needs to be part of our pulpit speech. While grace is most certainly the dominant note of the gospel, says Hilkert, "the word of grace that all human beings, not only churchgoers, long to hear cannot be spoken too quickly."[10] At the heart of gospel preaching stands the cross. Christian hope is anchored in a God who has entered utterly into suffering and grief.[11] News of grace and resurrection rings hollow disconnected from daily realities of loss, dispossession, and yearning for justice. Testifying to the God of Easter requires the language of lament.

Yet reclaiming specifically *biblical* lament in preaching means more than acknowledging grief and anger in the pulpit. Biblical lament prayers are a complex rhetoric that radically engages suffering, wrestling deeply with its effects on human relationships, including the human-divine relationship. Specific characteristic rhetorical elements, or tropes, recur in biblical laments, and while not every lament includes every element, many laments exhibit a relatively consistent two-part pattern, moving from plea to praise. The flow of these prayers from complaint, petition, and imprecation toward hope can be mapped as follows:[12]

I. Plea
   a. Address to God (called upon as one who hears and will help)
   b. Complaint (including cries of anguish as well as interrogation of God, sometimes holding God accountable for the trouble)
   c. Petition (action needed)
   d. Motivation clauses giving reasons warranting divine action (which may include protestations of righteousness on the part of the supplicant)
   e. Protest/Imprecation against adversaries

II. Praise
    a. Affirmation that God will hear
    b. Vow to praise when help has come
    c. Doxology[13]

Clearly then, while laments express mourning and anger, those who pray these prayers also interrogate the root causes of suffering, cry out for justice, and ask searching questions about God's attitude toward suffering and sufferers. While the psalmists at times protest their innocence before God, these protestations are often tempered with self-examination.

Some features of these psalms, such as curses against perceived adversaries and claims to personal blamelessness, make us hesitant to include these laments in public worship. Yet I would contend that when we allow our critical engagement with God and suffering to be informed by the full range of rhetorical tropes that comprise these prayers, we will stand a better chance of grappling honestly with suffering and our reactions to it. We will take suffering and its effects seriously, making it less likely that our experience will be prematurely "undercut by joy," to borrow Gail Ramshaw's arresting phrase.[14]

While biblical laments no doubt arose in specific situations, their fairly stereotypical language is an open invitation to appropriate them in our own prayer and theological reflection. Some bear editorial superscriptions identifying them, for example, with events in the life of David—a clear precedent for appropriating these laments in relationship to our own experience.[15] What is at stake, then, in preaching on a lament psalm, is not so much to "explain" the psalm—much less, to explain away language with which we are uncomfortable—but to allow the psalm to function as a hermeneutical lens through which preacher and congregation can interpret the complex web of feelings and impulses that attend present experiences of suffering and loss.

Lament can shape the sermon in at least four distinct ways. I will argue that a biblical lament as a whole can provide a hermeneutical framework, or map, for a sermon that journeys deeply into suffering and its many-sided effects on our relationships, including our relationship with God. However, depending on homiletical context and purpose, one particular feature of biblical lament may be dominant. A *pastoral* lament sermon whose purpose is to name and embrace the present experience of loss and disorientation will stress the cry of anguish and plea for help in biblical lament. The *critical-prophetic* lament sermon will accent biblical lament's tropes of protest, imprecation, and self-examination. The *theological-interrogatory* sermon will focus on the interrogation of the divine nature and purpose that is a feature of many laments.

Four sermons preached on September 16, 2001, the Sunday following the devastating terrorist attacks of September 11, will serve to illustrate these four approaches. The sermon text for all four sermons was Psalm 137, yet each preacher responded to the needs of a particular context. What emerged was four distinctly different sermons to help particular congregations find a way forward in those challenging days.

THE LAMENT PSALM AS HERMENEUTICAL MAP

One reason that lament prayers appear so infrequently in Christian worship is that they employ language that congregations today find foreign or even offensive. A preacher's first instinct, when confronted with a biblical prayer of lament, is to select certain elements of the psalm for preaching and leave others aside. Yet it is in grappling with the rhetoric of lament in all its strangeness that we and our congregations stand the best chance, not only of confronting the uglier aspects of our own reactions to suffering, but of understanding the suffering of others and the anger others feel.

A sermon following the pattern of a lament psalm will typically begin, like the lament psalm itself, by naming the juxtaposition of suffering and divine presence—at once the source of our hope and the source of our disquiet. Whatever our trouble, the lament tradition insists, it matters to God. Suffering plunges us into a high-stakes, nonoptional dialogue with God. Once we have placed ourselves squarely in the space bounded by God and trouble, the complaint itself begins. Naming suffering in concrete and unflinching terms is crucial. This can take the form of testimony from sufferers themselves (with the permission of those involved). We need to name trouble no less vividly than the psalmists, who use striking images and hyperbole to express the extremity of their distress.

When lament psalms move on from complaint to name and curse the "enemy," preachers and congregations flinch. Biblical sufferers do not hesitate to "name names," specify the injustices they have suffered, and invoke divine power against their detractors. I would contend that it is precisely our tendency to recoil at these rhetorical moves in the prayer of lament that makes them so valuable as lenses through which to examine the dark complexities of human suffering and its effects. These passages mirror for us our own impulse to blame and punish.

Larry Silva points out that imprecatory utterances figure in the vocabulary of Jesus and were intended "to call for radical change in the ways of those who heard him."[16] Jesus inveighs against the hypocrisy of leaders in the religious establishment and castigates his disciples for faithless waffling. Human agents, individual and collective, cause untold suffering. At the same time, we are put off—and rightly so—when a preacher pins the blame for natural disaster or epidemic on select members of society. Human sin and evil comprise a complex web that includes us all. Finger-pointing in the pulpit is not a new phenomenon. Even so sensitive a preacher as Martin Luther, who typically stressed empathy with sufferers and downplayed imprecation in the psalms of lament, occasionally made imprecation the springboard for anti-Semitic or anti-Catholic diatribes.[17]

Preachers need to keep in mind (and teach) that psalms of lament are *prayer*—not, in and of themselves, proclamation. By taking seriously imprecatory language, we lay the full destructive potential of our suffering before God. The psalmists rage against adversaries—and we recognize our own vindictive impulses, which need to be admitted and addressed in the company of the church. Today, "naming the enemy" can also mean anguishing over the unsolved riddles of disease, exposing the systems of power, social and economic, that cause or exacerbate suffering, and confessing our own complicity in webs of evil.

Nearly as difficult for contemporary worshippers as imprecation are passages where biblical sufferers rail against God's silence, inaction, or apparent absence and cite their own blamelessness as a spur to divine action.[18] Walter Brueggemann reminds us that the language of biblical lament is ruggedly dialogic. Laments are "the abrasive, insistent speech of faith that evokes the limit of God" in the face of chaos, says Brueggemann. Biblical faith does not meet trouble and abuse with mute submission. In lament, we accept our role as "mature covenant partners" with God who lay strident claim on the measureless Mercy poised just behind the silence. Struggling with God in our pain, we stand in a long tradition that includes Jesus himself, who wrestled in agony with God in the garden. "Biblical faith," writes Brueggemann, "is never in favor of pious silence. It is rather for direct, assertive, insistent demand that refuses to sit silently while the waters rise."[19]

Fundamentally, biblical laments are prayers of trust that God is ever attentive to the cry of the sufferer. The vast majority of biblical laments include expressions of trust in God and hope for a time when all shall be made right.[20] Yet the preacher's affirmation of divine care in a lament sermon needs to be appropriate and sensitive. We may need to whisper, not shout. Disease may continue its implacable advance. Mourners may dwell in the valley of shadows for many dark days before Easter's light touches them. Many battles for justice will not be won in our lifetime. Yet all Christian preaching is preaching in light of God's irrevocable promise in Jesus Christ to quench the powers that destroy creation and to wipe away our tears. To this promise, all preaching, even lament preaching, must ultimately bear witness.

The hope we declare needs to be distinctly Christian hope. Christian preachers do not announce the triumph of the human spirit (incredibly resilient though sufferers often prove to be) or that "love conquers all" (although love may indeed mitigate much evil). Faith-driven, God-directed lament, in laying its case on heaven's doorstep, seeks the ultimate healing of creation's suffering in its many forms not in the research lab, the United Nations, or innate human goodness, but in the God whose most eloquent pledge of fidelity is the cross, in One who promises to be with us through pain and beyond.

LAMENT AS HERMENEUTIC FOR SUFFERING: SEPTEMBER 16, 2001

What might it look like when a psalm of lament functions as the hermeneutical lens for confronting a situation of crisis and suffering? Just such a sermon was preached by Brant S. Copeland on September 16, 2001. Five days earlier, on September 11, terrorists seized the controls of four airliners, crashing them into the Pentagon, the World Trade Center towers, and the Pennsylvania countryside. On the Sunday following, congregations across the United States gathered in profound shock and grief, weeping, praying, and hoping against hope for a word from the pulpit to anchor them in the heaving tides of anger, grief, and fear.

In this critical moment, Copeland, pastor of First Presbyterian Church of Tallahassee, Florida, chose to preach on Psalm 137, a communal lament raw with sorrow and rage. Copeland allowed the psalm to guide him and his congregation as they sought a foothold amid the sorrow and dismay of those days. Copeland's sermon undertakes a sustained interpretation of the congregation's anguish, moving back and forth between the rhetoric of Psalm 137 and the congregation's experience.

Copeland begins by naming in simple terms the profound crisis and sorrow of the congregation and then turns immediately to the psalm, saying, "I know of no clearer guide to the journey than Psalm 137." As for Israel in exile, so for people of faith in the wake of September 11: "The landscape has changed, and they have lost their voice for singing." The lament for the city of Zion brings into focus the fallen walls and towers in New York and Washington. "We should never have placed our confidence in walls and towers and markets. They had no power to keep us safe. They were not proof of God's special blessings on us after all. Now those symbols, idols as much as icons, lie in ruins. . . . What shall we sing?" We have a choice, says Copeland. "Shall we try as best we can to reconstruct our former faith on those ruined symbols, or shall we invite God's Spirit to build our faith on something better, something everlasting?"

Certainly, Copeland affirms, the psalm gives vent to rage and acknowledges with shocking frankness the impulse toward revenge. (The psalm is well known for its petition that the infants of the enemy should be dashed against the rocks.) Indeed, says Copeland, one option is to "sing of revenge . . . of mass destruction . . . of hate for outsiders and expulsion of aliens among us." While Psalm 137:9 could be taken as warrant for such vengefulness, says Copeland, the very fact that it occurs in a psalm—in other words, *in prayer*—points to another option: "God invites us to sing these words so that we can offer them to God instead of putting them into practice. . . . As honest lament these words are sacred. As national policy they are the wrong road to follow." Handing our instincts for revenge over to God opens other possibilities, says Copeland—weeping with those who weep, moving ahead in the footsteps of Christ and the company of the saints, sustained by bread and wine. "God will show us the way home," Copeland concludes. "We will not dwell in Babylon forever."[21]

Copeland wisely allows Psalm 137 to interpret the congregation's experience at two levels. At one level, the images of the psalm function to illuminate aspects of this experience of suffering: grief, misplaced confidence in walls and towers, and human instincts for vengeance. Yet Copeland also helps the congregation recognize that Psalm 137 is indeed prayer and not warrant—much less, a template—for retaliatory action. Rather, in prayer, vengeance is relinquished to the One able to absorb grief's wrath and make us agents of transformation.

THE LAMENT SERMON AS CRY OF ANGUISH, CRY OF RESISTANCE, OR THEOLOGICAL INTERROGATION

The strategy of Copeland's sermon—a deliberate, intertextual rereading of present suffering guided by a psalm of lament—is but one way that biblical lament may shape the sermon. Distinctly different sermons suited to various contexts and purposes result when preachers foreground one element in the basic lament pattern. Three prominent features of the rhetoric of lament—anguished complaint, cries for justice, and interrogation of God—can become the guiding motif for the three types of lament sermon described earlier—pastoral, critical-prophetic, and theological-interrogatory.[22]

How the preacher appropriates a biblical lament for any occasion will depend on factors of timing and context. The validation of human grief and anger, mobilizing energies of protest and resistance, or examining God's relationship to sufferers and suffering are all aspects of the human struggle with pain and loss. Thus each mode of lament preaching may find its place as a preacher journeys with a congregation through suffering. Tears of grief and cries for justice are often closely linked; and both, unrequited, give way to deep struggles over the trustworthiness of God. Part of the preacher's task is to dwell deeply enough with both the suffering at hand and lament texts to discern the fitting "word of the Lord" for any given moment. Just such discernment in the days between September 11 and September 16, 2001, led three preachers to write quite different sermons on a single psalm text. All three chose, as did Copeland, Psalm 137 as the day's preaching text. Yet the different sermons that emerged demonstrate clearly the homiletical possibilities when pastoral, critical-prophetic, or theological-interrogatory aspects of lament rhetoric are stressed.

In Princeton, New Jersey, Dr. David A. Davis stepped to the pulpit of Nassau Presbyterian Church on September 16 knowing that he was facing a congregation in shock. New York City is but a short train commute from Princeton. Sitting in the pews were children who did not know if their schoolmates' mothers or fathers would ever come home. Some present had been in New York City when the planes hit. They themselves, or people they knew well, had fled the World Trade Center covered in ash and spattered with blood. Davis responded to the acute pastoral mandate of the occasion with a *pastoral* lament sermon on Psalm 137.

He began that morning by connecting the tears and outrage of Psalm 137 with the tears and outrage so palpable in the congregation before him. "By the rivers of Babylon," begins the psalm, "we sat down and wept." Weeping . . . a sense of captivity . . . disorientation in an unfamiliar landscape: in these images Davis found a mirror for the congregation's experience. Moving from there to the plaintive question of the psalm: "How shall we sing the LORD's song in a foreign land?" (v. 4 RSV), Davis asked, with the congregation, what could possibly be the Lord's song in such a land, in such a time? Acknowledging that he, and perhaps many in his congregation, were in a position for the first time truly to understand the raging cry for vengeance for which Psalm 137:9 is well-known ("Happy shall he be who takes your little ones and dashes them against the rock!" RSV), Davis nonetheless concluded that this all-too-human cry cannot be the theme of the Lord's song. Ultimately, said Davis, Psalm 137 is a song of tears, human tears and "the tears of God," mingled together. And though we weep now in a land made strange to us, "by the rivers of Babylon we will surely sing of that break of dawn that comes after the dark night of the soul."[23]

Guided by a profoundly pastoral purpose on the one hand and the raw outcry of Psalm 137 on the other, Davis entered with his congregation into the welter of soul-shredding emotion precipitated by the events of September 11, allowing the biblical lament to mirror and articulate inchoate anger and grief through the images of tears and displacement. Yet, guided hermeneutically by biblical lament, Davis allowed the psalm not only to give grief a voice, but to invoke a boundary on the human impulse to multiply evils in the face of evil. Like sufferers of old, we trust our broken, angry hearts to the God who weeps with us and will not abandon us or the world.

When Dr. Jeremiah A. Wright began his sermon before a largely African American congregation in Chicago on that same Sunday morning, differences of geography and social location shaped his interpretation of Psalm 137. Although Wright, like Davis, took very seriously the congregation's dismay and grief, he ultimately allowed the text to guide a *critical-prophetic* lament sermon that asked penetrating questions about the nature and origin of violence—violence sown and reaped.

Wright began his sermon by connecting the lament of Psalm 137, not with the events of September 11, but with the long history of the suffering of African American people. As Jerusalem's exiles sang by Babylon's waters, so have African exiles sung their laments in the tradition of the spirituals. Songs of exile provided a link for Wright between the psalm, the experience of African Americans, and the tumult of emotions rolling across America in the wake of the terrorist attacks.

For Wright's sermon, the center of gravity in Psalm 137 is the seventh verse ("Remember the day of Jerusalem's fall"). The violence of September 11, Wright suggested, belongs to a chain of violence to which America has added its own links. "We took Africans from their country to build our way of ease. . . . We bombed Grenada. . . . We bombed the black civilian community of Panama. . . . We bombed Iraq, we killed unarmed civilians. . . . We bombed Nagasaki." And now, says Wright, "We are indignant because the stuff we have done overseas is now brought right back into our own front yards. . . . Violence begets violence. Hatred begets hatred, and terrorism begets terrorism." Without denying the grief and outrage, Wright allows the imprecatory call for vengeance of Psalm 137:9 to occasion an inquiry into the roots of violence. "Rather than figure out who we gonna declare war on," says Wright, "maybe we need to declare war on racism. Maybe we need to declare war on injustice. Maybe we need to declare war on greed." Wright concludes that as we grieve, we also can thank God that we have been spared, given "another chance" to undertake self-examination, social transformation, and spiritual adoration.[24] For Wright and his congregation, Psalm 137 guides a forceful *critical-prophetic* inquiry into the complex factors that breed violence and reinvigorates the congregation's commitment to justice and change.

At Hampton Baptist Church, Hampton, Virginia, the morning of September 16, William Powell Tuck also chose Psalm 137 as his text. Although Tuck moved immediately to acknowledge and embrace the grief and outrage of the congregation, his sermon belongs fundamentally to the *theological-interrogatory* genre in lament preaching. Tuck began by explaining that psalms of lament like Psalm 137 "are confrontive and challenging in wanting to know where God is during the time of suffering, injustice, and evil." Taking these features of biblical lament as his point of departure, Tuck explored with his congregation several of the profound issues that acute suffering and evil raise for us. Consecutive sections of the sermon explored a valid view of anger, a valid concept of God's relationship to tragic events, a valid view of evil and of the world, and a valid understanding of the nature and scope of divine power. What we do *not* have in the wake of September 11, in Psalm 137 or elsewhere, said Tuck, is "the answer to the problem of evil and suffering." What we *do* have is "the *Presence* of the eternal God with us."[25] For Tuck, the psalmist's willingness to vocalize rage and interrogate God opens a space for the expression of our own deepest passions and questions.

Today's church needs to reclaim the voice of lament not only in its prayer but in its preaching. The sermons of Copeland, Davis, Wright, and Tuck demonstrate the power and range of lament preaching. To lament is not simply to grieve or mourn. Biblical lament, faith's outcry to God in the grip of trouble, is a rhetoric that wails and rages, protests and interrogates, and finally whispers its hope. Lament discloses at the heart of the biblical tradition a rhetoric of resistance and criticism that has yet to be fully explored, not only as a framework for prayer and preaching, but as a resource for critical and constructive theology. Equally important is the construction of worship practices shaped by lament, providing worshippers with language to forthrightly expose and lift to God in public worship the effects of loss and suffering, oppression and abuse.

No human life is ever exempt from loss and suffering. Today the church prays and bears witness in a world where deep enmities smolder around the globe. Tensions rooted in race, clan, religion, and glaring inequities of power and wealth erupt almost daily with deadly intensity. Amid such realities, a church shaped by biblical lament neither lashes out with brute force nor cowers in mute resignation, but commits itself in anguish and hope to One who bears the grief of all humanity and works with and among us, making all things new.

NOTES

1. Patrick D. Miller underscores that biblical lament is most fundamentally a prayer for divine help, and therefore interpretation of this genre must begin within the framework of biblical prayer. See *Interpreting the Psalms* (Philadelphia: Fortress Press,

1986), 18–28, 48–54. I argue, however, that while lament is first and foremost a form of prayer in the Scriptures, it also functions for the community of faith as a hermeneutical framework for constructive theological reflection in the presence of personal and social suffering.

2. Kathleen D. Billman and Daniel Migliore, *Rachel's Cry: Prayer of Lament and Rebirth of Hope* (Cleveland: United Church Press, 1999), 6.

3. See Miller, *They Cried to the Lord: The Form and Theology of Biblical Prayer* (Minneapolis: Fortress Press, 1994), esp. chap. 3, "Prayers for Help," and chap. 6, "Prayers Women Prayed."

4. For a list of psalms categorized either as individual or community laments and an indication of which verses of these lament psalms are included in the schedule of readings in various lectionaries, see Ivan T. Kaufman, "Undercut by Joy: The Sunday Lectionaries and the Psalms of Lament," in Jack C. Knight and Lawrence A. Sinclair, *The Psalms and Other Studies* (Cincinnati: Forward Movement Publications, 1990), 66–78. For a partial listing of laments outside the Psalter, see Bernard W. Anderson, *Out of the Depths: The Psalms Speak for Us Today*, 3rd edition (Louisville, KY: Westminster John Knox Press, 2000), 50–65. For a discussion of laments (prayers for help) outside the Psalter, see also Miller, *They Cried to the Lord,* chap. 3 and appendix I.

5. For a discussion of other NT laments, particularly in the Synoptic Gospels, see Richard Hughes, "Lament in Christian Theology," *Encounter*, vol. 61, no. 2 (2000): 191–97.

6. As Beth LaNeel Tanner has pointed out, this reality calls into question worship that trades in simplistic optimism and blithe expressions of praise. See "How Long, O Lord! Will Your People Suffer in Silence for Ever?" in Stephen Breck Reid, ed., *The Psalms and Practice* (Collegeville, MN: Liturgical Press, 2001), 144–45.

7. See especially Kaufman's illuminating analysis of the rhetorical and theological effects of lectionary verse selection in particular lament psalms, pp. 72–74.

8. On reclaiming the Psalms for preaching, see J. Clinton McCann Jr., "Thus Says the Lord: 'Thou Shalt Preach on the Psalms,'" in Stephen Breck Reid, ed., *The Psalms and Practice*, 111–22; J. Clinton McCann Jr. and James C. Howell, *Preaching the Psalms* (Nashville: Abingdon, 2001), esp. chap. 7, "The Problem of Pain"; and Thomas G. Long, *Preaching and the Literary Forms of the Bible* (Philadelphia: Fortress Press, 1989), chap. 3, "Preaching the Psalms."

9. See esp. Kathleen D. Billman and Daniel L. Migliore, *Rachel's Cry: Prayer of Lament and Rebirth of Hope*; also Donald Capps, *Biblical Approaches to Pastoral Counseling* (Philadelphia: Westminster Press, 1981), chap. 2, "The Use of Psalms in Grief Counseling"; Dan B. Allender, "The Hidden Hope in Lament," *Mars Hill Review*, vol. 1, no. 1 (Winter–Spring 1995): 25–37; Barbara A. Bozak, "Suffering and the Psalms of Lament," *Eglise et Theologie* 23 (1992): 325–38; Stephen P. McCutchan, "Illuminating the Dark: Using the Psalms of Lament," *Christian Ministry* 24 (March–April 1993): 14–17; Gail Ramshaw, "The Place of Lament within Praise: Theses for Discussion," *Worship,* vol. 61, no. 4 (July 1987): 317–22; Andre Resner, "Lament: Faith's Response to Loss," *Restoration Quarterly*, vol. 32, no. 3 (1990): 129–42; Ann Weems, *Psalms of Lament* (Louisville, KY: Westminster John Knox Press, 1995); and John D. Witvliet, "A Time to Weep," parts I and II, *Reformed Worship* 44 (June 1997): 22–26; and *Reformed Worship* 45 (September 1997): 22–25.

10. Mary Catherine Hilkert, *Naming Grace: Preaching and the Sacramental Imagination* (New York: Continuum, 2000), 109.

11. Ibid., 116–18. See also J. Clinton McCann Jr., *Preaching the Psalms*, chap. 7, "The Problem of Pain."

12. There are notable exceptions, of course. An example is Psalm 88, where the voice of complaint and anger expressed toward adversaries and toward God is unremitting.
13. Brueggemann, *The Message of the Psalms* (Minneapolis: Augsburg Press, 1984), 54–57. Brueggemann draws and builds upon the work of Hermann Gunkel, *The Psalms: A Form-Critical Introduction*, trans. Thomas M. Horner (Philadelphia: Fortress Press, 1967), 14, 20; and Claus Westermann, *The Living Psalms*, trans. J. R. Porter (Grand Rapids: Wm. B. Eerdmans Publishing Co., 1989), 26–35. Miller places the expectation of divine help in the "plea" section of the prayer. See *They Cried to the Lord*, 57, 86–96.
14. See Gail Ramshaw, "The Place of Lament within Praise: Theses for Discussion," 320.
15. Miller, *Interpreting the Psalms*, 22–28. Following this cue, Beth LaNeel Tanner undertakes feminist intertextual readings of psalms of lament with biblical narratives of women's suffering. See *The Book of Psalms through the Lens of Intertextuality* (New York: Peter Lang, 2001), 159–80; and "Hearing the Cries Unspoken: An Intertextual-Feminist Reading of Psalm 109," in Athalya Brenner and Carole Fontaine, eds., *Wisdom and Psalms: A Feminist Companion to the Bible*, 2nd series (Sheffield: Sheffield Academic Press, 1998), 283–301.
16. Larry Silva, "The Cursing Psalms as a Source of Blessing," in Stephen Breck Reid, ed., *The Psalms and Practice*, 223.
17. An example is Luther's lecture on Psalm 69. See Martin Luther, "First Lectures on the Psalms," Hilton C. Oswald, ed., *Luther's Works*, vol. 10 (St. Louis: Concordia Publishing House, 1974), 351–84. But see also Migliore's discussion of Luther's handling of psalms of lament in *Rachel's Cry*, 51–56.
18. Psalm 74 is a good example.
19. Walter Brueggemann, "Deep Waters" (sermon on Ps. 69:2, 13–15), in *The Threat of Life: Sermons on Pain, Power, and Weakness* (Minneapolis: Fortress Press, 1996), 101.
20. A widely noted exception is Psalm 88, where no flicker of hope mitigates the shadows of grief.
21. Brant S. Copeland, "The Lord's Song in Our Own Land," in Bertie Jeffress Powell, ed., . . . *On the Sabbath After* (Richmond: Brandylane Publishers, 2002), 125–27.
22. These three correlate, approximately, with Claus Westermann's three dimensions of the prayer of lament—the self, the others (enemies and witnesses), and God. See Westermann, *The Living Psalms*.
23. David A. Davis, "Sit and Weep," unpublished sermon, preached September 16, 2001, Nassau Presbyterian Church, Princeton, NJ.
24. Jeremiah A. Wright Jr., "The Day of Jerusalem's Fall," in Martha Simmons and Frank A. Thomas, eds., *9.11.01: African-American Leaders Respond to an American Tragedy* (Valley Forge, PA: Judson Press, 2001), 81–91.
25. William Powell Tuck, "Where Is God When Suffering and Evil Reign?" in William H. Duke Jr., ed., *For the Living of These Days: Responses to Terrorism* (Richmond: Center for Baptist Heritage and Studies, 2001), 112–16.

Chapter 4

The Shepherd's Song:
A Sermon

Nancy Lammers Gross

Introduction

The following sermon was prepared for a Lenten service in 2002. It was preached to a congregation located within forty miles of New York City, where many in the community worked. The ongoing grief and world-shattering aftershocks felt by this community as a result of the 9/11 attacks on the World Trade Center towers were compounded by the congregation's concern for their pastor, who was undergoing treatment for a deadly form of cancer—a condition from which he eventually recovered.

My concern in the sermon was to give voice to the sense of hopelessness and despair—the cry of woe—in Psalm 22 to which Psalm 23 is the answer. Psalm 23 is used liturgically, most often, as a balm for grief. I wanted the grief to be expressed and heard in worship, in order that subsequent renderings of Psalm 23 in the life of the church might more fully gather up those expressions of grief.

Today one rarely hears Psalms 22 and 23 yoked together liturgically. Yet in the early church, mourners in funeral processions regularly sang Psalms 22 and 23 on their way to the cemetery where the burial was to take place.[1] While the Roman custom was to hold funerals and burial at night with mourners wearing black clothing, the Christian custom was to wear white and to hold services in the day-light. The emphasis was on God's victory in the resurrection of Jesus Christ from the dead. The human suffering brought about by death and grief and expressed in Psalm 22 is integrally bound up with the hope in God expressed in Psalm 23.

SINGING THE SHEPHERD'S SONG
PSALMS 22 AND 23; JOHN 10:11–18

Psalm 23 is a trip-wired text. It is loaded with freight. It is a storehouse of per-sonal memories. It is a Scripture text that carries all the grief we've had to bear. Psalm 23 is where we go for comfort and reassurance. Psalm 23 is where we go for the age-old memory of the church's reassurance that God is with us, no mat-ter where, no matter what. In time of crisis, Psalm 23 doesn't need interpretation. Even city folk seem to know what it means for the Lord to be my shepherd.

C. S. Lewis remarked of the Psalms that they need "no historical adjustment." The emotion is readily apparent and available to us. And in the case of Psalm 23 it is uttered in situations that fill it with different kinds of meaning.

Whispered over a cell phone in a burning tower or on the air-phone of a doomed flight, Psalm 23 speaks one way. Spoken triumphantly at the memorial service of one of the great saints who has lived a long life of service to the Lord, Psalm 23 speaks another way. Uttered in the silence of one's bedroom in the mid-dle of the night, Psalm 23 speaks still another way. Psalm 23 carries it all—and it is trip-wired because the rendering of the psalm—any rendering of the psalm—can flood you with such memories.

Psalm 23 is the lectionary psalm selection for this, the fourth Sunday in Lent. The lectionary is a suggested list of Scripture readings for every Sunday over a rotating three-year period. In 150 Sundays, one might think all 150 psalms would be read. This is not the case. Some psalms are never read. And some psalms are read repeatedly. Psalm 23 is suggested six times in three years of Sundays; four of the six are either Sundays in Lent or Easter.

Lent and Easter, passion and power, trial and triumph, darkness and light, death and resurrection: Psalm 23.

> The Lord is my shepherd. I shall not want.[2]

Perhaps the most beautiful, most comforting, most familiar, and most mem-orized passage of scripture.

> He maketh me to lie down in green pastures; he leadeth me beside
> the still waters;

We need these words most, and we hear them most often, when life seems most bleak.

> He restoreth my soul.

We need these words most when what we want restored is lost forever.

In the Bible, Psalm 23 doesn't spring up out of nowhere. It has a context. And that context is Psalm 22. Psalm 23 speaks to us more resoundingly when we hear it as an answer to Psalm 22.

> My God, my God, why have you forsaken me?
> (Ps. 22:1)[3]

The anguish of the human condition; the inconsolable grief of the loss of a loved one; the profound helplessness in watching a loved one suffer; the hopelessness of falling into that black hole of despair and wondering if there will ever be a way out . . . these are the depths of human emotion to which Psalm 22 gives voice.

> My God, my God, why have you forsaken me?
> Why are you so far from helping me, from the words of my
>   groaning?
> O my God, I cry by day, but you do not answer;
> and by night, but find no rest.
> (Ps. 22:1, 2)

I was reading in the *New York Times* yesterday about residents of Middletown, New Jersey, who lost loved ones in the World Trade Center attacks. After New York City, Middletown suffered the single greatest loss of life, with thirty-four households losing a family member.

In the fall, the blur of shock and trauma, the public and political nature of their loved ones' deaths, and the outpouring of goodwill and charitable acts, all this gave way to the distractions of Thanksgiving and Christmas and New Year's.

As painful as those first Thanksgiving and Christmas and New Year's celebrations were, none of it compared to what many people are going through now—now that the numbness is wearing off; now that others are getting on with their lives; now that the reality is setting in; now that they have to live into the reality that the husband, wife, mother, father, daughter, son is not coming home.

As one woman reported, "Now it's sinking in that he's gone, and it just keeps getting worse and worse."

The psalmist says,

> I am poured out like water,
>   and all my bones are out of joint;
> my heart is like wax;
>   it is melted within my breast;
> my mouth is dried up like a potsherd,
>   and my tongue sticks to my jaws;
> you lay me in the dust of death.
> (Ps. 22:14, 15)

I am reminded of a conversation years ago in California with the mother of a suicide victim. I was the pastor to a family whose adult son had taken his own life. This mother described her son's experience of day-to-day life. His depression was so acute, he told her it was like falling deeper and deeper into a black hole from which he could not emerge. In the face of such hopelessness and despair, death was his welcome relief.

One of the surviving wives in Middletown, a mother of two toddlers, is now rarely left alone, ever since she confided to a friend last month her desire to "meet her husband in heaven," along with her children.

There may be many years when we take this Lenten journey and it feels more like a pleasant walk in the park. We have to remind ourselves that life isn't always good, when the pain of former grief has subsided.

There may be many years when we take this Lenten journey and never realize we're on a journey at all until we arrive at Easter Day, and the promise of spring and resurrection stands only in mild contrast to the mundaneness of everyday life.

But this isn't one of those years. This is one of those years when we cry out to God like the psalmist,

> Do not be far from me,
>   for trouble is near
> and there is no one to help.
>   (Ps. 22:11)

When a shepherd detected trouble was near his flock, he would gather them in a pen. The pen usually had a stone wall, and the top might be covered with briars. The opening to the pen could often be closed by rolling a big stone across it. This was called a sheepgate. But where there was no stone available, the shepherd himself would lie across the opening, rod in hand, in order to protect the sheep and be ready to club any predator who would dare to get at the sheep.

Shepherds used to actually know their sheep by name. They didn't just count their sheep; they named their sheep. And the sheep knew the shepherd's voice. A hired hand might be employed to watch the sheep for a time, but the hired hand was not obligated to lay down his life for the sheep. The hired hand was not obligated to protect the sheep from wild animal attack.

Jesus said,

> I know my own and my own know me,
> just as the Father knows me and I know the Father.
> And I lay down my life for the sheep.
>   (John 10:14, 15)

There are times in life when we are able to protect ourselves, to get ourselves out of scrapes, to bind up our own wounds, and to smooth over the rough terrain. There are times when the sound of our own voice, or perhaps the voice of a loved one or friend, is comfort enough.

But for so many, perhaps for you, this is not one of those times. The comfort of our families is no small comfort, but it isn't comfort enough. The warmth and goodwill of trusted friends is no small comfort, but it isn't comfort enough.

The sound of the voice of the Shepherd is the one thing needful. And nothing else will do.

But where does that voice come from and what does it sound like? How do we hear that voice in the darkness of night when the demons come, but sleep won't?

In the Old Testament, the various tribes of Israel were thought of as flocks. Jesus sought to reconcile the flocks of Israel. He said in John 10,

> I have other sheep that do not belong to this fold.
> I must bring them also, and they will listen to my voice.
> So there will be one flock, one shepherd.
> (John 10:16)

The voice of the Shepherd sounds like reconciliation. Our deepest distress often comes in the form of brokenness: broken relationship with God; broken relationship with another; brokenness within ourselves. The voice of our Shepherd sounds like reconciliation: healing, forgiveness, binding up old wounds. To hear this voice requires humility, accepting responsibility for ourselves and our actions, forbearing one another in love, even refusing to accept responsibility for another's wrongdoing.

The sound of the Shepherd's voice is the one thing needful. And nothing else will do. Sometimes the Shepherd's voice sounds like reconciliation.

Sometimes the Shepherd's voice sounds like the reminder that all of life is lived in the sphere of grace. That the blackest hole, the deepest despair, the most suffocating grief cannot separate us from the love of God.

In the midst of crying out to God, begging to know why God has forsaken him, the psalmist says,

> Yet it was you who took me from the womb;
>   you kept me safe on my mother's breast.
> On you I was cast from my birth,
>   and since my mother bore me you have been my God.
> (Ps. 22:9, 10)

Even the psalmist, in the midst of feeling desperately abandoned, knows that God is there, God has always been there. We live in the presence of God.

The apostle Paul says in Romans,

> If we live, we live to the Lord,
> and if we die, we die to the Lord;
> so then, whether we live or whether we die,
> we are the Lord's.
> For to this end Christ died and lived again,
> so that he might be Lord of both the dead and the living.
> (Romans 14:8, 9)

The sound of the Shepherd's voice is the one thing needful. And nothing else will do. Sometimes the Shepherd's voice sounds like reconciliation. Sometimes the Shepherd's voice sounds like the reminder that all of life is lived in the sphere of grace.

Sometimes the Shepherd's voice is heard in the glad tidings we receive in the Shepherd's song: You don't have to be afraid.

The psalmist says, I will fear no evil.

The angelic chorus told the frightened and cowering shepherds, Do not be afraid. The Shepherd's voice is heard echoed in the psalmist—I will fear no evil. The Shepherd's voice is heard echoed from the angels—Do not be afraid. And when the Shepherd departed this earth, he said to his disciples—Lo, I am with you always.

Between Do not be afraid and Lo, I am with you always is the very clear direction and guidance of the Shepherd's voice leading through the Scriptures, leading us through the witness of the Holy Spirit in our lives, leading as the community of faith together seeks to discern the will of God and live out the will of God together.

The sound of the Shepherd's voice is the one thing needful, and we will hear the Shepherd's voice increasingly clearly as we follow in the paths of righteousness. God has given us all things.

God the great Shepherd has given us life, God has given us a cool place to lie down, refreshing waters to drink. God restores our souls. We would not need restoration, were it not for the suffering of this earthly walk. God restores our souls precisely because we need it.

The Shepherd's voice is the calm reassurance that no matter where we are, no matter what circumstances conspire to destroy us or bring us down, no matter what danger befalls us, God the great Shepherd is with us. We need fear no evil.

Perhaps the best way to hear the Shepherd's voice is to sing the Shepherd's song. You will find it printed in your bulletin. Let us say it together. We are going to read it slowly, meditatively. I want you to envision the images, soak in the familiar phrases, allow the Shepherd's song to take root in you and do a healing work in you.

Let us read in unison.

Psalm 23

The LORD is my shepherd; I shall not want.
    He maketh me to lie down in green pastures:
        he leadeth me beside the still waters.
           He restoreth my soul:
        he leadeth me in the paths of righteousness for his name's sake.
Yea, though I walk through the valley of the shadow of death,
    I will fear no evil:
        for thou art with me;
           thy rod and thy staff they comfort me.
Thou preparest a table before me in the presence of mine enemies:
    thou anointest my head with oil;
        my cup runneth over.
Surely goodness and mercy shall follow me all the days of my life:
    and I will dwell in the house of the LORD for ever.

Let us pray.

O God, you have known us from our mother's wombs, and you have never left us or forsaken us. We do put our trust in you. We lay before you our burden of illness, of grief, of heavy sorrow, of physical pain and emotional turmoil. We lay before you the burden of worry over loved ones and broken relationships that we cannot seem to fix. We pray you will lift heavy burden, lead us in the paths of righteousness, and keep us all the days of our life in your gracious care, through Jesus Christ our Lord, the great Shepherd of the sheep. Amen.

NOTES

1. James F. White, *A Brief History of Christian Worship* (Nashville: Abingdon Press, 1993), 67.
2. All quotations of Psalm 23 are from the King James Version.
3. All quotations of Psalm 22 are from the New Revised Standard Version.

PART II
LOSS AND LAMENT, HUMAN AND DIVINE

Chapter 5

The Persistence of the Wounds

C. Clifton Black

> O God, what am I going to do?
> He's gone—and I'm left
> with an empty pit in my life. . . .
> How could you have allowed this to happen?
> I thought you protected your own!
> You are the power:
> Why didn't you use it?
> You are the glory,
> but there was no glory in his death.
> You are justice and mercy,
> yet there was no justice, no mercy for him. . . .
> O Holy One, I am confident
> that you will save me. . . .
> You are the power
> and the glory;
> You are justice
> and mercy.
> You are my God forever.[1]

Of all occasions for lament, the death of a child must stand as the parent's most searing. When Ann Weems penned these words after the death of her twenty-one-year-old son Todd, they had to have surfaced from the depths of an anguish that only parents like her could possibly plumb.

I

Rachel knew. So claimed the prophet Jeremiah in a lengthy poetic oracle that surveys the comprehensive slaughter of her grandson Ephraim's children—the northern kingdom, Israel, in 721 BCE—and the exile of her stepson Judah's children—the southern kingdom, in 587 BCE—from Ramah to Babylon (Jer. 30:4–31:22). According to one tradition (1 Sam. 10:2; cf. Gen. 35:20), Rachel had been buried five miles north of Jerusalem, near Ramah. Jeremiah imagines ghostly wailing: Mother Rachel, howling with inconsolable lamentation, for the murder and deportation of all her sons who were no more:

> Thus declared the LORD:
> A cry is heard in Ramah—
> Wailing, bitter weeping—
> Rachel, weeping for her children.
> She refuses to be comforted
> For her children, who are not.[2]
> (Jer. 31:15)

Who would dare restrain a mother from weeping for children who have ceased to be? In fact, according to the prophet, the Lord does just that:

> Thus declared the LORD:
> Restrain your voice from weeping,
> Your eyes from shedding tears;
> For your labor has its reward,
> Declares the LORD:
> They shall return from the enemy's land.
> There is hope for your future,
> Declares the LORD:
> And your children shall come back to their country.
> (Jer. 31:16–17)

Such restraint of a mother's tears lies only in the province of God, who alone can restore that which was not. Jeremiah promises Rachel that her pangs, at her children's death as at their birth, will not prove in vain. That assurance matches the profusion of comforting metaphors that spill out of this oracle: Jacob will be delivered from crushing tribulation (Jer. 30:7); Maiden Israel shall again learn the rhythm of the dance (31:4); Israel's remnant shall be gathered from the earth's farthest reaches (31:8); Jacob shall be redeemed (31:11); Ephraim, punished and moaning, shall be dandled by the constant Parent whose heart never stopped yearning for him (31:18–20). In brief (Jer. 30:3): "Behold, days are coming—

declares the LORD—when I shall restore the fortunes of my people, Israel and Judah, said the LORD; and I shall bring them back to the land that I gave to their fathers, and they shall possess it."

II

Turn the scriptural page. It is some four centuries later. The evangelist Matthew recounts the events surrounding Jesus' birth (1:18–2:23). Unlike Luke's version, in which the sword that will pierce Mary's soul (2:35) is all but submerged by blessings and joy (1:28, 42–48, 68; 2:10, 28), Matthew's infancy narrative bears ineradicable stains of intrigue and murder. The birth of Jesus, David's son and God's truly anointed (Matt. 1:1), is hurled in the teeth of Herod the Great, Israel's nominal and ruthless sovereign (2:1–3). When tricked by the magi, whom he deceived to direct him to Israel's genuine savior (1:22; 2:7–8), in fury Herod mandates infanticide, slaying all of Bethlehem's boys two years old or under (2:16). Gazing upon unspeakable slaughter, Matthew (2:18) hears afresh the voice of Jeremiah:

> *A voice was heard in Ramah,*
> *Loud wailing and grieving—*
> *Rachel, weeping for her children,*
> *And she would not be consoled, for they were not.*

The listener should pause to let the full weight of this lament sink in. Many are the distractions that would divert what must arrest us. Churchgoers may go for years without hearing a sermon that struggles with this passage. Matthew 2:13–23 appears only once in the Revised Common Lectionary: for use on the First Sunday after Christmas Day in Year A, "unless the readings for the Epiphany of the Lord"— which include Matthew 2:1–12—"are preferred."[3] I would wager that they almost always are. And so, if they hear any Scripture at all, worshippers in the pew celebrate Christmas with Luke's far happier story ringing in their by-then-weary ears.

Professional exegetes, without excuse for ignoring Matthew's very different account, may fall into traps of other kinds. For them, Matthew 2:18 has a most convenient pigeonhole: the first evangelist's well-known "formula quotations," five of which are clustered in his infancy narrative.[4] The scholar will also detect in Matthew 2 echoes of Exodus 1:15–2:10, 11:1–10, and 12:29–32. The commentator may note the resemblances of Matthew's scriptural interpretation to that in the Dead Sea Scrolls, murmur something critical or apologetic of its transgression of contemporary exegetical norms, then proceed to another topic. Meanwhile, Bethlehem's mothers join with Rachel in wailing for their children, disconsolate, for they had ceased to be.

A most noteworthy aspect of Matthew's remembrance of Jeremiah at this terrible point is what the evangelist chooses *not* to quote: namely, the prophet's *immediately subsequent* promise that Rachel's tears are dabbed away, because she will get her children back (Jer. 31:16–17).[5] One cannot explain this conspicuous gap with Matthew's inclination to keep things dark, since, as a matter of fact, his formula quotations incline toward sunny assurances:

> "His name shall be called Emmanuel," which is interpreted,
>   "God with us."
> (Matt. 1:23bc)

> "From you [O Bethlehem] shall come a ruler,
> Who will shepherd my people Israel."
> (2:6b)

> "The people who sat in darkness have seen great light,
> And for those who sat in Death's region and shadow
>   light has arisen on them."
> (4:16 [Isa. 9:2])

> "He took our infirmities,
> And he bore our diseases."
> (Matt. 8:17 [Isa. 53:4])

The evangelist's decision in 2:18 to leave Rachel weeping demands a better explanation.

A more satisfying answer lies embedded in the complex material surrounding Matthew's citation of Jeremiah. Before Herod enacts his pogrom, an angel of the Lord appears in a dream to Joseph, informing him of the plot against the child and instructing him to take the child and his mother to Egypt (Matt 2:13). Joseph complies (2:14–15). After Herod's own death, the Lord's messenger returns in a dream to Joseph, redirecting the child to the safety of Galilee, beyond the clutches of Herod's son Archelaus (2:19–23). To be sure, Matthew is strumming an unusually dense theological chord, which interlaces God's particular providence for the infant Jesus' welfare (narrated with the Elohist trappings of divine intervention via dreams and angelic intermediaries), Jesus as Israel *redivivus* (exiled into, then called out of, Egypt), and a rationale for relocating Bethlehem's newborn to Nazareth.

If we listen carefully, however, a dissonant note still penetrates: though Jesus narrowly escapes death by the hand of the political establishment, he isn't delivered to Egypt to hide out forever. The Lord calls his son out of Egypt, not merely to connect the dots with Hosea's oracle, but in order *to send him back* into Death's shadow,[6] where weeping mothers bury their infants for no reason other than that a tyrant felt threatened, into the region where the Messiah's people remain in acute need for salvation.[7] Matthew realizes that a dry-eyed Rachel would be grossly premature. Not only are her children still no more; before long, Mary's child will join them in the nothingness of death.

III

Indeed, the truth about Jesus' own end is harder than "nothingness," which could suggest human quietus as an Epicurean's painless, blissful insentience.[8] In Matthew, as in Mark (15:34), the crucified Jesus' final articulate cry is the psalmist's ultimate lament: "My God, my God, why have you left me in the lurch?" (Matt. 27:46; Ps. 22:1). As bitter a pill as nonexistence is for humans to swallow, it goes down more smoothly than the experience of death as God-forsakenness. Again, we must beware evasive maneuvers that would dull the knife-edged offense: for instance, the suggestion that a quotation from Psalm 22:1 is overwhelmed by that lament's confident conclusion (vv. 22–31). I confess that such an interpretation has never persuaded me. If anything in Psalm 22:22–31 lay nearer the heart of these evangelists' theologies, why, then, did they not put *those* words of hope on the dying Jesus' lips (as, in different ways, Luke and John have opted to do: Luke 23:34, 43, 46; John 19:28, 30)?

It seems to me equally suspect to rush to the Almighty's defense in Matthew and in Mark, protesting that the apocalyptic ambience of their crucifixion accounts demonstrates that God's beloved Son was truly not abandoned at three o'clock that afternoon (Matt. 27:45, 47–49, 51–54; Mark 15:33, 35–38). *Sub specie aeternitatis*, under the appearance of eternity (Spinoza), that is true. *Sub specie cruciatus*, under the aspect of torturous execution, it is no less true—from the evangelists' points of view—that Jesus ultimately, faithfully prayed to a God whose presence he could no longer perceive.

That, surely, is the point of Matthew's nightmare at Golgotha. "All of you will desert me this night" (26:31). All, without exception, did just that: Judas (26:14–16; 25, 46–50; 27:3–10); Peter (26:40, 69–75); Zebedee's sons (26:37, 40–45); the tatters of the Twelve (26:56); sinful dullards, into whose hands the Son of man was delivered (26:45; 27:47–49); Caiaphas and the Sanhedrin (26:57–68); Pilate and his wife (27:15–26); Jewish rabble and Roman guard (27:15, 21–23, 25, 27–31); élite and hoi polloi (27:39–43); crucified bandits, Jesus' fellow victims (27:38, 44). Finally, from the cross comes the cry: "*Eli, Eli, lama sabachthani?* My God, my God, why have you deserted me?" (27:46). Attuned to the undertone of that searing question, one still can hear Rachel's continuous lament for her other lost children: wailing unrelieved, devoid of palliative, lacking immediate answer or solace. At Golgotha, at the unfathomable convergence of human sin and divine intent, the last of Bethlehem's children was slain. The true heir to the throne whom Herod was really after (27:37), Pilate managed to destroy.

That would have been the end of that, had Albert Schweitzer been correct that Jesus' immeasurable greatness lay in his deluded yet heroic martyrdom for a lost cause that could only crush him.[9] Matthew, however, has no truck with such chilled Romanticism. For the first evangelist, Jesus' greatness lies not in a freedom fighter's ultimate self-sacrifice. Jesus was and is the Christ, son of David, son of Abraham, Son of God: the one on whom God's Spirit incomparably rests;

whose righteousness causes heavens to split and a supernal voice to announce to those with hearing ears, "*This* is my beloved Son, with whom I am well pleased" (Matt. 3:13–17). Moses and Elijah appear in the disciples' vision, but only Jesus is transfigured; to him alone must attention be paid, an injunction that collapses weak knees and throws faces to the ground (17:1–8). "All things have been delivered to me by my Father; and no one knows the Son except the Father, and no one knows the Father except the Son and any one to whom the Son chooses to reveal him" (11:27).

Whatever else the evangelist may mean by identifying Jesus as Emmanuel, "God with us" (1:23), surely it means, for Matthew, that Jesus is the solitary hinge on which pivot both heaven and earth, the unique link between God and the church. In Jesus the Christ, theology and ecclesiology are irrevocably joined. Only when we begin to comprehend the extraordinary dimensions of such a claim can we begin to appreciate how devastating the crucified Jesus' cry of dereliction really is. *God-with-us wails in God-forsakenness.* For such a paradox, there is no resolution. There can be only gross human misunderstanding (27:47–49), a dying outcry (27:50), and upheaval the like of which the world has never seen (27:51–53).

IV

Modern readers tend toward embarrassment at Matthew's Technicolor apocalypticism at Golgotha: the rip of the temple's curtain, the earthquake, the splitting of rocks, the graves' disgorgement of dead saints who appear in Jerusalem. Compared with contemporary sensibilities, compared even with the other Gospels, all this seems over the top.[10] Perhaps, however, there is proportion in Matthew's vision. When, crucified and derelict, God-with-us suffers death at its most accursed (Deut. 21:22–23), a single teardrop from heaven will not suffice. The scope of lament implied in Matthew 27:51–54—God's wailing over a tortured creation—corresponds to the magnitude of God's own loss. As André LaCocque observes, the Messiah's death throws the cosmos into convulsions.[11]

If, by chance, one of the saints raised in Jerusalem that day had been an infant butchered by Herod—a tiny, surrogate victim for the true King who had to die so that others would live (Matt. 20:28; 26:26–29)—that little one's resurrection would never have stilled Rachel's weeping. It would only have validated the reason that she too continued to cry. Were Todd Weems returned to the arms of his mother Ann, her lament—even joy-crazed—would persist, precisely because there was neither justice nor mercy, neither power nor glory, in her son's death to start with. So it was with the Father's own beloved Son. And yet, God's actions in Matthew 27:51–53 bespeak no flailing incoherence. There is sense in it, and purpose. The righteousness of Jesus, denied by his taunters—for surely God would rescue the righteous (Wis. 2:17–24)—finds vindication in the raising of the saints. No longer does God sit in his holy temple (Ps. 11:4), whose destruction the ripped curtain epitomizes. God remains with us, crucified with us and for us.[12]

Eventually, however, all exegetical fillips fail, and every theological common-place is burnt away, for lament leads human creatures into the inmost heart of God, in whose image we are indelibly crafted. As long as we live with God in a world destined for glory yet still unredeemed, at times unspeakably blasphemed, we shall lament even as we rejoice. Well-intentioned but mistaken psychothera-pists have confused grief with lament, implying that lamentation expresses a definable stage in a predictable grieving process. A person or family proceeds through "stages of grief," which, if executed successfully—that is to say, in accor-dance with psychotherapeutic protocols—eventuate in a mentally reconstituted individual or group. Others must speak to the cogency of that model.[13] This I know, by faith and from experience: grief may wane or become numbed, but lament is not a "stage" from which children destined for the glory of God evolve, then leave behind (Col. 1:24–29).

For Christians, as long as every Friday recollects Good Friday, just as each Sun-day instantiates the Day of Resurrection, our life in God telescopes time beyond discrete stages in sequence. Because that is so, the only life we know is entwined with death, and the only joy is interlaminated with lament. Until the consum-mation of the ages, God and Rachel and all the company of saints will weep for their children, because they were not.

There is no explaining such mystery. There can be only testimonies to it.

V

Alas—
Lonely sits the city
Once so crowded with people.
She that was great among nations
Has become like a widow.
The princess among cities
Has become a slave.
. . . .
My teeth he has broken on gravel;
He has ground me into the dust.
My life is bereft of peace;
I forgot what happiness is.
. . . .
But this do I call to mind,
And so I have hope:
The LORD'S steadfast love has not ended,
His compassion is not spent.
                    (Lam. 1:1; 3:16–17, 21–22)

I reckon the sufferings of the present season incomparable to the coming glory to be revealed to us. For creation waits with intense yearning for God's adoptees to be disclosed. . . . For we know that all creation moans as one and until now collectively suffers labor pains—and not only that: but we ourselves, who have the Spirit's firstfruits, we too moan inwardly while

awaiting our adoption, the redemption of our bodies. For in hope we were
saved. (Rom. 8:18–19, 22–24a)

Poet and apostle bear witness to the corporate dimension of lament. A metrop-
olis is laid waste. A survivor stumbles through smoldering rubble, offering an
elegy for Jerusalem. Centuries later, on this side of Easter, Paul invites the church
in Rome to wait with him in a birthing room. It is the cosmos, God's creation in
its entirety, that writhes in travail, beginning to give birth to a glory only glimpsed
and to this day not yet fully delivered. Like the poet and the apostle, we are not
detached spectators. We too are seized by besetting, universal pangs: the ache—
subsiding only long enough to redouble its inexpressible intensity—that empties
all memory of happiness.

Yet the spine of lament is hope: not the vacuous optimism that "things will
get better," which in the short run is usually a lie,[14] but the deep and irrepressible conviction, in the teeth of present evidence, that God has not severed the
umbilical cord that has always bound us to the Lord. Anguish concealed God
from both psalmist (Ps. 22:1) and the Crucified One (Matt. 27:46), but neither
could finally let go of his adoption. The God who forsakes was and remains "*My
God, my God.*" And somehow our God suffers our own God-forsakenness.[15]

VI

How long, O Lord? Will you forever ignore me?
How long will you hide your face from me?
How long shall my mind be troubled,
And grief in my deepest self the day long?
How long shall my enemy have the upper hand?
Look at me—answer me, O Lord, my God.
. . . .
But in your fidelity I trust;
In your deliverance my inmost self shall rejoice.
(Ps. 13:1–3a, 5)

We are in all ways pressed but not crushed, at a loss but not despairing,
hounded but not forsaken, thrown down but not destroyed, always carrying about in the body the killing of Jesus, so that also the life of Jesus may
be manifested in our body. For we the living are constantly handed over to
death for Jesus' sake, so that Jesus' life may also be manifested in our mortal body. So death is operative in us, but life in you. (2 Cor. 4:8–12)

In late December a few years ago, I returned to the town where I had grown
up, to the cemetery where my family is buried. Not far from my parents' graves,
the sunlight caught something that twinkled. Walking over for a better look, I
discovered a Christmas tree: a foot tall, meticulously ornamented. Beside that
miniature sat a tiny bear immaculately dressed. Though I saw no one else nearby,
both decorations looked fresh enough to have been placed at the grave only five

minutes earlier. I peered at the epitaph, wondering if I would recognize the child's name. I didn't—but was thunderstruck by the inscribed dates: 1957–1959. In an eternal moment, the gravestone shuddered; tree and bear wept for a full forty years of relentless loss.

So it is with lament. Its very nature is constant and durative. An impatient, death-denying society demands that sufferers "get over it." Across millennia, by contrast, the psalmist asks over and again, "How long, O LORD? How long?" In this life are things for which there's no getting over; such belong to the land of lament. With maturity, by God's grace, the scales of woe and trust become balanced. In the meanwhile, we pray that we shall rejoice over deliverance yet to come, as we adorn the graves of those dead and loved and remembered.

Psalmist and apostle also remind us that lamentation, though never privatistic, is intensely personal. Indeed, in a startling reversal of expectation, Paul transposes the whole of his ministry into the key of lament. In his view, life is no dirge; rather, it has been transfigured, root and branch, by Jesus' cross and resurrection. For the sake of the Crucified, "we the living are forever handed over to death," so that our besieged and corruptible bodies may reveal the indestructible life that Christ now lives. For the Christian who believes, "You have died, and your life is hid with Christ in God" (Col. 3:3), lament is not an occasional tune, hummed by others. It has become the signature theme of every life in Christ.

VII

Since Jews demand signs and Greeks search for wisdom, we proclaim Christ who is crucified, a snare for Jews and folly for Gentiles—but to those called, both Jews and Greeks—Christ: God's power and God's wisdom. For God's foolishness is wiser than people, and God's weakness mightier than people. (1 Cor. 1:22–25)

Then one of the elders said to me, "Don't cry. Look—the lion of the tribe of Judah, the root of David, has conquered, to open the book and its seven seals." And I saw, between the throne and the four living creatures and the elders, a lamb, standing as if slaughtered, with seven horns and seven eyes which are the spirits of God that have been dispatched into all the earth. And he came and took it from the right hand of the one seated on the throne. And when he took the book, the four living creatures and the four-and-twenty elders fell down before the lamb, each with a harp and golden bowls full of incense, which are the prayers of the saints. And they sang a new song, saying:

> Worthy are you to take the book
> And to open its seals:
> For you were slaughtered, and you bought for God with your blood,
> From every tribe and tongue and people and nation,
> And made them for our God a dominion and priests,
> And they shall reign on earth.
> . . . .

Worthy is the slaughtered lamb to receive
The power and wealth and wisdom and might
and honor and glory and blessing.
                                    (Rev. 5:5–10, 12)

And the eleven disciples went to Galilee, to the mountain where [the risen]
Jesus had directed them. And when they saw him, they bowed down, though
some had doubts about it. (Matt. 28:16–17)

I don't know that a name was ever coined for it, but the functional avoidance
of Good Friday among many Christians is a heresy of long standing. Its tacit justification seems to be that Easter Sunday signals a victory so complete that God
effectively annihilated Golgotha. Such confusion makes for a theology that is not
merely bad, but heartless and even dangerous. In place of the Christian gospel of
God's triumph, it substitutes the bad news of human triumphalism. It stills the
voice of lament—often throwing the additional burden of guilt on the plaintive—and dares to attempt what even God refused: obliterating the wounds of
Christ Crucified.

Christians should occasionally pause to marvel that God raised Jesus from
death itself but did not wipe away his lacerations. "Look at my hands and my
feet—it's really me. Touch me and see—a spirit doesn't have flesh and bones, as
you see me have" (Luke 24:39). To Thomas: "Put your finger here and look at
my hands, and bring your hand and thrust it into my side; and stop being faithless, but believe it" (John 20:27; cf. 19:31–37). Ending with only the promise
that Jesus has been raised and will reunite with his disciples, Mark's Gospel has
no need for a story so told: the last of Jesus we see in that Gospel is the one hang-
ing, then buried. Matthew's disciples regard the Risen Crucified with mixed feelings: They worshipped, yes, but had their doubts. In the seer's vision, the lamb
worthy to unseal the book, to purchase a people, and to receive all reverence
in heaven and on earth resembles in some respects the militant horned ram of
1 Enoch 90 but is altogether unlike that bellwether in one crucial aspect: Christ,
Agnus Dei, remains slaughtered. Revelation insists upon that lamb—victorious
yet butchered—with unmistakable repetition. Paul makes the same point more
subtly in 1 Corinthians 1–2: "For I determined to know among you nothing save
Jesus Christ, *who indeed continues to be the one crucified*" (2:2, whose appositive
emphasizes a perfect passive participle). The New Testament is remarkably consistent on this point: By raising Jesus from the dead, God did not eradicate the
scars of his death but, instead, vindicated this Crucified One, and no other, as
the Messiah.

Just there lies the most important reason for the practice of lament. Without it,
whether they know it or not, Christians again deny the One whom God has both
vindicated and forever verified as Christ on the cross. The wounds of the Messiah's
crucifixion are the inexpungible identification by which God has embodied himself for us, for our healing, for the salvation of all. Until that day when every tear
has been wiped away and death shall be no more (Rev. 21:4), all of God's people—

Rachel and Ann, Jesus and Paul, all of us without exception—unite their voices in lament, hopeful but without closure. Among them is yet another parent who lost a child: philosopher Nicholas Wolterstorff, whose twenty-five-year-old Eric died in a mountaineering accident:

> So I shall struggle to live the reality of Christ's rising and death's dying. In my living, my son's dying will not be the last word. But as I rise up, I bear the wounds of his death. My rising does not remove them. They mark me. If you want to know who I am, put your hand in.[16]

NOTES

1. Ann Weems, *Psalms of Lament* (Louisville, KY: Westminster John Knox Press, 1995), 20.
2. All translations in this chapter are my own.
3. *The Revised Common Lectionary: Consultation on Common Texts* (Nashville: Abingdon Press, 1992), 26.
4. Matthew 1:23 (citing the Greek version of Isa. 7:14 and 8:8, 10); 2:6 (Mic. 5:2); 2:15 (Hos. 11:1); 2:18 (Jer. 31:15); 2:23 (whose referent may be Isa. 11:1 or 53:2 but remains ambiguous).
5. For a perceptive analysis of Matthew's use of Jeremiah at this and other points, consult Michael Knowles, *Jeremiah in Matthew's Gospel: The Rejected-Prophet Motif in Matthean Redaction*, JSNTSup 68 (Sheffield: Sheffield Academic Press, 1993). Matthew's interpretation of Jer. 31:15–17 also deviates from subsequent rabbinic readings of that text, whose outlook is preponderantly positive (Knowles, 33–52).
6. So Richard J. Erickson: "The one who escaped at Bethlehem comes back to endure it all himself, *and to reverse it!*" ("Divine Injustice? Matthew's Narrative Strategy and the Slaughter of the Innocents (Matthew 2.13–23)," *Journal for the Study of the New Testament* 64 [1996]: 5–27; quotation, with Erickson's emphasis, 26).
7. Transcribing the comments of his third-world parishioners, Ernesto Cardenal offers bracing points of view on Matthew's narrative in *The Gospel in Solentiname* (Maryknoll, NY: Orbis, 1976), esp. 70–86. "It's very rough," says one woman, "but what happened then has gone on in every age. . . . And more Herods will come along, because whenever there's someone struggling for liberation there's someone who wants to kill him, and if they can kill him they will" (71–72).
8. As Epicurus (ca. 342–270 BCE) wrote to Menoeceus: "For all good and evil consists in sensation, but death is deprivation of sensation. . . . So death, the most terrifying of ills, is nothing to us, since so long as we exist, death is not with us; but when death comes, then we do not exist" (quoted in C. K. Barrett, ed., *The New Testament Background: Writings from Ancient Greece and the Roman Empire That Illuminate Christian Origins* (rev. ed.; San Francisco: HarperCollins, 1989), 79–80.
9. Albert Schweitzer, *The Quest of the Historical Jesus: A Critical Study of Its Progress from Reimarus to Wrede* (New York: Macmillan, 1968), esp. 370–71.
10. True to Matthean form, however, these circumstances echo apocalyptic images in the Old Testament: Isa. 26:19; Ezek. 37:12; Dan. 12:2; Joel 2:10; Nah. 1:5–6. They also provide a bookend for the astronomical aberrations in his infancy narrative: Matt. 2:1–2 (cf. Num. 22–24).

11. André LaCocque, "The Great Cry of Jesus in Matthew 27:50," in *Putting Body and Soul Together: Essays in Honor of Robin Scroggs*, ed. Virginia Wiles, Alexandra Brown, and Graydon F. Snyder (Valley Forge, PA: Trinity Press International, 1997), 138–64.

12. For further discussion, see Paul S. Minear, "The Messiah Forsaken . . . Why?" *Horizons in Biblical Theology* 17 (1995): 62–83.

13. Nicholas Wolterstorff: "I skimmed some books on grief. They offered ways of not looking at death and pain in the face, ways of turning away from death out there to one's own inner 'grief process' and then, on that, laying the heavy hand of rationality. I will not have it so. I will not look away. I will indeed remind myself that there's more to life than pain. I will accept joy. But I will not look away from Eric dead. Its demonic awfulness I will not ignore. I owe that—to him and to God" (*Lament for a Son* [Grand Rapids: Wm. B. Eerdmans Publishing Co., 1987], 54).

14. "I hoped for happiness, but evil came; I looked for light, but there was darkness" (Job 30:26).

15. See James L. Mays, "Prayer and Christology: Psalm 22 as Perspective on the Passion," *Theology Today* 42 (1985): 322–31; Terence E. Fretheim, *The Suffering of God: An Old Testament Perspective*, Overtures to Biblical Theology (Philadelphia: Fortress Press, 1984).

16. Wolterstorff, *Lament for a Son*, 92–93.

Chapter 6

Rending the Curtain: Lament as an Act of Vulnerable Aggression

Robert C. Dykstra

Among many striking depictions of lament throughout the Bible, none is as powerful as God's own fierce lament over the death of Jesus in Gospel accounts of the rending of the curtain in the temple (Mark 15:38; Matt. 27:51). As Jesus "gave a loud cry and breathed his last," the Gospel of Mark recounts, "the curtain of the temple was torn (*eschisthē*) in two, from top to bottom." Matthew elaborates, "The earth shook, and the rocks were split." To split is to split open, and this, I suggest, is the deeper meaning, the profound significance, of the rending of the curtain of the temple. The rending of the curtain signifies the unveiling of God. The One who was hidden, the unknown and unknowable God, is suddenly now revealed. No, the word *revealed* is too tame, too familiar to our Christian way of hearing, so accustomed are we to speaking of the revelation of God in Jesus Christ as though it were a mere announcement. Instead we should say that the One who was hidden, the unknown and unknowable God, *exposed* himself, and did so, that terrible day, in no uncertain terms. The time for hide-and-seek—that shadow on the rock, that thunderous voice, that backside of God which Moses saw and heard—was over. The time had come for God to be seen on full display.

In Brian K. Blount and Gary W. Charles's *Preaching Mark in Two Voices*, Charles suggests that "the passive voice of the verb *schizō* indicates that this rending is the

59

divine response to the death of Jesus; the tense and meaning of this verb suggest a violent, completed, and decisive action. As God rends the veil (*katapetasma*) of the sanctuary (*naos*), *that which divided the holy from the profane is removed.*"[1] In thus rending the veil of the sanctuary, God responds to Jesus' own naked cry of lament from the cross—"My God, my God, why have you forsaken me?" (Mark 15:34; Matt. 27:46)—by God's own reciprocal stripping down. The rending of the curtain to the Holy of Holies signifies the exposure of the very Self of God. In a moment of excruciating sorrow, God the Father lays bare the divine Self, becoming in turn as vulnerable as the crucified Son. Blount and Charles point out that the verb *schizō* used to describe the rending of the temple curtain is the same one used in Mark's depiction of Jesus' baptism (Mark 1:10).[2] As Jesus descended, here too fully naked, into the waters of death, the heavens were torn apart (*schizomenous*), and God was revealed. This, though, was a blessed event— "You are my Son, the Beloved; with you I am well pleased" (Mark 1:11)—while the second was a cursed event, a day of absolute horror. In the former, God's voice came, as it were, out of nowhere—a disembodied voice. In the latter, God split the curtain to become fully visible, as if to say, *You have longed to see me. You have used all your human cunning to lure me into the open. It was not even enough that I sent you my Son, my beloved. So take a good look. Here I am!*

In this essay, I seek to explore some of the meanings that this dramatic act of divine exhibition has in particular for men of faith today. In doing so, I am fully aware that other meanings may be drawn from this event. I have been invited here, however, to write on the subject of lament, and this invitation prompts me to seek to relate this act of divine self-exposure to the laments of ordinary men, especially those who for various reasons have found themselves fearful of the consequences of their own self-exposure.

GOD'S BODY

The rending of the curtain on that terrible Friday afternoon links divine lament with divine self-exposure. This rending stands in striking contrast to the strong prohibitions against seeing God's body—hence, God's nakedness and vulnerability—throughout the Hebrew Scriptures. In *God's Phallus and Other Problems for Men and Monotheism*, Rabbi Howard Eilberg-Schwartz argues that despite numerous references in the Hebrew Scriptures to God's *having* a body, there is a great deal of resistance within ancient Judaism even to speculating on the specific *nature* of that body. Especially problematic—thus, taboo—is speculation on the anatomical characteristics of the Jewish God that relate to sexuality. He writes:

> We find a great deal of information is available about the gender of the monotheistic God, but the sex of this God is carefully obscured. In [biblical] accounts of God sightings, the gaze is averted from the face and front, parts of the anatomy that are critical to an identification of a body's sex. Not only is there no indication that this God has a penis, but we do not even

know whether this being has secondary sexual characteristics such as facial hair. We have no information about the divine anatomy.[3]

Eilberg-Schwartz argues that despite the overwhelming use of male gender imagery in biblical depictions of God (as king, father, shepherd, man of war, and so on), the fact that the divine sex is always veiled suggests that the rendering of God as sexually male was for some reason inherently problematic for ancient Israel. While many feminists have rightly recognized ways in which the Bible's preponderance of male attributes for God has been detrimental to women, Eilberg-Schwartz contends that such attributes also prove highly problematic for men. Why? Because while on the one hand the characterization of God as specifically male can be seen as enhancing men by legitimating masculinity and male supremacy, on the other hand it proves detrimental to them by rendering "the meaning of masculinity unstable."[4]

This destabilization centers especially on the problem of "homoeroticism, the love of a male human for a male God":

> The issue of homoeroticism arises in ancient Israel because the divine-human relationship is often described in erotic and sexual terms. Marriage and sexuality are frequent biblical metaphors for describing God's relationship with Israel. God is imagined as the husband to Israel the wife; espousal and even sexual intercourse are metaphors for the covenant. Israel's relationship with God is thus conceptualized as a monogamous sexual relation, and idolatry as adultery. But the heterosexual metaphors in the ancient texts belie the nature of the relationship in question: it is human males, not females, who are imagined to have the primary intimate relations with the deity. The Israel that is collectively imagined as a woman is actually constituted by men—men like Moses and the patriarchs. And these men love, in ways that are imagined erotically and sensually, a male deity.[5]

How are men to love, to the point even of considering themselves betrothed to, a male God, particularly in a culture such as Israel's which denounces homoeroticism as an abomination? Israel resolved this presumably unconscious dilemma, Eilberg-Schwartz argues, in part by suppressing or repressing natural questions concerning the defining sexual characteristics of God, questions about God's body that any curious child would be inclined to ask.[6] Why resist or repress such natural questions? Eilberg-Schwartz suggests that if God's sexual anatomy remains veiled, the male-female complementarity at the heart of Israel's understanding of human relations and of its favored status as a nation "espoused" to God remains intact, while at the same time enabling men to retain their dominance in Israel's social hierarchy. If God's sexual anatomy were identified as male, then this very complementarity could conceivably lead to the elevation of Israel's women over its men as "the natural partners of a divine male."[7] Thus the veiling of God may serve as a theological legitimation of male hegemony. Unable to identify God's sex, Israel's men maintain their status as God's beloved, while at the same time remaining safe from insinuation of homoeroticism.

If Eilberg-Schwartz's provocative thesis about ancient Judaism's prohibitions against speculation about God's sexual anatomy is correct, I suggest that Gospel accounts of the rending of the temple curtain change all this, and that lament is at the very heart of this decisive, even earth-shattering change. Divine lament suddenly usurps divine modesty and the long-standing—and long-suffering—ancient prohibition concerning unveiling. This rending of the curtain not only signifies a dramatic shift in terms of what attributes of God people of faith are allowed to "see"; it also undermines by association a clandestine source of Israel's legitimation of male dominance. In the act of lamenting the death of Jesus—himself utterly naked and exposed there on the cross—God's own nakedness is at last revealed. In this, God the Father fully identifies with God the Son. As a result, men who love and worship a God whom they overwhelmingly perceive to be male may now be pressed to confront, perhaps for the first time, the homo-erotic implications of God's self-revelation in Jesus; they can no longer so read-ily dismiss as inferior that which they deem feminine, passive, or vulnerable.

I am not trying to suggest that most men of faith have consciously wrestled with homoerotic concerns related to their conceiving of God the Father, and cer-tainly Jesus the Son, in primarily male gender terms. I would contend, however, that ample historical and anecdotal evidence reinforces the perception that men, more than women, characteristically find themselves hesitant or self-conscious concerning matters of faith and its practice. For centuries, for example, women have disproportionately filled the membership rolls and pews of most churches. So recurring historical movements such as so-called "muscular Christianity" in American Protestantism between 1880 and 1920, in reaction to what Ann Doug-las and others have described as the increasing feminization of church and soci-ety in that era, and the more recent Promise Keepers and other men's movements of the 1990s collectively point to an enduring underlying anxiety among men that faith somehow threatens masculinity.[8]

God's lament, then, drives God—and this underlying anxiety among men of faith—from the closet; an unbearable grief, shame, and rage in response to Jesus' death compel God to step out from behind the curtain in all God's desperate glory. In Jesus' death, we at last get a full frontal glimpse of God. God's lament removes the dividing line between the holy and the profane. As the curtain is rent in two, so too the old division between sacred and profane is forever torn apart.

LAMENT AS NAKED AGGRESSION

To this point, I have represented the rending of the curtain as an act of divine vulnerability, the very vulnerability that is reflected in the figure of Jesus nailed to the cross, and the very vulnerability that those who are bereaved of a beloved family member or friend cannot conceal from others, however valiantly they try to maintain their customary composure. The rending of the curtain, however, was also a vulnerably *violent* act—*eschisthē* is a form of the verb to "tear" (which, not incidentally, conjures in English the "shedding of tears"), so it would be hopelessly inapt to think of it as taking a pair of scissors and carefully cutting a piece of cloth in two. No, according to Blount and Charles's reading of the text, this was a decisive, an even violent act, an act of naked aggression, and, as such, it reveals an aspect of God—God's very vulnerability—that we, in our desperate need to think of vulnerability as an act of humble acquiescence to circumstances beyond our control, tend to downplay and to treat as ephemeral. This is *our* form of repression and prohibition, and it is no less self-protective than the prohibitions and repressions we have seen in the case of ancient Israel.

But if such vulnerability takes the form of naked aggression, against what or whom does it aggress? I suggest that it is largely *self*-directed. In rending the curtain, God himself bears the full weight of the violence, vulnerability, and shame of his action. Lament, then, is an always visceral, sensual, therefore in the broad sense a necessarily sexual eruption of vengeance or despair that aggressively targets the lamenter's own self. The paradigmatic kinetic expression that accompanies a lament's vocal cry from the heart is a reflexive rending of the lamenter's own clothing, a spontaneous form of exhibitionism that intensifies the stricken person's vulnerability. Dozens of examples of such rending can be found in the biblical witness. To lament is to protest some circumstance perceived as especially shaming or otherwise damaging to the self by intentionally shaming oneself in kind, in part through the wild response of laying oneself bare. Those who lament paradoxically insist on their own nakedness and vulnerability as the only suitable "covering" by which to redress their humiliating self-exposure at the hand of another. Lament thus breaches the self's usual modesty and decorum, transgressing internal boundaries between one's tenderness and rage, one's intimacy and aggression—a territory so constitutive of the self's psychological core that lament likely becomes the optimal, perhaps the only, path to restoration and healing in the face of overwhelming humiliation or violation.

However, as noted, in necessarily exposing the intimate but usually unconscious link between sexuality and aggression—invoking the physical, even sexual, body in an inherently aggressive manner—the practice of lament has fared rather poorly in Christian theology and church history. Certainly lament must be numbered among the church's most endangered practices, relegated to the role of a despised or neglected step-sibling to other more ethereal practices of Christian love or spirituality.[9] *Good Christians*, so we come to believe, *are not supposed to lament*, just as—and because—we are not to delight in things sensual or to express anger or aggression. Lament meanwhile insists on this delight and this expression. Christians—and here I am especially concerned with and for Christian men, who know that they are to refrain from lament, who have learned, so to speak, to remain always properly attired, to hold themselves together under duress—tend, as a result, to experience a diminished capacity for intimacy, mutuality, and authentic forgiveness with God and one another. When God's naked aggression—God's finally allowing, even daring, us to take a good look and witness his vulnerable self—is itself ignored, our gaze reflexively averted, our very chance to know intimacy and mutuality with God is sacrificed on the altar of decorum.

RENDING BARRIERS BETWEEN
THE HOLY AND THE PROFANE

Some vignettes from film and literature can serve to support this view of lament as a naked aggression that intensifies the lamenter's vulnerability, even while enhancing the possibility for catharsis and restored intimacy in the face of unbearable shame, self-depletion, and despair:

Recall, for example, the sensual physicality of the lament of Joseph Cinque, the African protagonist of Steven Spielberg's *Amistad*, a film based on historic events in the aftermath of an 1839 revolt against the ship's crew by a group of slaves undergoing brutal transport from Africa. In a memorable scene late in the film, Cinque (played by Djimon Hounsou), the leader of the revolt, is imprisoned in New Haven with others of his companions while undergoing trial for murder in the mutiny. Though the court eventually rules in favor of the Africans, the case is subsequently appealed to the U.S. Supreme Court by President Martin Van Buren, depicted as fearing an uprising by the South as well as retribution from Spain, which presumed jurisdiction, in response to the verdict. On being told of this appeal by his lawyer, Roger Baldwin (Matthew McConaughey), in the immediate aftermath of the initial court victory, Cinque impulsively tears off all his clothing and screams in a fiery mantra, "What kind of place is this where you *almost* mean what you say? Where laws *almost* work? How can you live like that?"[10] The one who laments here is highly vulnerable, for he is fully unclothed, yet is simultaneously angry and aggressive, raging against a terrible injustice. His cry seemingly demands his nakedness, his aggression and vulnerability melded into an indiscrete, riveting whole.

So too does naked aggression conjoin with lament at a pivotal moment in Paul Monette's award-winning autobiography *Becoming a Man: Half a Life Story*, an unflinching account of the young man's struggle to come to terms with his homosexuality. Monette describes a season following his graduation from college in which desperation over his sexual quandary and hopelessness concerning his prospects for employment converge in a poignant cry of despair. Driving away from a job interview at an unknown prep school in Vermont, "horrified," he writes,

> at the thought of being trapped there all winter, I got lost on the country roads, arched over by the delirious red and gold of October. I stopped beside a lake and walked all the way around it, slogging through the marsh and then upland fields. I took off all my clothes and sat on a rock in the chilly sun. Trying to feel free, or daring, or something. And I suddenly threw back my head and screamed: "Somebody find me!"
>
> It echoed across the fields and lost itself in the woods, the cry of an animal dying in a trap. Nobody came, of course, not even a hunter to put a bullet through my misery. I put my clothes back on and drove home in silence, to paint another porch and read in my room with half a heart.[11]

Though Monette's lament, unlike Cinque's, is removed from public view, his nakedness and his cry from the heart are clearly intertwined, of one piece. Naked, he screams his longing to be found, to anyone and no one. His exhibitionism, an act of vulnerable aggression, is a desperate plea for intimacy, mutuality, and authentic forgiveness. "My God, my God, why have you forsaken me?" his Son cries from the cross, and as he cries, the Father rends the curtain and himself declares, "Here I am, my Son; today we are one." What human beings have split asunder, lament has joined—rejoined—together.

The exhibitionism inherent in the laments of Cinque and Monette contributes to their ambiguous appeal; they are at once disturbing and mesmerizing. While on the one hand their raw displays of shame, rage, and aggression would normally lead an observer to want to turn away, hiding one's eyes, on the other hand their nakedness and vulnerability make it more difficult to avert one's gaze; their exhibitionism invites our voyeurism. The exhibitionism evident in these painful circumstances, however, like that of God's own self-revelation on the day his Son hung exposed on the cross, is a far cry from that of a sexual predator, whose nakedness threatens and violates an unsuspecting victim. No, the lamenter's violence is *self*-inflicted, his nakedness violating only himself, while befittingly revealing his *own* victimization. This is a vulnerability that we witnesses actually need and long to see, an exhibitionism that carries both victim and witness alike beyond victimization and isolation to the hope of restored connection and vitality in their life together. This leads then to my concluding point, that the capacity to lament is integral to the capacity to love.

LAMENT AND THE TENSIONS OF LOVE

In *Can Love Last? The Fate of Romance over Time*,[12] published posthumously, Stephen A. Mitchell reflects on the seemingly inevitable decline of romance in long-term, committed relationships. Mitchell, a prolific author on contemporary psychoanalysis and a practicing psychotherapist in New York City until his recent death at age fifty-four, suspects that this ebbing of passion is the result not of familiarity breeding contempt but of its breeding a sense of danger.

Passion, for Mitchell, does not merely fade away but is instead intentionally killed. Why? Because passion consists in tension, specifically a tension between *love* and *desire* that becomes increasingly difficult to sustain over time. Monogamy intensifies our sense of dependency on just one partner, leading us to attempt to "guarantee that love" and thus "pretend to ourselves that we have, somehow, minimized our risks and guaranteed our safety—thereby undermining the preconditions of desire, which requires robust imagination to breathe and thrive."[13] Citing a paper by Freud entitled "On the Universal Tendency to Debasement in the Sphere of Love" (1912), Mitchell writes:

> Perhaps the most striking feature of Freud's clinical observation was that the condition most likely to interfere with complete potency, a full experience of desire, was love itself. . . . Freud's patients could love, and they could desire, but they could not experience both love and desire with the same person at

the same time. "Where they love, they have no desire," Freud noted; "where they desire, they cannot love."[14]

Love and desire are so difficult to reconcile, Mitchell argues, because while love seeks the comfort and familiarity of a "home,"[15] desire beckons one to leave home in quest of the exotic and new. Whereas love inspires an attitude of "worshipful conscientiousness," desire insists on "a kind of reckless exploitation."[16] Thus, while "love and desire are both thoroughly human," they nonetheless "orient us toward very different goals. Love seeks control, stability, continuity, certainty. Desire seeks surrender, adventure, novelty, the unknown."[17]

Romantic passion, meanwhile, is generated by the intoxicating "arc of tension"[18] between the two. Love and desire must both be sustained if love indeed is to last, but this is precisely what proves so difficult in committed relationships over time.

The destabilizing effects of erotic desire eventually motivate partners to attempt to regain equilibrium by asserting control over themselves and their loved one through "strategies for false security that suffocate desire."[19] An extreme form of such a strategy is sexual perversion, "the central feature of which is the degradation of the other to an object under one's omnipotent control, so that the sexual act becomes a perseverative script in which nothing new can ever happen." Far more subtle strategies of control, however, are evident in every long-term bond. Thus, "ironically enough, attachment is the great enemy of eroticism."[20]

Though harboring no illusions about reversing this pattern on a broad scale, Mitchell nevertheless does seek to bring those he counsels to a place where they can begin to restore and sustain the tension between love and desire, at first simply by allowing them to acknowledge to themselves and their partners the sense of danger they may feel in becoming so fully "known" by the other. This sense of danger often surfaces in an occasional flare of aggression, a natural response to one's feeling endangered. Thus, for him, "the survival of romance depends not on skill in avoiding aggression but on the capacity to contain it alongside love. . . . A love that has endured episodic aggression has a depth and resilience obtainable in no other way," which accounts for the sense of "profound relief" that lovers often report at their love having survived "the dreaded first real knock-down, drag-out fight."[21] Mitchell concludes that "the degradation of romance is due not to the contamination of love by aggression but to the inability to sustain the necessary tension between them."[22]

Mitchell's commending to us the tension between love and aggression strengthens the case for reclaiming lament in the church, lament here conceived as a divinely sanctioned act of vulnerable aggression in the face of perceived danger necessary to love. Not unlike monogamous love, monotheistic faith—the mutual commitment of a particular covenant people and just one God—can only intensify the dependency between that people and God, escalating as a result the sense of danger inherent in their becoming so fully known by another (an Other). Monotheism makes for a dangerous faith. Would we not then expect to find various problematic tendencies in monotheistic faith, whereby God and God's people would attempt to secure their relationship and guarantee their love? In extreme form, such "strategies for false security that suffocate desire," as Mitchell describes them, would suggest the theological equivalent of sexual perversion, usually referred to as "idolatry" in the biblical witness. Idolatry in this sense, however, would be understood less as a covenant people's rampant pursuit of sexual or other pleasures, as it is often portrayed in so-called "orthodox" theologies, than to the contrary as their attempt to *eliminate* "excess, enigma, and mystery"—that is, to excise eroticism—from a faith "that is, by its very nature, elusive and shifting."[23] Idolatry here becomes a preoccupation with an orthodoxy that rationalizes away God's body and, with it, any chance for intimacy. To intentionally kill the likes of erotic desire between God and God's people is to transform a wondrous, passionate, childlike faith into "a perseverative script in which nothing new can ever happen."

Returning, then, to the beginning of this essay, ancient Israel's injunction against seeing God's body suggests itself as one such strategy for false security that kills desire in the guise of love. This veiling of God, according to Eilberg-Schwartz, minimizes any hint of erotic tension in the passionate bond, especially between Israel's men and the God they overwhelmingly perceive to be male. As Mitchell points out, however, such strategies for false security, while not unexpected in committed relationships over time, come at a cost, initially in this case, we may assume, to God and Israel's men themselves, who sacrifice a depth of intimacy and mutuality for the sake of bolstering a threatened masculinity. The collateral damage, however, extends even more disproportionately to Israel's women, children,[24] and various tangential men compelled daily to embody the indignities of a patriarchy siphoned of passion or compassion.

Nor has the Christian church escaped the temptation to resist the dangers of its covenantal love. By distancing itself from the rending of the curtain and God's own act of vulnerable aggression, the church promotes its own false strategy for securing a faith under its control, one with consequences for all men, but especially for the disenfranchised. The laments of Joseph Cinque, Paul Monette, and others like them stand in judgment on the church's perverse denials of their passions and very manhood, even as they expose the threat of impropriety, indeed seeming blasphemy, inherent in every honest lament. A church that can no longer lament has surrendered the hatred necessary to love.

The Gospel writers portray God as wildly and decisively rejecting this rejection of passionate intimacy with God in the rending of the curtain of the temple at the moment of Jesus' death. They suggest a God who hates the fallout among the dispossessed, with whom in this death God too must now be numbered, that results from the veiling of God's nakedness, that is, from theological systems that promote an elusive, invulnerable, unseen God. In rending the curtain, it is as though God cries out, *Enough! Enough with hiddenness, with veiling, with distancing, with separation, with patriarchy, with homophobia, with the worshipful conscientiousness of love at the expense of the reckless exploitation of desire! Enough!*

Here is a God now suddenly revealed in lament, angry and aggressive while naked and vulnerable, a God engaging in a sacred exhibitionism. Would that those men who have the most to lose could love a God like this, could love God like this, could finally, in the end, simply love like this.

NOTES

1. Brian K. Blount and Gary W. Charles, *Preaching Mark in Two Voices* (Louisville, KY: Westminster John Knox Press, 2002), 240, my emphasis.
2. Cf. ibid., 20–21, where Blount finds in Mark's account of the rending of the heavens in Jesus' baptism "a foreboding image of the eschatological schizophrenia human history has now become."
3. Howard Eilberg-Schwartz, *God's Phallus and Other Problems for Men and Monotheism* (Boston: Beacon Press, 1994), 24. See also Eilberg-Schwartz's chapter, "God's Phallus and the Dilemmas of Masculinity," in Stephen B. Boyd, W. Merle Longwood, and Mark W. Muesse, eds., *Redeeming Men: Religion and Masculinities* (Louisville, KY: Westminster John Knox Press, 1996), 36–47.
4. Eilberg-Schwartz, *God's Phallus*, 2.
5. Ibid., 4. See, e.g., Hos. 1–2, Jer. 2:2, Ezek. 16:8.
6. Ibid., 80.
7. Ibid., 4.
8. Ann Douglas, *The Feminization of American Culture* (New York: Doubleday Anchor Press, 1988). Cf. also Daniel Boyarin, *Unheroic Conduct: The Rise of Heterosexuality and the Invention of the Jewish Man* (Berkeley: University of California Press, 1997); Donald Capps, *Men and Their Religion: Honor, Hope, and Humor* (Harrisburg, PA: Trinity Press International, 2002); and Clifford Putney, *Muscular Christianity: Manhood and Sports in Protestant America, 1880–1920* (Cambridge, MA: Harvard University Press, 2001).
9. E.g., in Dorothy C. Bass, ed., *Practicing Our Faith: A Way of Life for a Searching People* (San Francisco: Jossey-Bass, 1997), an ambitious and influential book based on a project funded by the Lilly Endowment that seeks to reclaim for Christians various neglected or misunderstood practices of faith (honoring the body, keeping the Sabbath, giving one's testimony, singing hymns, among many others), just two paragraphs are devoted to lament (167–68), these in a chapter by Amy Plantinga Pauw on the topic of "dying well." Immediately thereafter, however, the author reverts to a more sublime appeal in the subsequent paragraph: "Lament must, however, be balanced by hope and thanksgiving. . . . The approach of death can be a time of thanksgiving for all of God's good gifts in our earthly life" (169).
10. David Franzoni, *Amistad*, directed by Steven Spielberg, DreamWorks Pictures, 1998, videocassette.
11. Paul Monette, *Becoming a Man: Half a Life Story* (San Francisco: HarperSanFrancisco, 1992), 190.
12. Stephen A. Mitchell, *Can Love Last? The Fate of Romance over Time* (New York: W. W. Norton & Co., 2002).
13. Ibid., 47.
14. Ibid., 34.
15. Ibid., 36.
16. Ibid., 189.
17. Ibid., 91–92.

18. Ibid., 53.
19. Ibid., 92.
20. Ibid., 87.
21. Ibid., 120.
22. Ibid., 144.
23. Ibid., 87, 79.
24. E.g., referring to the impact of patriarchy, particularly on boys, in *Driven by Hope: Men and Meaning* (Louisville, KY: Westminster John Knox Press, 1996), pastoral theologian James E. Dittes writes, "Patriarchy is enemy to sonhood as resoundingly as to womanhood. Sonship is a victim of cultural bias that favors fatherhood and exalts manhood (or at least the prevailing stereotype of fatherhood and manhood) fully as much as is femininity a victim, and perhaps with even more devastating damage to actual manhood and to the culture that so idolizes it" (131).

Chapter 7

Nervous Laughter: Lament, Death Anxiety, and Humor

Donald Capps

Ecclesiastes tells us that "for everything there is a season, and a time for every matter under heaven." There is "a time to be born, and a time to die; a time to plant,
and a time to pluck up what is planted; a time to kill, and a time to heal; a time
to break down, and a time to build up; *a time to weep, and a time to laugh*" (3:1–4).
Given its inclusion in this recital of contrasting events, "a time to weep and a time
to laugh" conveys the impression that these, too, are very distinct occasions. Yet
many have had painful experiences when they "didn't know whether to laugh or
cry." This uncertainty is especially likely when the experience also seems ridiculous or absurd.

Drawing on this ambiguity between crying and laughing, I want to focus here
on the rather curious fact that death is a topic that inspires humor. If there is one
experience for which laughing seems positively alien, this is death. Yet there are
probably more jokes about death than about any other subject or topic. There
are many reasons for this, but I want to propose that it has much to do with the
fact that humor is one of the resources to which we turn when we are anxious,
that is, when we have the feeling of being powerless and unable to cope with a
threatening event. Since there is no more threatening event than death—after all,
death means the extinction of our very being—it isn't surprising that humor is

one of the resources to which some of us turn to help us cope with our anxieties relating to death.

To set the stage for my consideration of humor's role in coping with the prospect of our own death, I will briefly discuss the biblical lament form and Elisabeth Kübler-Ross's theory of the stages of grieving to make the point that her theory does not address the chronic state of death anxiety that we routinely experience as one of the prices we pay for life itself. Thus we need a similar construct to hers for death anxiety. The construct that I offer here may seem, as it were, a far cry from the biblical lament, but, given the association noted between crying and laughing, it may well be the case that many of us will be helped to avail ourselves of the unique benefits of the biblical form of lamenting when we have first entertained the idea that death is, in fact, a laughing matter.

THE LAMENT FORM AND STAGES OF GRIEF

In his 1977 article "The Formfulness of Grief," Walter Brueggemann compared the structure of psalms of lament with Elisabeth Kübler-Ross's suggestion that the grief process has five stages.[1] He contended that the basic *intention* of the lament in psalms and other biblical writings is to rehabilitate and restore those who are suffering, and that the *form* of the lament helps to realize this objective. It does this when it "*enhances* experience and brings it to articulation and also *limits* the experience of suffering so that it can be received and coped with according to the perspectives, perceptions, and resources of the community." Thus the form of the lament defines the experience of suffering: "It tells the experiencer the shape of the experience which it is legitimate to experience." What makes the lament effective in dealing with situations of misery, hurt, and agony is the fact that it provides a *form* for understanding and experiencing these miseries, hurts, and agonies: "The form not only describes what is, but articulates what is expected and insisted upon."

In Brueggemann's view, we moderns find it difficult to appreciate this formative influence of the psalm of lament because we lack the forms that enable us to understand our experiences of grief: "Technical medicine, like urban consciousness generally, is resistant to form, denies the formfulness of experiences, and resists the notion that grief or any other experience is formful." Kübler-Ross's view that the death-grief process involves five elements (denial and isolation, anger, bargaining, depression, and acceptance) is an attempt to recover the formfulness of the grief experience.[2] But while Brueggemann supports her effort to describe the formfulness of this experience, and recognizes similarities between the lament and her stages (the major parallel is that both allow expression of anger), he emphasizes the very significant differences between them. (See the chart below for purposes of comparison.) The differences are due primarily to the fact that the lament expresses confidence in God's ability to intervene in the lives of the sufferers. Thus the major dissimilarity in the two structures is that *confession of trust* leads to *petition*—which, not incidentally, is the form of prayer that

Jesus employed and recommended to his disciples[3]—at precisely the point where, in Kübler-Ross's structure, *bargaining* is followed by *depression*. This major structural difference has a very decisive effect on the subsequent elements in the sequence. The lament moves from petition to confidence and praise, while Kübler-Ross's model moves from depression to acceptance.[4]

Brueggemann acknowledges that this move from depression to acceptance marks a shift as dramatic as when the lament moves from petition to confidence, but "it is unclear concerning Kübler-Ross whether 'acceptance' is affirmation or whether it is resignation. I believe she, herself, is not clear."

STAGES IN THE GRIEF PROCESS

Biblical Lament	*Kübler-Ross*
Address to God	Denial and Isolation
Complaint	Anger
Confession of Trust	Bargaining
Petition	Depression
Words of Assurance	Acceptance
Vow to Praise	

In the case of the lament, "the form itself centers in intervention, whereas Kübler-Ross must treat the intervention ambiguously and gingerly because the context of modernity must by definition screen it out." When the grieving or dying person is able to move from depression to acceptance, this is usually because of the support of a friend, relative, or member of the medical health team. Such intervention, no matter how consoling, lacks "the presence of a sovereign God" who can "powerfully intrude to transform."

Brueggemann's purpose is not to criticize those who are engaged in charting the stages of grief and dying. Rather, his intention is to illustrate how, for ancient Israel, it was the *form* of the lament that made possible the "transforming intervention" of God. Contemporary stage theories of grief and dying differ most from the lament in their failure to include this transformative dimension in the grief experience itself. Why they do not do so is less a reflection on the personal convictions of these authors and more a commentary on the fact that modern consciousness and its ideologies (including psychological ideologies) resist the *limitations* that traditional forms such as the lament place on human experience. For moderns, the form of the lament is simply too structured, its movement from complaint to petition to assurance to praise is too predictably pat. The very ambiguity that Brueggemann sees in Kübler-Ross's stages of *acceptance* is reflective of the desire of moderns for forms that are open-ended, their outcome clothed in mystery.

But while the basic structure of the traditional lament form did not change, this is not to say that the lament was a rigid form. In the course of time, its cry for vengeance against one's enemies was accompanied by petition in their behalf (a change that reaches its epitome in Jesus' cry from the cross, "Father, forgive them, for they know not what they do"). Also, the personal lament was augmented by the lament of the mediator (which first appears in the lament of Moses, recurs in the lament of Elisha, and reaches a high point in the laments of Jeremiah and the songs of the Suffering Servant in Deutero-Isaiah); and the truly revolutionary lament of God in Isaiah, Hosea, and Jeremiah (where God wrestles with his own decision to give his rebellious people over into the hands of their enemies). The lament of God was an especially significant development, because it simultaneously *enhanced* the lamenter's experience of God and severely *limited* the lament's effectiveness in making the grief experience comprehensible. In my view, the lament of God enables the traditional lament form to articulate with the ambiguity of modern consciousness while retaining the traditional model's capacity to "powerfully intrude to transform" the experience of loss.

Thus, while Brueggemann's warning against our easy acceptance of "the frames of reference of the psychological disciplines which are insensitive to form" is thoroughly appropriate, we should avoid the opposite error of assuming that the alternative choice is a rigid traditional form. In point of fact, the traditional lament form was not invulnerable to changing conditions in human experience. One reason that the personal lament form has survived for so many centuries is that the original form was not specific about the conditions that gave rise to the psalmist's lament, enabling it to adapt itself to new circumstances that were unanticipated by the early psalmists. Another, and more profound, reason for its survival was that it was augmented by new variations (the lament of the mediator and the lament of God), changes that introduced new complexities and ambiguities into its original form.

Kübler-Ross's model was extremely popular at the time Brueggemann wrote his essay on the formfulness of grief. While there is less direct mention of it today, it continues to be influential; it has become, as it were, a permanent resident in the house of modern consciousness. It is worth noting that the empirical basis for the model was interviews with patients suffering from a terminal illness conducted by Kübler-Ross, a member of the psychiatry faculty of the University of Chicago; Carl A. Nighswonger, the head chaplain at the University of Chicago Hospital; and Herman Cook, his associate. Nighswonger wrote a brief article, published in the *Journal of Thanatology*, on the six stages of terminal illness.[5] These stages are (1) denial versus panic (the "Not me!" stage); (2) catharsis versus depression (the "Why me?" stage); (3) bargaining versus selling out (the "Maybe not me!" stage); (4) realistic hope versus despair (the "If it's me, then . . ." stage); (5) acceptance versus resignation (the "Yes, it's me! Now . . ." stage); and (6) fulfillment versus forlornness (the "Yes!" stage). He also suggests that these stages involve the playing out of a series of dramas: shock, emotion, negotiation, cognition, commitment, and completion. This model employs a dialectical structure similar to Erik H. Erikson's well-known life-cycle model, and because it *is* dialectical, it seems closer, in spirit at least, to the lament structure. Kübler-Ross's model became popular; and Nighswonger's was known to only a few of his chaplaincy colleagues. His untimely death prohibited him from completing his own book based on the interviews with terminally ill patients.

The fact that both models were originally derived from interviews with the terminally ill was largely lost sight of as the Kübler-Ross model gained currency as a description, instead, of the five stages of grief. I am concerned in this essay, therefore, with the issue with which the original Kübler-Ross and Nighswonger interviews were concerned, that of patients' responses from the time they were informed that their illness was terminal until the time of death. We may assume that these patients were experiencing *acute* forms of death anxiety. We may also assume that the rest of us experience a more *chronic* state of death anxiety. I would guess—though I know of no study in support—that few of us go through a day in our lives without thinking that we will die, that our lives will not continue forever. We may not be obsessed with the thought that we will die someday, but few of us are total strangers to a sort of chronic, low-grade death anxiety. And this, I believe, is where humor has a therapeutic role to play.

In a study of worry and sense of humor, William Kelly, then a counselor located, appropriately enough, in Las Vegas, found that worry was negatively related to sense of humor.[6] Persons with a high sense of humor tend, in a sense, to treat frustrating life situations as something to joke about, while persons with a lower sense of humor tend instead to worry about these situations. Kelly suggested that worriers might be encouraged to develop a greater sense of humor. On the other hand, he also found—and this was completely unexpected—that both humor and worry were useful coping strategies against anxiety. In other words, some people minimize anxiety through humor, others minimize anxiety by worrying.

HUMOR AND THE FIVE STAGES OF DEATH ANXIETY

I will leave it to someone who is an expert worrier to explain how worrying might be helpful for coping with death anxiety and will instead focus on how humor enables us to express and share our chronic death anxieties and thereby get a better grip on them. Having spent the past several months studying joke books, I am in a position to declare that there are five stages of death anxiety. Jokes are designed to help us cope with these five stages of death anxiety by providing guidance on how to conduct ourselves at each stage in the process. We may think of them as a sort of etiquette manual for the dying and their loved ones.

The five stages of death anxiety include (1) how to react to being informed that one is much closer to death than one had thought or planned for; (2) how to manage the inevitable awkwardness of the deathbed scenario; (3) how to conduct ourselves at funerals; (4) how to wrap our minds around the unknown that follows death; and (5) how to come to terms with the fact that our loved ones will outlive us or, expressed more gracefully, how they will manage when we are gone. While my study of the literature confirms that there are dozens of jokes in most categories, I present here only two or three jokes in each category, as my purpose is simply to illustrate the model.

Stage 1: Announcement of Terminal Illness   The "bad news and even worse news" format is common: "Yeah, Doc, what's the news?" answered Fred when his doctor called with his test results. "I have some bad news and some really bad news," admitted the doctor. "The bad news is that you only have twenty-four hours to live." "Oh, no," gasped Fred, sinking to his knees. "What could be worse news than that?" "I couldn't get hold of you yesterday."

Reassurances that fail to have their intended effect are also typical: After his annual physical exam, an elderly patient asked his doctor, "Tell me, how long am I going to live?" "Don't worry," his doctor replied, "You'll probably live to be eighty." "But, doctor, I *am* eighty," he said. "See, what did I tell you?"

Stage 2: The Deathbed Scene   Most jokes in this category represent the dying person as ill disposed to going gently into that good night. For example: A man was in his bed dying, slipping in and out of consciousness. His wife came into the room with his doctor and the parish priest. "Mrs. Casey, you realize that the bill for my services is one thousand dollars," the doctor whispered. "Fine," she responded, "I'll see to it that you are paid from my husband's savings." Then the priest whispered, "And don't forget, Mary, the funeral and casket will cost one thousand dollars." "Don't worry, Father, I'll see to it that you're paid as well." The three walked over to the bed. The doctor stood on one side of the bed and the priest stood on the other. Mr. Casey wearily opened his eyes and motioned to the priest to come closer. In a hoarse voice he said, "Father, would you tell the people at my funeral that I died as Jesus died?" "Do you mean pure of heart and poor in spirit, Tom?" "No, I mean between two thieves!"

And this: A priest was preparing a man for his long day's journey into night. Whispering firmly, the priest said, "Denounce the devil. Let him know how little you think of his evil!" The dying man said nothing. The priest repeated his instructions. Still the dying man said nothing. The priest asked, "Why do you refuse to denounce the devil and his evil works?" The dying man murmured, "Until I know where I'm heading, I don't think I should mix in."

Stage 3: The Funeral   Jokes in this category reflect the idea that, because a funeral involves death, it really ought to go awry. Thus: A minister, a priest, and a rabbi die in a car crash. They go to heaven for orientation. They are all asked, "When you are in your casket, and friends, family, and congregants are mourning over you, what would you like to hear them say?" The minister says, "I would like to hear them say that I was a wonderful husband, a fine spiritual leader, and a great family man." The priest says, "I would like to hear that I was a wonderful teacher and a servant of God who made a huge difference in people's lives." The rabbi replies, "I would like to hear them say, 'Look, he's moving!'"

Or this Scandinavian joke: Ole and Lars were shipwrecked on a small island in the Pacific. Also stranded was an Irishman named Kelly. As time went on, the three men grew accustomed to being marooned and had a good life on the island. Finally, the Irishman died. The two Norwegians were puzzled about how to give

Kelly a proper funeral, since they hadn't gone to church since childhood. But Ole said he thought he could remember how it's done and volunteered to do the service if Lars would dig the grave. So after Lars dug a big hole, Ole put on his best ministerial tone: "In da name of da Father, da Son, and (shoving Kelly's body with his boot) in da hole he goes!"[7]

Stage 4: The Great Unknown   If a dramatic shift occurs in both the traditional lament and the Kübler-Ross models, one occurs in this model too, between stages three and four. The old life is over, the new one is about to begin. The most common joke format is awaiting admission through the pearly gates (the heavenly equivalent of a border crossing or standing in line at a hotel registration desk). Less common are jokes about the deceptive advertising and the lousy living conditions of hell. The following joke is typical of the more common form: Two men waiting at the pearly gates strike up a conversation. "How'd you die?" the first man asks the second. "I froze to death. So, how did you die?" "I had a heart attack. You see, I knew my wife was cheating on me, so one day I showed up at home unexpectedly. I ran up to the bedroom and found her alone, knitting. I ran down to the basement, but no one was hiding there. I ran up to the second floor, but no one was hiding there, either. I ran as fast as I could to the attic, and just as I got there, I had a massive heart attack and died." The second guy shakes his head. "That's so ironic. If you had only stopped to look in the freezer, we'd both still be alive."

These two, lamenting their deaths, haven't yet discovered what the elderly couple in the following joke learned, namely, that trying to prolong their lives on earth was a big mistake: An eighty-year-old couple died in a car crash. They had been in good health the last ten years, mainly as a result of her interest in health food and exercise. When they reached the pearly gates, Peter took them to their mansion, which was decked out with a beautiful kitchen and a master bath suite with a sauna and Jacuzzi. As they oohed and aahed, the old man asked Peter how much all of this was going to cost. "It's free," Peter replied, "This is heaven." Next they went to survey the championship golf course that their home backed up to. When the old guy asked the price of the green fees, Peter replied, "This is heaven, you play for free." Next they went to the clubhouse and saw the lavish buffet lunch with the cuisines of the world laid out. "How much to eat?" the old man asked. "Don't you understand yet? This is heaven. It's free," Peter replied with some exasperation. "Well, where are the low-fat and low-cholesterol tables?" the old man asked timidly. Peter responded, "That's the best part. You can eat as much as you like or whatever you like and you never get fat and you never get sick. This is heaven!" With that, the old guy threw down his hat, stomped on it, and began cursing. Peter and his wife tried to calm him down, asking him what was wrong. He glowered at his wife and said, "This is all your fault. If it weren't for your blasted bran muffins, I could have been here ten years ago!"

The question of what kind of car the old guy would drive didn't come up in the preceding story but is the central issue in the following: Three guys were met at the pearly gates by Peter. He said to them, "I know that you guys are forgiven because you're here, but before I let you in, I have to ask you something. Your answer will determine what kind of car you get, and you'll need a car, because heaven is getting more and more populated." Peter asks the first guy, "How long were you married?" "Twenty-four years." "Did you ever cheat on your wife?" "Yeah, seven times, but you said I was forgiven." Peter replies, "Yes, but that's not too good. Here's a Pinto for you to drive." The second guy is asked the same question. He replies, "I was married for forty-one years and cheated on her only once, but that was our first year and we really worked it out well." Peter replies, "I'm pleased to hear that; here's a Lincoln for you." The third guy walked up and said, "Peter, I know what you're going to ask. I was married for sixty-three years and didn't even look at another woman. I treated my wife like a queen!" Peter said, "That's what I like to hear. Here's a Jaguar for you." A little while later, the two guys with the Pinto and the Lincoln saw the guy with the Jaguar crying on the golden sidewalk. They went over to see what was the matter. "What's the trouble? Why are you crying?" He looked up and replied, "I just saw my wife. She was on a skateboard!"

Stage 5: How Will They Manage When I Am Gone?   The death anxiety model begins and ends on a note of reassurance. Stage five jokes reassure us that the survivors will take the death in stride and that their loved ones will not be missed nearly as much as they assume. For example: Two old ladies met in the park. After inquiring about each other's health, the topic of conversation turned to their respective husbands. "Oh," said one, "Harry died last week. He went out to the garden to get a cabbage for dinner, had a heart attack, and dropped dead in the middle of the vegetable patch." "Oh, my," said the other. "What did you do?" "I opened a can of peas instead."

And this: Lena was dying, and in her final hours she sympathetically wished her husband, Ole, a happy life when she was gone. "In fact, Ole," she said, "When I am gone, I tink you should get yourself anudder vife. And you can even give her my dresses." "Von't work," answered Ole, "She's a 6 and you're an 18."

Finally, here's an example of a stage five joke that could also be placed among stage three (funeral) jokes, thus making the point that the stages are somewhat fluid: Ole enters a funeral home. "What can I do for you?" asks the undertaker. "I vant to make arrangements for my funeral. I vant to be buried at sea." "Why would you want to be buried at sea?" asks the puzzled undertaker. "Did you serve in the Swedish navy?" "Naw, it's nuthin' like dat. I vant to get back at my vife. She said that vhen I died, she vas going to dance on my grave!"

CONCLUSION

The point of the foregoing is not that jokes about death may help someone who is grieving the loss of a loved one. Nor is it to make a case for the sensitive use of humor in funerals.[8] Instead, their value relates to the fact that almost everyone has anxieties about death that are never far from our consciousness; yet we do not talk about them much. In the psychological literature on anxiety disorders, anxiety is commonly defined as "anticipatory dread." In some cases, we know that our anticipatory dread is exaggerated, that the dreaded event is unlikely to be as onerous, irksome, or fraught with peril as we imagine it will be. While this may also be true of death, our attempts to reassure ourselves on this point seem like so much whistling in the dark.

I suggest, therefore, that humor is useful for our more chronic state of death anxiety. The very fact that it is *not* recommended, or is recommended only with great caution, for situations of acute grief implies its value for the more chronic state of death anxiety that hovers around us even when—perhaps especially when—we are feeling happy and contented, when we find ourselves thinking to ourselves or exclaiming to one another, "If only this happiness and contentment would last forever!" The painful emotions that humor in this case may spare us are not, therefore, the stabbing pains of grief, but the more persisting pain of realizing that life as we know it ends in death.

This volume of essays and sermons is concerned to reclaim the practice of lament. My reflections here might be summed up this way: When we behold the pale horse approaching with Death in the saddle (Rev. 6:8), it may help us to howl Woe (Ezek. 30:2 KJV) if we have first become accustomed to hollering, "Whoa!"[9]

NOTES

1. Walter Brueggemann, "The Formfulness of Grief," *Interpretation* 31 (1977): 263–75. The following discussion of the lament structure and the stages of grief is excerpted from my *Biblical Approaches to Pastoral Counseling* (Philadelphia: Westminster Press, 1981; republished Eugene, OR: Wipf & Stock, 2003), chap. 2.
2. Elisabeth Kübler-Ross, *On Death and Dying* (New York: Macmillan Co., 1969).
3. Donald Capps, "The Psychology of Petitionary Prayer," *Theology Today* 39 (1982): 130–41; "Praying in Our Own Behalf: Toward the Revitalization of Petitionary Prayer," *Second Opinion* 19 (1993): 21–39; "Don't Forget to Pray for Yourself," *U.S. Catholic* 60 (1995): 13–19.
4. In *On Death and Dying*, Kübler-Ross has a brief chapter on hope following her chapter on acceptance. It is clear, however, that she does not view hope as the sixth stage in the grief process, but rather as an expression that may occur at various stages, though it appears to be most commonly linked to the fifth stage of acceptance.
5. Carl A. Nighswonger, "Ministry to the Dying as a Learning Encounter," *Journal of Thanatology* 1 (1971): 101–8.
6. William E. Kelly, "An Investigation of Worry and Sense of Humor," *Journal of Psychology* 136 (2002): 657–66.
7. When I told this joke in a class, only a few students laughed, leaving me to wonder whether the joke itself isn't especially funny or whether seminarians today wouldn't know that Ole and Lars lived in an era when the third person of the

Trinity was more ghost than spirit, and that when people died, they gave theirs up. Another possibility, of course, is that they understood the joke, thought it was pretty funny, but were inhibited from laughing because it made humorous use of an ancient Christian doctrine.

8. Kenn Filkins makes such a case in "Funeral for a Funny Lady: Humor and the Funeral Message," *Preaching* 9 (1994): 25–26.

9. The following joke illustrates this point: A man has been walking in the hot desert for about two weeks. Finally, just as he's about to collapse from heat exhaustion, he sees the home of a missionary. Tired and weak, he crawls up to the house and falls on the doorstep. The missionary finds him and nurses him back to health. Feeling better, the man thanks the missionary and continues on his trek through the desert. On his way out the door he sees a horse. He goes back to the house and asks the missionary, "Could I borrow your horse and give it back when I reach the nearest town?" The missionary says, "Yes, but there is a special thing about this horse. You have to say 'Thank God' to make it go, and 'Amen' to make it stop." Feeling elated and not paying much attention, the man says, "Sure. Okay." So he gets on the horse, says, "Thank God," and the horse starts walking. Then he says, "Thank God, thank God," and the horse starts trotting. Feeling secure, the man says, "Thank God, thank God, thank God, thank God," and the horse starts to gallop. Pretty soon he sees a cliff coming up, and he begins doing everything he can to make the horse stop. "Whoa, stop, hold on!" Finally he remembers and shouts, "Amen!" The horse stops four inches from the cliff. Then the man leans back in the saddle, wipes his brow, and says, "Thank God."

Chapter 8

Jesus' Cry, God's Cry, and Ours

William Stacy Johnson

In his dying moments from the cross Jesus of Nazareth raised up a loud cry to God.[1] Many contemporary theologians have interpreted this cry as a declaration of despair. They believe that God determined to forsake unreservedly this one who called him "Abba, Father" and, moreover, that this God-forsakenness marks the pivotal and defining moment in the drama of human salvation. In some circles this thesis of God-abandonment has risen to the level of an axiom, a belief merely assumed rather than needing an explicit argument to sustain it.[2]

Despite the contemporary appeal of this divine abandonment thesis, it is marked by serious exegetical, theological, and pastoral flaws. I want to challenge this thesis by insisting that the good news of the gospel points in a different direction. The defining premise of the gospel is that God did *not* abandon Jesus when he cried out. Rather, the God who is *for* us and *with* us in Jesus Christ refused to abandon Jesus in his affliction and instead raised him up. It is precisely because God was united with Jesus in his agony and refused to abandon him that we can be assured of God's refusal to abandon us. In Jesus' cry, God cries too; and in Jesus' cry, our own cries are validated by God and will be redeemed. In short, God is at work in Jesus' cry to hear us, to save us, and to empower us, so that in response to this God who refuses to let us go, we too, by the Spirit's power, can resolve *not* to abandon one another.

GOD HEARS US: FINDING PURPOSE IN JESUS' CRY

The thesis of Jesus' utter God-abandonment owes much of its current strength to Jürgen Moltmann's 1972 classic, *The Crucified God*.[3] For Moltmann everything turns on a particular exegesis of the so-called "cry of dereliction" in the Gospel of Mark. Twice in Mark's Gospel Jesus cries out with a loud voice. The first time, his cry comprises the very first line of the Twenty-second Psalm, "My God, my God, why have you forsaken me?"[4] The second time, the cry is inarticulate, and Jesus dies. That Jesus is invoking a psalm here seems to make little difference to Moltmann, who thinks he hears in this cry an assertion that God is absent.[5] For Moltmann, Jesus' statement is construed not so much through the genre of biblical lament, in which God is still presumed to be present and able to save, as through the lens of modern atheistic protest.[6] Moltmann asserts, first, that Jesus died in despair, not devotion to his cause; second, that his cry asserted God's absence, not faith in God's presence; and, third, that, because he was absolutely cut off from God, Jesus' death was more horrendous than any other death imaginable.

Jesus' death was a heaving, panting wretchedness. There can be no question about that, since crucifixion was a brutal form of death by torture. Yet each of the three points Moltmann wants to make is difficult to sustain upon a careful reading of the biblical text. First, let us consider the purpose of Jesus' cry, and especially the way it functions in the telling of Jesus' story.[7] In the Synoptic Gospels Jesus' cry is not an assertion about God's absence, as Moltmann insists, but an invocation of God's presence. After all, the psalm Jesus invokes in Mark falls within the genre of a cry for help.[8] Though the supplicant in Psalm 22 is suffering bodily affliction to the point of death, he entrusts his cause to God.[9] It is a cry directed not *against* God but *to* God.[10]

Not only is this a cry for help, but the prayer in Psalm 22 is one that receives a definite answer. For both the psalmist and the evangelist, God is a God who saves the righteous. This theology of deliverance is written into the very structure of the psalm. The first part—the lament of verses 2–21a—recalls how righteous ones in the past have cried out to God and have been delivered (vv. 4–5). The second part—the thanksgiving of verses 21b–31—declares that God "did not hide his face from me, but heard when I cried to him" (v. 24b).

Whereas Moltmann focuses his interpretation solely on the first line of the psalm—the cry—it is actually the whole psalm to which Mark and Matthew allude in order to explain Jesus' passion. At one level, this is simply literary common sense. The first line of the psalm brings to mind for knowledgeable readers the entire psalm, much as a Christian's recitation of the words "Our Father, who art in heaven" brings to mind the rest of the Lord's Prayer.[11] Yet the list of more explicit literary parallels between the psalm and Mark's retelling of the passion is impressive, so much so that the recounting of Jesus' crucifixion echoes quite specifically what occurs in the psalm.[12]

The psalmist is reviled by his tormentors (Ps. 22:6), and so is Jesus (Mark 15:29, 31–32; Matt. 27:39, 41–43; cf. Luke 23:35–36). In both the psalm and the passion narrative, people pass by "wagging their heads" at the afflicted one (Ps. 22:7; cf. Mark 15:29; Matt. 27:39). The psalmist trusts in God to deliver him (Ps. 22:8), just as those who are deriding Jesus say, "He trusts in God; let God deliver him now, if he wants to; for he said, 'I am God's Son'" (Matt. 27:43; cf. Mark 15:31–32). In the same way that the psalmist has evildoers encircling him (Ps. 22:16), Jesus has brigands to his right and to his left (Mark 15:27; Matt. 27:38, 44; cf. Luke 23:32, 33b, 39). The psalmist laments that the perpetrators divide his clothes and cast lots for them (Ps. 22:18), a circumstance that is repeated at the crucifixion (Mark 15:24; Matt. 27:35; cf. Luke 23:34b).

The psalmist indicates that in the darkness of night he has shouted before the Lord (Ps. 22:2), in the same way that darkness covers the whole earth before Jesus utters his cry (Mark 15:33–34; Matt. 27:45–46; cf. Luke 23:44–45a). Moreover, the psalmist shouts out to God a second time, whereupon God hears him (Ps. 22:19–21, 24b). Similarly, Jesus cries out a second time before he dies (Mark 15:37), at which point the curtain of the temple is torn in two (Mark 15:38). Finally, in the psalm it is said that the Gentiles shall worship the Lord, who delivers the one who was afflicted (Ps. 22:27); and in all three Synoptic Gospels a Gentile centurion makes a statement concerning Jesus' divine sonship immediately after Jesus invokes the psalm (Mark 15:39; Matt. 27:54; Luke 23:47).[13] The cumulative weight of these parallels is quite impressive, making it hard to avoid the conclusion that the whole psalm is being invoked by Mark to make his theological point: Jesus cried out to God not in despair but for deliverance.

This way of understanding Jesus' cry accords with the collective witness of the biblical writers. If the words from the cross in Mark and Matthew bespeak Jesus' agony as he cries out for deliverance, then Luke accentuates Jesus' trust in that deliverance itself. Quoting not Psalm 22:1 but Psalm 31:6, the Lukan Jesus dies saying, "Father, into your hands I commit my spirit" (Luke 23:46 RSV). In Luke, furthermore, Jesus issues words of forgiveness to those who have done him in (Luke 23:34a) and a statement of comfort to those who are dying with him (Luke 23:43). Far from giving us a portrait of divine abandonment, the combined witness of the New Testament is one of a divine presence through a savior who identifies with the afflicted one on the cross and who reaches out to embrace the afflictions of us all. This divine outreach to humanity becomes intensified in John's Gospel, in which Jesus, who is the embodiment of God's word of grace, assures his followers that "I am not alone because the Father is with me" (John 16:32). In addition, Jesus' final words in John are an expression not of despair but of devotion to his mission of divine graciousness: "It is finished" (John 19:30).[14] Perhaps the best summary of what motivated Jesus' cry is provided by the letter to the Hebrews: "In the days of his flesh, Jesus offered up prayers and supplications, with loud cries and tears, to the one who was able to save him from death, and he was heard because of his reverent submission" (Heb. 5:7).

Second, there is the question of God's role in Jesus' death and vindication. Moltmann's claim is that God positively abandoned Jesus in his time of agony. Yet this is the very claim that Jesus' tormentors are making against him as he dies; for that matter, it is the very claim that the Gospel writers are aiming to refute. To be sure, in some sense the Gospel writers do consider the death of Jesus to have occurred, as do all events, under the will of God.[15] In addition, Moltmann rightly appeals to the teaching of the apostle Paul that Jesus was "handed over" (*paradidōmi*) by God into the custody of evildoers (Rom. 8:32; cf. Rom. 1:18ff.) and that Jesus surrendered himself so as to occupy the place of sinners for our sakes (Gal. 2:20, 3:13; 1 Cor. 5:21). Yet sending one's agent into harm's way is by no means the same thing as "abandoning" or "forsaking" him. A general sends a loyal soldier into battle knowing that the soldier's life is at risk, but this is not the same thing as willing the soldier's death.

Mark is very clear about this: "The Son of Man is to be betrayed into *human* hands, and *they* will kill him" (Mark 9:31, emphasis added).[16] He perceives what happens to Jesus as following an ancient pattern; for, as indicated in the allegorical parable of the Wicked Tenants (Mark 12:1–12; cf. Matt. 21:33–46; Luke 20:9–19), the owner of the vineyard (God) has sent many servants in the past and now sends the beloved son hoping that, finally, those who occupy the land will listen.[17] Accordingly it is the conflicts Jesus provokes with human authorities in carrying out his mission that lead to his death, conflicts evidenced for Mark in Jesus' apocalyptic actions against the temple (Mark 11:1–11, 15–18; 13:1–8), his oblique words against the blasphemous claims of the Roman political authority (Mark 13:14–23), and his popularity among the riot-prone crowds (Mark 11:8–10; 14:2). These actions were enough to confirm his status as politically controversial; they were even inflammatory enough to get him crucified between two *lēistai* (Mark 15:27)—a word which is best translated not (as many traditional versions have it) "thieves" but "brigands" or "bandits."[18] The biblical witnesses present Jesus as being executed right alongside two figures whom the Romans considered to be insurrectionists.[19]

This sheds light on yet another reason that the Markan Jesus appeals to Psalm 22. In both the Hebrew original and the Septuagint translation into Greek, the wording of Psalm 22 places a question before God concerning purpose: for what *reason* (Mark 15:34, *eis ti*), the supplicant asks, or to what *purpose* (Matt. 27:46, *hinati*), am I dying? This grammatical observation gives a vital clue into the function and meaning of the cry in both Mark and Matthew. The psalmist is framing the very question that Jesus' ignominious death actually posed to the earliest Christian community, namely, why did the Messiah have to die?

The answer to this question—that the Messiah died on account of the faithful life he led—leads us to the third point, namely, the question of the relationship between Jesus' suffering and the afflictions suffered by other human beings.

Moltmann claims that, because he has been forsaken by God, Jesus suffered a death that was unique in kind, not like that of any other person before or since.[20] "Just as there was a unique fellowship with God in his life . . . so in his death there was a unique abandonment by God."[21] Yet here again Moltmann's interpretation is confuted by the very way in which Jesus' cry is presented by the biblical writers.

Jesus, in lifting up the lament from Psalm 22, is situating himself directly within that long line of servants who have suffered unjustly for God's sake and whom God will *not* abandon. In praying the psalm, as James L. Mays puts it, Jesus "joins the multitudinous company of the afflicted and becomes one with them in their suffering."[22] This is not a suffering that the Gospel writers set out to glorify or that they consider to be redemptive because it is suffering for suffering's sake. Rather, this is an unjust human suffering that bears a connection with all unjust suffering everywhere and that is decried by God. This same sort of suffering, as it turns out, is going to be visited upon Jesus' disciples, which is why Mark advises his readers to persevere and take heart in the knowledge that the one who endures suffering until the end will be saved (Mark 13:13).

To summarize, the God-abandonment thesis misconstrues the nature of Jesus' cry, skews the relationship of God to this cry, and obscures the relationship of Jesus' cry to the cries of others. It will no longer do, therefore, for theologians simply to assume without further justification that this God-abandonment perspective represents the best way to exegete Jesus' cry. Not only this, but in the case of Moltmann the God-abandonment exegesis is interwoven with a broader theological perspective that in its own right is problematic. Those who are tempted to embrace the God-abandonment approach need to think this through more carefully.

First, Moltmann's exegesis of the cry is in the service of a rather extreme theology of creation, a theology that alleges the world stands under complete and unrelenting alienation, darkness, and despair. Moltmann argues that in creating the world, God had to "withdraw" to make a place for the creature.[23] Moltmann then goes on to make the questionable claim that by withdrawing in this fashion, "the space which comes into being and is set free by God's self-limitation is a literally God-forsaken space."[24] It is in this God-forsaken space that the created world is situated. Moltmann does allow that in a desire to overcome this God-forsakenness, God is suffering along with the world in Jesus Christ, but until the eschatological renewal of all things, the world we inhabit remains bereft of God's true power. Hence we human beings can do no more than place our hope in a new world that is yet to come. Given Moltmann's presuppositions, it is clear that if Jesus is to occupy our place in the darkness of the present world, then Jesus *must* suffer God-abandonment. In other words, his philosophical presuppositions drive his exegesis. The question, of course, is whether Moltmann's presuppositions here make any sense. I believe they fail to do justice to the biblical teaching that, despite its fall into sin, the world was created "good" (Gen. 1:4, 10b, 12b, 18b, 25b, 31) and that it is still a domain in which God is actively at work to save.

Second, and more serious, it is not clear why anyone would want to trust the "god" that Moltmann describes. If, as Moltmann insists, God abandoned this one son of Israel long ago, then what would keep God from abandoning nearly six million children of Israel during the dark years from 1933 to 1945? Or the 1.5 million children of God in Armenia during the First World War? Or the 20 million children of God under Joseph Stalin in the former Soviet Union? Or up to 72 million children of God under Mao Zedong in Communist China? Or the 1–1.7 million children of God under the Khmer Rouge in Cambodia?[25] Or who-knows-how-many Native Americans at the hands of European settlers in North America? Moltmann's response is that in abandoning Jesus, God was in reality subjecting God's own self, in the person of the Son, to abandonment. Yet this does not really answer the question. The question is whether, as such, divine "abandonment" of the other—in this case, Jesus—is a godly strategy under any circumstances. Moltmann's claim that God is intimately present with those who suffer atrocities rings hollow if God the Father left Jesus—who cried out to him in the earth-bound frailty of his human flesh—to darkness and despair in his hour of greatest need.

It is no wonder that Moltmann's thesis of God-abandonment has prompted the famous objection, especially prominent among feminist theologians, that a God who would proactively abandon the Son is actually engaged in a brand of "cosmic child abuse."[26] Moltmann's answer to this charge hardly provides any theological comfort. God's abandonment of Jesus differs from child abuse, according to Moltmann, in that Jesus is not the mere passive object of God's rejection but is rather an acting subject. In fact, God the Father and God the Son have, so to speak, entered a "pact" with one another concerning this arrangement. Jesus, who is one in divinity with the Father, has consented to his fate in an act of gracious self-surrender.[27] Yet, if indeed God the Father is the one who abandons the Son to this affliction, it is difficult to see how Jesus' consent to his own death by torture can absolve God of blame. Would a court of law absolve a human father, were this rationale of the child's consent to be offered in defense? Let us pray not. Moreover, the defense Moltmann offers to this charge of abuse does not square with the rest of his account, for one of the chief features of Moltmann's theology is that Jesus' cry precipitated an unfathomable "rift" in the very life of God. Why would there be a rift if this is all prearranged? It is a rift, because Jesus "died as one rejected by his God and his Father."[28]

It must be acknowledged that Moltmann desperately wants to find what he thinks is fatherly mercy and grace in the events of Jesus' story. In abandoning Jesus the Son, Moltmann argues, God the Father also suffers a severe loss, which is the loss of the Son to death. Yet how this loss on God's part is supposed to be redemptive, or why we should sympathize with a God who enters into a pact with the Son to consent to such an injustice, is not clear. This twofold sense of loss is predicated on Moltmann's view that God's being as Father, Son, and Spirit consists in three individual centers of consciousness, three I's, each of whom experiences Jesus' death in a different way. Moltmann leaves us with an interesting piece of theological speculation. However, it is not, so far as I can see, the most per-suasive way to articulate the gospel. Moltmann stands in a long line of Western theologians who maintain that God can be *for us* only by being *against Jesus*. To this line of thinking, it is time to say no.

The central conviction of the gospel is that it is precisely because God hears Jesus' cry that our cries also are heard. It is because of God's yes to Jesus Christ by the Spirit's power that there is now no condemnation for any who are in Christ Jesus (Rom. 8: 1). When Jesus cried out to God for deliverance, he did so in agony but not in despair. He died forsaken by all around him, but not by God. And he suffered and died so that, by the power of the resurrection, suffering and death would not have the last word.

GOD SAVES US: JESUS' CRY AS GOD'S CRY

There is always more to a biblical text than appears on the surface. On one level, the Scriptures present Jesus' death cry as that of a thoroughly human figure—frail, vulnerable, defeated. His is the cry of one whose life—sadly, mercilessly, unjustly—is being snuffed out by violent men. Yet on another level, the church has come to hear still more in Jesus' cry. In the voice of this Jesus who is dying, by faith we can also hear the very voice of the God of life. If it is true that in Jesus Christ the eternal Word became flesh, then in Jesus' cry of death, the God of life is also crying out. Although I cannot here present a complete theology of salva-tion, I do want to state briefly three theological implications that flow from the confession that, in being one with Jesus in his agony, the incarnate God cries out from the cross.

First, Jesus' cry is replete with Trinitarian significance. As the third-century theologian Gregory Nazianzus recognized, Jesus' cry expresses the agony of God the Son being lifted up to God the Father through the mediation of God the Spirit.[29] It is not, as Moltmann claims, an agony that caused some sort of rup-ture in the life of God but an act by which the agony of us all is lifted up into the sphere of divine healing. Jesus' cry is the decisive divine embrace of the fragility, suffering, and despair that mark the human condition. Indeed, God is never more divine than in God's determination to be our God even unto incarnation, humil-iation, and death.

Based on this togetherness of the Father with the Son through the Spirit, patristic exegesis in both the East and the West reached a remarkable unanimity concerning the cry, a unanimity the church needs to recapture. They took Psalm 22 as a hermeneutical key in interpreting Jesus' death, and, on Trinitarian and christological grounds, they rejected the idea that Jesus' cry signaled God's aban-donment.[30] In the East this was articulated by none other than Athanasius, that great architect of Nicene orthodoxy, who interpreted the ominous signs that sur-rounded Jesus' cry—the earthquake, the rending of the veil, the eclipse of the sun, the dead appearing from the graves, and the affirmation of Jesus' righteousness in the centurion's confession—as clear evidence that God was present at the time of Jesus' death.[31] Chrysostom went a step further, identifying the numinous events that accompany Jesus' death as signals of God's presence in wrath—a wrath directed not against Jesus but against the human beings who killed him.[32] The divine abandonment idea was also rejected in the early days of the Latin West when Augustine insisted that, while Jesus was abandoned by those who ridiculed him in his death, he in no way was forsaken by God.[33] In fact, Augustine considered it impossible that the God who dwells in the selfsame unity of Father, Son, and Holy Spirit could be guilty of such a contradiction.[34]

Yet this affirmation of God's solidarity with Jesus even unto death left patristic interpretation with a conundrum. While these theologians insisted on God's incarnate presence with Jesus in his death, they were equally insistent that it was impossible for God to suffer. In order to make sense of this impasse, the consensus view was that Jesus suffered not in his divinity but only in his humanity. Thus Athanasius maintained that when Jesus in the garden said, "Let this cup pass from me," and from the cross, "Why have you forsaken me?" it was his humanity speaking, not his divinity.[35]

What are we to make of this? No doubt there is an element of truth in this patristic reticence to declare God a suffering God. By definition, God is not mortal. Yet at the same time patristic theology let certain Greek ideas about God's inability to be moved, to change, or to be affected by God's creatures color its interpretation of the gospel. If there is no capacity in God to embrace our suffering and to make it God's own, then the biblical witness to God's intimate care and concern for our salvation is vitiated. Moreover, as Gregory Nazianzus famously argued, if any part of our humanity remains unassumed by God, then that part of our humanity also remains unsaved.[36] If God does not embrace our suffering, then it remains a suffering without hope. Patristic interpretation saw correctly that God was for and with Jesus in his cry, but patristic theology failed to draw the appropriate conclusion, namely, that God is for and with us in our suffering.

In order to correct this incongruity in ancient Christian teaching, the twentieth-century theologian Karl Barth developed a bolder view of the triune God's relationship to the suffering that Jesus endured. Barth proclaimed that in Jesus' suffering, God suffers too. And this, in turn, led to a bolder view of God's relationship to Jesus' cry, a view in which the ancient assumption that God is incapable of suffering is brought fundamentally into question and transformed.[37] In Jesus' cry of abjection we learn that something is at stake, not only for Jesus and for us, but also for God. God enters into the suffering of Jesus, such that something momentous takes place for God in Jesus' dying moments from Golgotha. Something grievous is being transacted in Jesus' cry, something painful is being communicated here: between God—and God![38]

Unfortunately, like Moltmann, Barth construes Jesus' forsakenness on the cross as a *God*-forsakenness. To be sure, the division between the Father and the Son is not as stark in Barth, since, unlike Moltmann, Barth views God not as three I's but as a single subject, a single I intimately at work in three activities.

Still, Barth perpetuates a divine abandonment theology that fails, because it teaches that God is able to be *with* God's children in their suffering only by being *against* Jesus at the time of his cry.

Second, Jesus' cry is part of an unfolding drama in which, through the divine and human togetherness in Jesus Christ, something is at stake both for human beings and for God. What does this mean? According to the ecumenical councils of Nicaea (325 CE) and Chalcedon (481 CE), Jesus Christ is both fully human and fully divine.[39] This does not mean that Jesus is 50 percent human and 50 percent divine, or that Jesus is merely in certain ways human and in certain other ways divine. Rather, if we take the doctrine seriously, it means that the whole drama of Jesus' life—the way he was born, the way he lived, the way he died, and the way he lives again today—constitutes a togetherness of the human and the divine, in which both parties are united in one incarnate subject, with both, so to speak, having something on the line.

What is on the line for human beings is their redemption; what is at stake for God is the accomplishment of this redemption. The latter concern, whether the word of God accomplishes what it sets out to accomplish (see Isa. 55:11), is not merely the posing of a hypothetical question. Paul, in effect, raises it in Romans when he raises the issue whether it it possible that the word of God has failed in the case of Israel (Rom. 9:6). The answer the apostle gives, of course, is "By no means!" (cf. Rom. 9:14). Yet the "By no means!" here represents the assurance of things hoped for. It is a true answer the apostle gives, but an eschatological one. Living into the mystery of Jesus' cry, then, means to allow both the question— real and harrowing as it is—and the answer—truly an answer but also an eschatological one—to play their necessary and legitimate roles. It is only by living into the experiential gap between question and answer, between promise and fulfillment, that we can truly embrace the cry rather than squelch it.

To put it a different way, what happens in Jesus of Nazareth is the coming together of two stories into one. The story of Jesus in all its humanity—its twists and turns, its defeats and its victories—is at the very same time the story of God. If the ending of the story is eschatological for us, there is a real sense—if we can say it reverently—that the story is also eschatological for God. The story is real, both for God and for us, but its plot is still unfolding. It is not that the Scriptures are telling a story *about* God, as though the story being told here were merely an allegory or fable. Rather, what we learn in the symbolic constellation of events and signs that surround the life, death, and resurrection of Jesus of Nazareth is this: God is as Jesus is; God does as Jesus does; God suffers as Jesus suffers; indeed, God cries as Jesus cries. Or as John puts it, "And the Word became flesh and lived among us, and we have seen his glory, the glory as of a father's only son, full of grace and truth" (John 1:14). And again as Paul explains, "God was in Christ reconciling the world to himself, not counting their trespasses against them, and entrusting the message of reconciliation to us" (2 Cor. 5:19).

Understanding the Gospels as a still-unfolding divine and human story raises a third issue. Divine abandonment theology makes the mistake of focusing narrowly on the saving significance of Jesus' death. Rather than being an isolated moment in time, however, Jesus' death cry stands in relationship to the whole sweep of the drama of salvation. It is as though divine-abandonment theologians freeze-frame the drama of salvation at a single point and assert that this moment is to be elevated above all the others. Yet the meaning of Jesus' cry of death can be properly viewed only in relation to what preceded it and what followed it, and these other moments also contribute to the saving significance of Jesus' person.

In the first place, Jesus' cry at death is intimately connected to the cries that preceded it. For example, Ignatius of Antioch emphasized early on that Jesus' death cry is part of the same mystery in which Mary cried out in childbirth and Jesus himself let out his very first cry of life.[40] For Jesus and for each human being, the cry at birth is the most vulnerable, the most involuntary of cries; it is a sign of our utter need of grace. This cry of Jesus at birth, on the analysis I have presented here, is no less a divine and human cry than the cry from the cross. By determining to become human, God embraced this birth cry too, in all its frailty, and made it God's own. Both this earliest cry of Jesus and the cry he uttered in death, moreover, were uttered in solidarity with the cries of many others that accompanied him on his earthly journey—the cry of Rachel weeping for the slaughtered innocents (Matt. 2:16–18), the cry of John the Baptist preparing the way in the wilderness (Mark 1:2–6; Matt. 3:1–6: Luke 3:1–6; John 1:19–23), the cries of the Jerusalem crowds who hailed him as king (Mark 11:9–10; Matt. 21:9; Luke 19:38; John 12:13). Even the cries of the demon-possessed (e.g., Mark 10:46–52; Matt. 9:27–31; Luke 18:35–43), and the angry cries of "Crucify him!" (Mark 15:13–14; Matt. 27:22–23; Luke 23:21–23; cf. John 18:40) contribute to make his story what it is. All these cries—and the cries of each one of us—are gathered up, judged, and blessed in his cry from the cross.

In the second place, the New Testament is also bold to declare that one day the risen Christ will cry out a final time, this time not in the vulnerability of birth or the agony of death, but in victory. The risen Christ will cry out again on that day when our redemption is to become complete. "For the Lord [Jesus] himself, with a cry of command, with the archangel's call and with the sound of God's trumpet, will descend from heaven, and the dead in Christ will rise first" (1 Thess. 4:16).[41] Again, if the Chalcedonian character of Jesus' life is to be thought through consistently, then even this eschatological shout of victory is both a divine and human cry, and one that is already adumbrated in Jesus' cry from the cross. This final shout is divine, for only divinity is capable of such a cry. Yet this victory cry is also human, because in the resurrection of Jesus Christ our very humanity too has been raised up.

GOD EMPOWERS US: JESUS' CRY AND OUR CRIES

What we say about Jesus' cry, whether God was absent or present to Jesus in his death, makes a significant difference in how we respond to the cries of others.

This is illustrated in a poignant way in Ingmar Bergman's 1962 film *Winter Light*. Set during a snow-covered midwinter, the story focuses on the plight of Tomas Ericsson, a Lutheran pastor who, following the death of his wife, loses all faith in a deity who cares or can save. He confides in Jonas, a parishioner contemplating suicide, that he has come to see "god" as but a fiction, an "echo-god" of his own creation. Tomas advises Jonas to let go of the false comforts of a supernatural realm, to admit that there is no explanation for evil, and to embrace whatever goodness in life can be found.

The conversation between Tomas and Jonas takes place underneath a large crucifix. After Jonas leaves, Tomas, becoming agitated, declares once and for all his belief that God is absent, crying out, "God, my God, why have you deserted me?" Like the crucifixion of Jesus itself in the Gospels, the film's story begins at 9:00 in the morning and ends at 3:00 in the afternoon. It begins rather bleakly with Tomas officiating at a sparsely attended worship service. It ends more bleakly still as Tomas intones the words of the prayer book at an afternoon service. Having just learned that after leaving his office, Jonas shot himself, Tomas goes through the motions of worship in a near-empty church.

Why Tomas persists in leading the worship service when almost all have deserted the church is unclear. What is clear throughout the film is that Tomas exemplifies in his own self-absorbed, cold, and abusive relationships with others the very despairing traits he imagines in his portrait of "god." Just as he considers God to be indifferent, so Tomas himself withholds any feeling, care, or concern from those around him. Just as he believes God to be absent from the lives of the faithful, so Tomas is himself powerless to reach out to those who need him. The film is a tragic parable of the emptiness that divine-abandonment theology, so prevalent in the churches of Europe that Ingmar Bergman knew, could produce. In making this film, Bergman signaled his own alienation from this version of the Christian faith.

To leave this version of the Christian faith, however, need not lead one to give up on the gospel. Quite the contrary. In contrast to divine-abandonment theology's fixation upon despair and death, the revelation that is ours in Jesus Christ embodies and proclaims a dynamic movement from death to life. Not unlike the centurion who stood facing Jesus when he cried out from the cross (Mark 15:39; cf. Matt. 27:54), we are enabled to participate in this life-giving movement. Believing, by the Spirit's power, that God is present in the person of Jesus Christ when he cries out, we have confidence that our own cries are joined to Jesus' cry and redeemed. Insofar as Jesus is the pioneer and perfecter of our faith (Heb. 12:2; 2:10), he recapitulates the cries of all people everywhere, the cries of all who ever have suffered or ever will suffer. Because Jesus' cry is human, we know that Jesus participates in our situation. Because Jesus' cry is divine, we know that God reaches out to save our situation. In this one cry, by which divinity is revealed in humanity and humanity redeemed in divinity, all other cries take on a new and urgent significance. Precisely because God did *not* abandon Jesus in his time of trial, we come to see that God draws near in grace to all who are poor, weak, defeated, or lost.

And because God has made our situation God's own, God is urging us to pay heed to the cries of our neighbors. It is not enough to confront the cry of Jesus Christ with the resources of exegetical and theological wisdom. To heed Jesus' cry is to give ourselves to it in passionate, pastoral, practical response. Just as God hears our cries in Jesus Christ, so too by the Spirit's power are we called to hear the cries of one another. Just as God embraces our cries to save us, so too are we called to participate in and contribute to God's great deliverance. Through Jesus' cry, we are given both a power and a promise. It is the power to respond to the needs of the other; it is the promise that "just as you did it to one of the least of these who are members of my family, you did it to me" (Matt. 25:40). Knowing that God is *for* us, because God is for the crucified; and knowing that God is *with* us, because God is with Jesus in his cry; so we also know, by the power of the resurrection, that God is always at work among us, calling us to be *for* and *with* one another.

NOTES

1. This, at least, according to three of the canonical Gospels as well as the non-canonical *Gospel of Peter* (Mark 15:33–17; Matt. 27:45–50; Luke 23:44–46; *Gospel of Peter* 5:15–19).

2. Three recent examples will suffice: Robert W. Jenson, *Systematic Theology*, vol. 1, *The Triune God* (New York: Oxford University Press, 1997), 49; Alan E. Lewis, *Between Cross and Resurrection: A Theology of Holy Saturday* (Grand Rapids: Wm. B. Eerdmans Publishing Co., 2001), 53–54, 82–83; Miroslav Volf, *Exclusion and Embrace: A Theological Exploration of Identity, Otherness, and Reconciliation* (Nashville: Abingdon Press, 1996), 9. Each of these otherwise excellent books assumes, without argument, that Jesus' cry was a signal not merely of forsakenness by human beings but forsakenness by God. Important predecessor works that operate from this assumption include Karl Barth, *Church Dogmatics*, ed. G. W. Bromiley and T. F. Torrance (Edinburgh: T & T Clark, 1956–62), vols. I/1 to IV/4, esp. IV/1; Hans Urs von Balthasar, *Mysterium Pascale: The Mystery of Easter*, trans. Aidan Nichols (Grand Rapids: Wm. B. Eerdmans Publishing Co., 1993); Jürgen Moltmann, *The Crucified God: The Cross of Christ as the Foundation and Criticism of Christian Theology*, trans. R. A. Wilson and John Bowden (London: SCM Press, 1974); Eberhard Jüngel, *God as the Mystery of the World*, trans. Darrell Guder (Grand Rapids: Wm. B. Eerdmans Publishing Co., 1983).

3. Jürgen Moltmann, *Der gekreuzigte Gott* (Munich: Christian Kaiser Verlag, 1972, 1973) [ET: *The Crucified God: The Cross of Christ as the Foundation and Criticism of Christian Theology*].

4. It is possible that Psalm 22 first became associated with the crucifixion of Jesus because of the lament of the psalmist in v. 17: "They have pierced my hands and my feet." Although this line is neither quoted nor alluded to by Mark or Matthew, the pierced hands and feet of Jesus are mentioned in the resurrection appearance stories in both Luke and John (Luke 24:39; John 20:25, 27).

5. Moltmann draws a problematic contrast between the psalmist, who is calling upon the God of Israel for self-vindication, and Jesus, who, he alleges, demands that the one he has called "Father" should rise up to vindicate not only Jesus but also "himself"—i.e., God (*The Crucified God*, 150–51). This contrast is questionable, both because of the erroneous distinction it presupposes between the

God of Israel and the triune God, and because it removes Jesus' cry from the genre of biblical lament. For a perspective that does not make this mistake, see James L. Mays, "Prayer and Christology: Psalm 22 as Perspective on the Passion," *Theology Today* 42 (October 1985): 322–33.

6. On this point, cf. John Roth, "A Theodicy of Protest," in *Encountering Evil: Live Options in Theodicy*, ed. Stephen T. Davis (Atlanta: John Knox Press, 1981), 7–22.

7. A comprehensive treatment of the cry is available in Raymond E. Brown, *The Death of the Messiah: From Gethsemane to the Grave: A Commentary on the Passion Narratives in the Four Gospels,* 2 vols. (New York: Doubleday, 1994), 2:40–42. See also the treatment of the words from the cross in Kenneth Grayston, *Dying, We Live: A New Enquiry into the Death of Christ in the New Testament* (New York: Oxford University Press, 1990), 222–28.

8. See Mays, "Prayer and Christology," 22.

9. Trust in God is made clear in vv. 4–5: "In you our ancestors trusted: they trusted and you delivered them. To you they cried, and were saved; in you they trusted, and were not put to shame." For the description of the psalmist's afflictions, see vv. 6, 14–15, 16b–17.

10. My construal of the relationship between the psalm and the passion narratives is informed by the materials collected in Brown, *The Death of the Messiah*, 2:1455–57.

11. I have been informed by conversations with John Muddiman, who suggests that Mark was essentially a set of notes used for oral recitation. If this were so, then not all of those hearing the story would necessarily have been familiar with the psalm that lay behind Jesus' prayer. Even those who heard the prayer in the story itself mistook it as an invocation of Elijah (Mark 15:35). It is also quite possible that Mark's purpose is ironic. The cry may have been misunderstood by those witnessing Jesus' death, as so many things are misunderstood by characters in Mark's Gospel, yet there is also a deeper meaning available to those who know the psalm. For an ironic reading of Mark, see Donald H. Juel, *The Gospel of Mark*, Interpreting Biblical Texts (Nashville: Abingdon Press, 1999).

12. Raymond Brown mentions all of these parallels, though he is not convinced all of them are intended by Mark. See Brown, *The Death of the Messiah,* 2:1455–57.

13. For purposes of my argument, it makes no difference whether the centurion's statement is a confession or a sarcasm ("Yeah, right, this is the Son of God"). If it is a confession, then the divine abandonment hypothesis becomes virtually impossible. Why, if the centurion saw Jesus questioning God's presence, would it engender faith? If, on the other hand, the centurion speaks ironically, he still speaks the truth, though unintentionally. Hence his mockery becomes a negative witness to Jesus' solidarity with God. It is not a warrant for an atonement theology based on God-forsakenness. On the latter point, see Donald Juel, *Messianic Exegesis: Christological Interpretation of the Old Testament in Early Christianity* (Philadelphia: Fortress Press, 1988), 114–17; and *The Gospel of Mark,* 146–47.

14. The argument of Moltmann and others trades on the idea that in John one is dealing with a repudiation of the Markan theology based on Psalm 22. Yet it is significant that the importance of Psalm 22 lingers in all four Gospels. See Brown, *The Death of the Messiah,* 2:1455–57.

15. See Juel, *The Gospel of Mark,* chap. 8.

16. It is also human agency Mark sees at work in Jesus' other two passion predictions. "Then he began to teach them that the Son of Man must undergo great suffering, and be rejected by the elders, the chief priests, and the scribes, and be killed, and after three days rise again" (Mark 8:31). "See, we are going up to Jerusalem, and the Son of Man will be handed over (*paradothēsetai*) to the chief priests and

the scribes, and they will condemn him to death; then they will hand him over (*paradōsousin*) to the Gentiles" (Mark 10:33).

17. On this theme, see Jon Levenson, *The Death and Resurrection of the Beloved Son: The Transformation of Child Sacrifice in Judaism and Christianity* (New Haven, CT: Yale University Press, 1995).

18. See Benjamin Isaac, "Banditry," in *Anchor Bible Dictionary*, ed. David Noel Freedman, 6 vols. (New York: Doubleday, 1992), 1:575–80; Richard A. Horsley and John S. Hanson, *Bandits, Prophets, and Messiahs* (Minneapolis: Winston Press, 1985).

19. Nonetheless, Jesus seems to have remained a figure committed to nonviolent forms of resistance. The Gospels are careful to distinguish Jesus from movements that did resort to violence to overthrow Roman rule. For a general treatment, see Richard A. Horsley, *Jesus and the Spiral of Violence: Popular Jewish Resistance in Roman Palestine* (Minneapolis: Fortress, 1992).

20. Here Moltmann is following a tradition best represented in recent theology by Karl Barth, who writes flamboyantly and alarmingly: "God has never forsaken, and does not and will not forsake any [one] as [God] forsook this man. And 'forsook' means that [God] turned against [Jesus] as never before or since against any—against the One who was for [God] as none other, just as God for [God's] part was for [Jesus]. . . . But the very fact that [God] was for [Jesus] . . . entailed that [God] was wholly against [Jesus] as the One who took our place as the place of evildoers" (*Church Dogmatics* IV/3.1:414).

21. Moltmann, *The Crucified God*, 149.

22. Mays, "Prayer and Christology," 23.

23. Here Moltmann is appropriating the teaching of the sixteenth-century rabbi Isaac Luria (Yitzhak ben Solomon Ashkenazi, 1534–72), who held that God withdraws in order to create the world, and is assimilating that teaching to the divine abandonment theology. See Gershom Scholem, *Kabbalah* (New York: Quadrangle, 1974).

24. Jürgen Moltmann, *God in Creation: A New Theology of Creation and the Spirit of God,* trans. Margaret Kohl (Minneapolis: Fortress Press, 1985), 87.

25. For further reflection, see William Stacy Johnson, "Religion, Violence, and Genocide," in *Encyclopedia of Religion and War,* ed. Gabriel Palmer Fernandez (New York: Routledge, 2004), 368–73.

26. The paradigmatic form of the cosmic child-abuse argument is advanced in Rita Nakashima Brock, *Journeys by Heart: A Christology of Erotic Power* (New York: Crossroad, 1992), esp. 53–57.

27. This argument appears in Jürgen Moltmann, *The Way of Jesus Christ: Christology in Messianic Dimensions*, trans. Margaret Kohl (New York: Harper Collins, 1990), 175–78.

28. Moltmann, *The Crucified God,* 152.

29. "It was not [Jesus, the Son] who was forsaken either by the Father, or by His own Godhead, as some have thought, as if It [the Godhead] were afraid of the Passion, and therefore withdrew Itself from Him in His Sufferings (for who compelled Him either to be born on earth at all, or to be lifted up on the Cross?). But as I said, He was in His own Person representing us. For we were the forsaken and despised before, but now by the Sufferings of Him Who could not suffer, we were taken up and saved. Similarly, He makes His own our folly and our transgressions; and says what follows in the Psalm: for it is very evident that the [Twenty-second] Psalm refers to Christ" (Gregory Nazianzus, *The Fourth Theological Oration*, in Philip Schaff and Henry Wace, eds., *A Select Library of Nicene and Post-Nicene Fathers of the Christian Church,* 2nd series, vol. 12, *S. Cyril of Jerusalem, S. Gregory Nazianzen* (Grand Rapids: Wm. B. Eerdmans Publishing Co., 1989), 311.

30. For early affirmations of the importance of Psalm 22 see Justin Martyr, *Dialogue with Trypho,* in Alexander Roberts and James Donaldson, eds., *The Ante-Nicene Fathers,* vol. 1, *The Apostolic Fathers* (Grand Rapids: Wm. B. Eerdmans Publishing Co., 1989), 248; and Tertullian, *Against Marcion,* in *The Ante-Nicene Fathers,* vol. 3, *Latin Christianity,* 337. For two early examples of the rejection of divine abandonment, see Irenaeus, *Against Heresies,* in *The Ante-Nicene Fathers,* vol. 1, *The Apostolic Fathers,* 327; and Origen, *Against Celsus,* in *The Ante-Nicene Fathers,* vol. 4, 477.

31. Athanasius, *Four Discourses against the Arians,* in *A Select Library of Nicene and Post-Nicene Fathers of the Christian Church,* vol. 4, *St. Athanasius: Select Works and Letters,* 424.

32. John Chrysostom, *Homilies on the Gospel of Saint Matthew,* in *A Select Library of Nicene and Post-Nicene Fathers of the Christian Church,* vol. 10, *The Works of Saint Chrysostom,* 520–24.

33. Augustine, *On the Creed,* in *A Select Library of the Nicene and Post-Nicene Fathers of the Christian Church,* vol. 3, *St. Augustine: On the Holy Trinity, Doctrinal Treatises, Moral Treatises,* 373.

34. Augustine, *On the Psalms,* in *A Select Library of the Nicene and Post-Nicene Fathers of the Christian Church,* vol. 8, *St. Augustine: Expositions on the Book of Psalms,* 111.

35. Athanasius, *Four Discourses against the Arians,* 424. So too for Augustine, the cry of dereliction cannot be, in the final analysis, the cry of the God for whom it is impossible to suffer but a cry coming forth solely from Jesus' humanity itself (Augustine, *On the Psalms,* 111). Perhaps the most sophisticated patristic treatment of the "impassible" suffering of the eternal Word in Jesus Christ is that of Cyril of Alexandria. See the helpful study of Steven A. McKinion, *Words, Imagery, and the Mystery of Christ: A Reconstruction of Cyril of Alexandria's Christology* (Leiden: Brill, 2000), esp. 212–14.

36. Gregory Nazianzus, *Nicene and Post-Nicene Fathers,* vol. 12, 440. This argument was first pressed against the heresy of Apollinaris, who held that the mind or *nous* of Jesus was fully divine in such a way that it had displaced the human mind. The objection to this line of thought was that if Jesus did not have a human mind, then the human mind remains untouched by salvation. By this same logic, if God were to remain completely aloof from the frailty and brokenness of the human condition, then humanity would remain devoid of salvation.

37. See Karl Barth, *Church Dogmatics* II/1:370–71.

38. This is grounded in the doctrine of election, Karl Barth, *Church Dogmatics* II/2: esp. 33.

39. For a text of these creedal statements, see John H. Leith, ed., *Creeds of the Churches: A Reader in Christian Doctrine from the Bible to the Present,* 3rd edition (Atlanta: John Knox Press, 1982), 28–40.

40. Ignatius of Antioch, *Epistle to the Ephesians,* chap. 19, verse 1, in *The Ante-Nicene Fathers,* vol. 1, *The Apostolic Fathers,* 57. See also William R. Shoedel, *Ignatius of Antioch,* Hermeneia (Philadelphia: Fortress Press, 1985), 87–94. Shoedel's translation of the pertinent passage is more literal. It reads: "The virginity of Mary and her giving birth eluded the ruler of this age, likewise also the death of the Lord— three mysteries of a cry which were done in the stillness of God" (ibid., 87).

41. Cf. also Rev. 6:10; 7:10; 8:13; 12:2; 14:9; 18:18–19; 19:6; 21:4.

Chapter 9

May We Trust God and (Still) Lament? Can We Lament and (Still) Trust God?

Ellen T. Charry

Trust in God is based on the conviction that God is working good for us and is effective in bringing it about. May we, on this doctrine of providence, lament what we consider to be the tragedies of life? Conversely, can we trust divine providence in the face of senseless tragedy? This essay will attempt to wrestle with these old questions by considering the healing grace and blessing that can accompany lament when it is publicly shared.

THE PROBLEM

Lament expresses bewilderment and shock. Something has gone wrong for which we cannot account. The event must not be unnoticed; it must be shared. What is senseless to us confounds our expectations of order, rightness, and fairness. Lament is caused by what Walter Brueggemann notes are disorienting events or circumstances that make unsense of the world we strive so hard to render sensible. He thinks out of a theological cast of mind. He sees the world as basically orderly because it is created by a good and powerful God. The first note the Bible strikes is that the world is ordered by God. Tragedy interrupts that order and assaults the assumptions about God. John Kekes, of a secular philosophical cast of mind, assumes a noncoherence to the world caused by what he calls "permanent adversities" that are the result of contingency, conflict, and evil that cannot be otherwise.

The question of coherence versus chaos or at least chance is posed by both theologian and philosopher, but with an important difference. The theologian asks how we can regain stable footing when things are no longer as they ought to be, while the atheist philosopher asks how we are to live once we conclude that life does not and will not conform to meaningful patterns at all. The more stoically minded cannot experience disorientation at all, because for them there is no order to be disrupted. On this view, complaining is out of bounds. There is only endurance.

The theist has the advantage over the atheist of having set out from a stance of hope rather than despair, although the atheist would say that this hope is at the price of self-delusion. Indeed, that very hope only intensifies the psychological distress, the jarring effect of having things erupt in one's face when tragedy strikes from nowhere. The atheist, lacking hope that things even might be different, must fall back on pure fortitude. The best that one can hope for is to bear it with dignity and a cheerful countenance. There is greater disappointment for the theologian than for the philosopher who never expected much to begin with.

Trust that the world is orderly, then, divides believer from skeptic. Lament is the province only of the believer, because it shatters that trust. Without hope, one cannot lament, for there is no meaningful pattern to life to be disrupted. Lament is the outraged cry of the believer when anticipated order collapses. It is a protest against being brought up short in the face of the expectation that life is fair, that if we live a godly, righteous, and sober life to the honor and glory of God, we will be rewarded with a full and contented life, or at least not be victims of tragedy or calamity.

For the Christian believer, if one holds that all that happens is according to God's will and his will for us is good, the sense of shock and betrayal in the face of calamity is more complicated. On the view that God's goodness, knowledge, and power are absolute, shock and anger in the face of tragedy are unseemly because they appear to doubt God. On a very strong belief in God's powerful goodness, what happens must be for our good, and we should rejoice gratefully, even if we are being punished. For such persons, lament is also precluded because it conveys a questioning of divine goodness. It is inappropriate to supplicate God or to ask that things be different, for that is asking God to change his plan.

A strong or "high" doctrine of providence claims that God is able, ready, and indeed does provide what we need. On this view, death at an early age, permanent injury or disfigurement from accident, and other calamitous or tragic events threaten to undermine the presumption that what happens to us is the will of God. Events that take our lives in dramatically unfortunate directions confound our understanding of God if we believe that God is interested in us, intends good for us, and is able to effect his beneficent desires for us.

The Bible does not know of this theology. Moses cries out to God to deliver the Israelites from Egyptian bondage, so that they can worship him freely, and he pleads with God to heal his sister Miriam of leprosy. The psalmists cry out for deliverance from enemies, sickness, abandonment, and despair. In contrast to the later high Christian doctrine of the absoluteness of the divine will, their assumption seems to be that it is acceptable to bring important matters to God's attention. It is even acceptable to point out that rescue of the afflicted is a good public relations move on God's part, because then there will be great rejoicing, and praise for God will be broadcast far and wide.

As has often been pointed out, the church has been slow to appreciate psalms that complain to and directly confront God with his failure to redress terrible situations. They affront divine authority and a strong doctrine of providence that dictates that persons should be grateful for whatever happens to them, because it is God's will. There are two sides to this question, then. May we trust God and (still) lament? Can we lament and (still) trust God? An exuberant doctrine of providence will say no to both. Skepticism about divine providence will also say no to both.

Through a case study, I hope to suggest that we may trust God and lament and we can lament and still trust God, but more modestly than high Calvinists can, and certainly more than the rigorous atheist will admit. A somewhat broader way to put this is to say that we can admit that life can be harsh, yet not despair of its beauty.

DANA: A CASE STUDY

When he was at the height of his powers, my fifty-six-year-old husband, Dana, my beloved companion of forty years, was diagnosed with stage IV lung cancer. He had not smoked for twenty years and had never been a serious smoker. He had never been sick a day in his life. He worked out twenty-five minutes a day, four days a week. He was extremely careful in medical matters, always checking out any possible problems right away. He had been one year in the best job of his career, providing mental health services to the indigent through public and private service agencies.

He was completely symptom-free until his collarbone broke one day without cause. At our initial interview with the oncologist, the doctor told us that he could offer us only palliative treatment. It was too late for surgery. It would be a matter of months, maybe as many as eighteen, one doctor told me.

We quickly came to see how inadequate modern medicine is before the scourge of cancer. There had been no real breakthrough in lung cancer treatment in at least twenty years, although new therapies were under development. Sixty percent of people respond to the standard chemotherapy, but after three three-week cycles of infusions, it was evident that Dana was not one of them. A world-wide prayer network sprang up for him spontaneously.

It turned out that he had only eight months. No treatment had any positive effect. We were involved with four hospitals, at least fifteen medical practices, and twenty-five medications, in addition to many hours in the emergency room. He was hospitalized because of oversedation and dehydration—having lost almost twenty-five pounds in about six weeks—and was confused, aphasic, and even hallucinating. We tried radiation treatments, chemotherapy, and an experimental biological therapy, all to no avail. As more metastases appeared in his bones, he suffered more and more pain on lying down, sometimes for ten hours at a time, and he could only lie on his back. It took two pain management practices and two months to get the various types of pain under control, but he still could not lie on his right or left side or stomach because of pain from the broken collarbone that never healed, as well as rib metastases. Sleeping and eating were sometimes difficult. Life consisted of nothing but coping with the illness and dealing with insurance company bureaucracies. My employer changed insurance companies in the middle of our struggle. Eventually, his blood became unable to extract oxygen from the air, and again nothing the doctors tried helped at all. They did not even know why it was happening. He died in the ICU within two and a half hours of taking him off the ventilator, amidst a vigil of prayer and hymns that sang him into God's waiting arms.

Perhaps the most poignant point is that five years earlier, a chest X-ray and CT scan revealed a cloudy area in the periphery of his right lung, exactly where the primary lesion later would be. He was told that it was old scar tissue—although from what was never asked—but that it was nothing to worry about. It was not monitored. Chest X-rays as part of an annual physical examination had long since been abandoned as not cost-effective.

Dana was a man of prayer, and a lover of the Psalms. He said his prayers in the shower and as he commuted to work. He had a long list of people he prayed for every day, which got longer and longer because he could not bear to eliminate anyone. He recited prayers from childhood, and psalms in Hebrew by heart, especially Psalm 30, which became his standard-bearer during the illness.

Shortly after receiving the pathology report that confirmed the diagnosis, he wrote a round-robin letter to most of his friends and family across the country and around the world telling them what had happened. After he started treatment, he wrote another. I became a little uncomfortable with the letters, thinking that they might be telling people more than they wanted or needed to know, and scrutinizing who was on this list. He insisted that people wanted to know, because many wrote back encouraging letters in response.

I came to see that Dana's letters were his way of dealing with the shock of the diagnosis and lamenting his wonderful life and gifts that were about to end. His parents were both in their eighties when they died, and he had no reason to expect that he would be any different. His whole life had been a ministry of nurturing others, and his way of bemoaning his own lost life was to nurture those who wanted to support him through this crisis. People began hearing about the list, and asked to have their names added—including people who had originally been on it, but whom I had urged Dana to take off!

Until he was too weak to write, just under a month before he died, he sent more than a dozen letters, apprising his friends and family of the progress and stumbling blocks in his treatment, and reflecting on what he needed and did not need from them. For the first four months of his fight, he was hopeful that some treatment would help at least slow down the progress of the disease. When this proved not to be the case, he lost the energy to hope for improvement, because he wanted only to be painfree. He did not want visitors and could not return calls from well-wishers. He became increasingly absorbed in his symptoms and pains and measuring out the medications designed to relieve them.

We worked hard on the theological dimension of his circumstance. The biblical view that this was punishment for sin made no sense in this case. It was easier to accept the helplessness of God or that God set the world to operate under its own rules and that this was simply a random occurrence than that. He shared his fear of ceasing to be. I suggested that, because of his baptism into Christ's death and therefore into God's drama of salvation for the cosmos, his whole life would be taken up into the life of God, where it would endure forever. He seemed to find this comforting. Still, eventually he lost the ability to pray or to find comfort in Scripture. The illness took everything.

GRACE AND HEALING THROUGH LAMENT

Dana's letters were his way of ministering to those who loved him. Further, he taught them how to respond to people in crisis. Many admitted their gratitude for his openness and direction. Caring for the sick and dying is not something we do well. His lament itself comforted people. It told people what to pray for and enabled them to feel close to him, even when they were separated by continents and oceans. Here are some excerpts from the letters.

Christmas 2002

Dear Friends and Family,

How we wish we could send you a Christmas letter this year filled with joy and hope, telling you of the wonderful things that have happened to our family. Indeed, the greatest thing is one which you probably know about already: Rebecca and Vido's wonderful wedding in the spring and their joyful married life in Dubrovnik. . . .

But overshadowing this for the moment is a piece of unbelievably bad news that has suddenly come to us. After fifty-six years of excellent health, with no symptoms indicative of anything serious, Dana has been diagnosed with advanced lung cancer. As of now, we know that he has a primary tumor in the lung, with three small visible points of spread in the bones. . . .

And yet it seems clear that God's answer—so far—is not the one we were hoping for. This is a test of our faith which we will have to ponder in the months to come. We have read the works of Jewish and Christian sages who point out that God's answer may at times be "no." In time the reason may be clear.

This much we know: We have experienced more love, joy, professional fulfillment, religious treasure, wonderful people, and the presence of God in these fifty-six years than most people in this world experience in a lifetime. We have a fairytale marriage to our childhood sweethearts and have seen our daughters grow into wonderful women. Ellen and I love each other as much as on the day we met.

Is this not joyous news of the season?

Please join the many people who are praying for us. We welcome your e-mails and notes and cards. If you have a picture that you can send, it will be added to the "prayer mural" that Tamar is making to show all the people who are praying for us.

We wish you and your loved ones the most beautiful of Christmas seasons.

In God's Love and Peace,
Dana & Ellen

January 1, 2003

Dear Friends and Family,

Lately it has been somewhat of a roller coaster ride. Just when we think we understand what's going on medically, something else crops up to raise new questions and cast new shadows over the little bit of optimism that we've been able to build up. There is definite good news: my liver and brain are unaffected, my colon and upper GI tract are intact, my left lung is fine, I only have three small metastatic areas in my bones (collarbone and two ribs).

Ellen and I continue to pray together, weep together, comfort each other, and learn wisdom from each other as we have done for the last forty years that we have been together. Tamar has also been a glorious gift from God, without whom we would both probably be a wreck. This crisis has brought her back into the heart of our family and all of her goodness and love and sense of humor has come to the fore. . . . Rebecca is far away but we talk every day and she is fully with us in heart and soul and spirit.

There are so many of you who have written and called and are keeping us in your daily prayers that we cannot help but feel encouraged.

We are truly in God's hands.

Thank you for your many expressions of prayer and support. We'll let you know what happens, and may God bless you and your families in the New Year.

Dana

January 16, 2003

My Dearest Gerry,

How I wish I could have spared you this news. And yet, how very happy I am that you know, and that you are storming heaven on my behalf. I pray every day that God may hear the fervent prayers of his people, and I do believe he does.

So much has happened to us since December 8, when all of this started to become clear. Our old life has ended, and a new life has begun—not supplanting the old one, but now with a whole different focus. In many ways the new life is just like the old—its purpose is to serve God and serve his creatures, only we must now take an inordinate amount of the spotlight for our own immediate needs.

The bottom line is that I am receiving chemotherapy and radiation—the former once every three weeks, the latter daily (fifteen minutes) for the next ten days or so. The main tumor is in my right lung, with metastases to the collarbone and two spots on the ribs on the left side. The chemo addresses everything and hopes to shrink the tumor and destroy other tumor cells elsewhere in the body; the radiation is aimed specifically at the three bone points.

By the way, the chemotherapy reaches every part of the body except for one—the brain. There is a special "blood-brain barrier" around the brain that prevents the chemotherapy chemicals from entering but unfortunately doesn't prevent all tumor cells from getting in. If you want to say a special imaged prayer, pray that Jesus wrap his hands tightly around all the organs of my body, but especially my brain, and with his loving gaze and healing touch drive out all sickness. Then pray that he erect a special barrier of his love around my brain that no evil may enter in. It's my greatest vulnerability, and I have never felt so completely in God's hands before. I wish I could say I have no fear at all, but I'm getting there.

'Nuff said. Read the messages for more details, and we'll stay in touch. God is in the midst of the fray along with all our doctors, throwing everything he's got at this demon.

Update February 11, 2003

Dear Friends and Family,

I have not written in a while. I'm doing well with the chemotherapy this week and last—and about to get hit again on Friday with the third round. The cancer support group leader (see below) told me that many people find the second round the hardest. Here's hoping. Several weeks after that round we'll have another set of scans and see where we stand.

I have a new theological approach to this, which is helping me a lot. My old concept of God not being responsible for this illness led to too much frustration and lack of confidence. I now believe that God for some absolutely inconceivable reason has determined that this should happen; and if so, my calling is to be faithful to his will and carry out my life with as much dignity and grace as I can, helping others every day. I am certainly not about to reject God who has given me so many wonderful things and changed my life significantly (in good ways) over the years. So I believe he is always with me and will heal me according to his will. It's a tough theology, but either way is tough, so you choose the least difficult.

What can I do? Things only make sense to me in theological terms, and this way of seeing it has brought a degree of calmness that I sorely needed.

Keep me in your prayers as I head into the third chemo, and especially for the tests which are to follow two weeks later. Thank you for all your support and love. Hope you're all well.

Dana

Update February 27, 2003

Dear Friends and Family,

Just a quick update, since it's past my bedtime and I'm fading fast. I have come through the third round of chemo. The intestinal effects lasted longer and were a little more pronounced than the second round, but I was in a better frame of mind and was able to deal with them pretty calmly and keep functioning as much as possible.

I take great comfort in your messages and your prayers. The people here around us in Princeton continue to shower us with offers of assistance, food, and expressions of love and concern. Rebecca is visiting with us—she's been here a week and will stay one more—and she is a joy to be with. Some of you may not know that she is pregnant, and expecting in July! She and Vido were planning already to spend the summer and early fall here with us, so the baby will be born here. What a thing to look forward to!

Our love to all of you from all of us,
Dana

Update March 5, 2003

Dear Family and Friends,

I imagine you are all eager to know the outcome of the set of tests which I had two days ago. We've seen the preliminary reports and we'll get the full reports tomorrow, but here are the main points.

It's a mixed picture, and not quite the miracle we had hoped for. On the positive side, the primary tumor has decreased in size! . . . But on the other side, the bone lesions have not responded to chemotherapy or to radiation, and apparently have gotten a little bigger than they were. . . .

When I let myself think about it, I do wonder what God has in mind with all these problems. As I've said to you before, the one good which we can see coming out of this is that so many people have poured out so much love and concern and support. There must be other good which we cannot yet see. I still feel very close to God, and I'm not struggling theologically or emotionally. What I want most of all is some good quality time. . . . I pray that God will grant me that. . . .

Love from both of us,
Dana

Update March 15, 2000

Dear Family and Friends,

Here's the situation. On Monday Ellen and I went down to the Fox Chase Cancer Center for a consultation and second opinion. The doctor there was very kind, courteous and obviously very knowledgeable about lung cancer. After evaluating all the reports, he recommended that my best option would be to enter a clinical trial of an experimental drug which they are conducting there at Fox Chase. . . .

We continue to be unspeakably grateful for the outpouring of love and support and assistance from all those around us and from all of you. I especially need your prayers now, because I feel that this experimental treatment may be the last chance I have. If you are inclined to recite Psalms with your prayers, you might say Psalm 30, which I have recited daily for the past seventeen years. I hope and pray that I too will be able to say that God has lifted me up and brought me back from the brink.

Blessings to all of you and your families,
Dana

Update March 27, 2003

Dear Family and Friends,

There's one thing we have learned in dealing with this illness: No piece of good news ever comes along without having some bad news attached.

It happened again today. We reached the Big Day and went down to Fox Chase ready to get the medication. When we met with Dr. Cohen, he reviewed an MRI of the pelvis that I had taken yesterday, and told us that it showed that I now have metastases in both femurs (the long thigh bones). So, this means that I am at risk for a broken hip, which could necessitate a hip pinning and put me out of commission for a month or more.

Of course Ellen and I are so frustrated that we could scream, and we do at times. But most of the time we settle into a "get the job done" mode, because every day brings its own challenges. For example, the radiation will be given at Hunterdon Medical Center (where I had my first round of radiation), which is about forty-five minutes drive from here. I hope to be able to drive myself each time, but if I can't, then Ellen has to change her plans and help me. And so it goes. Nothing is simple.

But I continue to have hope for the treatment, once I finally get on it. Dr. Cohen told us today that they expect a 30–40% success rate with this drug. That's good to hear.

Update April 23, 2003

Dear Friends and Family,

I'm happy to tell you some good news. On Monday (two days ago) we made our way down to the Philadelphia Surgical Center, and I had an epidural injection (into the space around the nerves) in my lower back. The procedure went well, and since that time I've been able to lie down without any pains down my leg. What a great blessing that is! I can now stay up into the evening again, and Ellen and I celebrated by going out to dinner last night at our favorite Indian restaurant.

(I just took my two "magic pills" for the day—always with a special prayer.)

I must admit that we have been "clobbered" so many times with new problems and setbacks that sometimes it's a scary prospect just to get through the day. Anything can happen anytime. Rebuilding a sense of confidence in your own physical integrity is quite difficult, and yet you have to have it if you're going to venture back out into the world. I have read about this, but now I can see firsthand how great a problem this poses.

I hope you all had a joyous Easter, Passover, or just plain holiday weekend. The coming of spring here on the East Coast brings new beauty and new life. May it be a blessing for all of us.

> Love from us,
> Dana

Update April 29, 2003

Dear Friends and Family,

There is one thing that has changed recently about my attitude. Since the time my cancer was discovered, there have been a remarkable succession of positive things that have happened in our lives, as though God was responding to the crisis by sending every possible support our way. Hundreds of cards and letters and e-mails have come in; people from all over have come forward to help us and show their support; our younger daughter has reestablished her close connections with us and has become a great source of strength; both Ellen's colleagues and mine at Catholic Charities have gone out of their way to make it easy for us.

But until now, I had not been truly grateful for these things. Not that I didn't thank everyone, and really mean it, but my thanks was tinged with jealousy— "Easy enough for you to do that; you're going to go on living and I may not." It was a terrible attitude and I hope you will not hold this confession against me. But now I find that I'm able to be truly thankful for the good things that have come from my illness, and to let go of the jealous part. Because whether or not I survive, these good things will go on into the future. This is especially true of family relationships that are being renewed and solidified around this concern. Our children, for example, have drawn much closer to their cousins in the last six months, and those ties will hold. I haven't done anything specific to make this change of attitude happen on my part; it just seemed ready to take place, by the grace of God. I suppose it shows my growing acceptance of the situation, although I have not for a moment stopped praying for healing.

So we go on, thanking God for each day. Thank you, all of you, for your love and support and prayers and messages. Enjoy the springtime, and God's blessings be upon you and your families.

                              Love from all of us,
                              Dana

Update June 5, 2003

Dear Friends and Family,

It has been such a long time since I have written to you and of course I must apologize for keeping you in the dark, but those of you who know about what happened will understand that there is a very good reason for this. I have just gone through a period of five days in the hospital which culminated two weeks of increasing symptoms and serious medication side effects.

I was being treated by a pain management specialty group that was highly recommended to us, and my doctor in that group believed in using medications aggressively. When my leg pains failed to respond, he raised the opiate medication to a very high dose, and this dose started to cause serious side effects: abdominal symptoms, confusion, drowsiness, and aphasia. The mental effects were very striking, although of course like most organic mental problems, you don't recognize them when you are in them. I didn't know it, but I was slowly becoming more and more disoriented, losing memory and not being able to find words properly and even developing irrational ideas.

After weeks of this, I think it broke through to all of us that we were on a runaway train without a competent person at the controls. We started taking steps: we contacted Dr. Cohen at Fox Chase and discussed this with him. He agreed that it looked like the experimental drug was not working and that my idea to get radiation for the leg pain would be a good idea.

Dr. Fine, the radiotherapist, was contacted and said he would be glad to resume radiation, but there was still the problem of all the medications I was on, with all of their own side effects and problems. On top of this, I had become dehydrated and weak from not eating.

We finally went to my oncologist, Dr. Yi, last Tuesday, and asked for his help. His suggestion was that I needed some time in the hospital, and I was promptly admitted to Princeton Medical Center oncology unit for a complete reevaluation of my medication and a process of rehydration. This was my first experience of ever being in the hospital, so you can imagine how it was for me, particularly in a confused and disoriented state. I now know what it is like to be hallucinating and completely out of touch with one's surroundings and even have paranoid ideas about those around you, which later seem to be perfectly ridiculous.

Once again, thanks to you all for your good wishes, your prayers, your help in so many ways. I know it has been frustrating to you not to be able to visit me, but please understand that the time alone or with just a very few people is really essential for recovery. I hope to begin visiting with those of you in the area, and in the meantime I will keep all of you in my prayers every day.

God's blessings and peace to all of you and your families.

Love,
Dana

Update June 17, 2003

Dear Friends and Family,

I have been in a difficult place, and that's why you haven't heard from me. When I got out of the hospital three weeks ago, my functioning had dropped considerably since before I went in. Over the weeks prior to admission, I had lost more than twenty pounds, plus considerable muscle strength due to lying in bed for so many hours with leg pain. I felt an all-pervasive weakness for the first time; there was no longer any area I could cordon off as "The illness" and function normally in the rest. I am now essentially homebound. Furthermore, I simply look sick, as I never have before.

Couple this all with the decision I made that the time had come to officially resign my job. Short of a miracle, my working days are over.

Everything suddenly got busier and more complicated. We now talk in terms of home health aides and walkers, wheelchairs and disability. The telephone seems to be ringing constantly with calls from health care providers, visiting nurses, pharmacies, and endless dealings with insurance companies.

All of this hit me very hard and continues to do so. It tests my understanding of God and evil in the world, and raises many new questions about living day to day, and the purpose of it all. The one ray of hope is that today I'm starting on Iressa, an oral anticancer medication which may make a difference. It's an older version of the Fox Chase medication that I was on.

My response to all this has been to withdraw. I don't have the energy to tell the story to people, and I have nothing positive to say right now, except that I am unspeakably grateful to Ellen and Rebecca, who continue to help me in every way possible, and to all of you for all your love and support. Much more than that I can't say right now. I read e-mails very infrequently and answer equally infrequently. I don't take phone calls and I don't really want visitors.

But please understand that I am not in any way pushing you away. Perhaps if things pick up with the Iressa, my frame of mind will change. Meanwhile, if you call us, please understand that it may take a long time to return your call—or it may not be returned at all. I'm not taking calls, and Ellen has only limited energy to deal with all the healthcare personnel and insurance companies.

Hope you and your families are all well.

God's blessings,
Dana

Update July 11, 2003

Dear Family and Friends,

First of all, thank you for your patience and faithfulness in sticking with us through the ups and downs of my emotional and spiritual state. Sometimes I feel like I jerk you around on a string: one day I want your calls, the next day I don't; one day I read your e-mails, then I don't for the next week. I don't deserve your patience.

But the fact is I'm feeling better, after going through a weeklong bout of severe abdominal pains. I'm on a different medication (along with my many usual ones) which seems to be working well. The last four or five days I've felt good energy, good appetite, and have been very much up and around. The day before yesterday, at my suggestion, we all piled into the car and went to the beach for the afternoon and evening. A great time was had by all.

When I am like this, relatively free of pain, the whole world looks more positive and life is more worth living. I can look forward with relish to the birth of our grandson in about two weeks, and having as much time as possible with him.

In many ways pain is the determining factor. I've found to my chagrin that pain has the raw power to wear down faith and hope and the will to live. It's true for me, at least—perhaps there are others who can bear it better than I. It'll just suffice to say that I've suffered a whole lot of it.

We live one day at a time, cautiously. We never know what symptoms will come. I have not forgotten all the good that God has done for us and continues to do. But I have a much more sober attitude about his ability to do anything about the big problem. I don't spend much time theologizing these days. We give thanks for the good days.

I love you all and hope that you are receiving all of God's blessings in your lives.

Much love,
Dana

ON TRUSTING AND LAMENTING

Dana's struggle with God during his illness suggests, I think, a way through the extremes of high Calvinism and atheism, so that we can both trust God and lament the calamities of life. Like Moses and the psalmists he loved, Dana lamented his fate and cried out to God for deliverance. He wanted God to heal him, but God didn't. This is not to say that there was no healing, however. Dana himself noted in the letters that his illness brought healing within our immediate family, as well as a closer relationship among the extended family. We discovered the depth of feeling and eloquence of one of his nephews for the first time through his responses to Dana's letters, for example. Beyond this, there was deep healing among estranged members of the family. After he could no longer write letters, a niece in Europe from whom we had heard nothing for more than a decade wrote an elegant and deeply touching letter asking Dana's forgiveness for having treated him badly. Fortunately, she wrote it just in time. There was to be much more healing within the family after he died. Why did it take his death to do that? This is the same question we might ask about Jesus' death. It takes so much to move us beyond pride and hurt.

Aside from the healing within the family, however, was the deep healing that Dana himself experienced in the course of his illness. He had always been somewhat insecure. He was perpetually searching for more friends, fearful that he was slow of mind and wit. He felt that he could not keep up with other people's clever conversation. The great outpouring of support for us during his illness finally healed that empty place that had haunted him all his life. He died knowing that he was loved.

Is this an example of divine providence? Who is to say it is not? Does this demonstrate order, rightness, and fairness in the world? Dana experienced healing in parts of his life that had gone begging for decades and about which he had long since given up trying. Fortunately, as he attested in one of the later letters, he was able to celebrate this while he yet had life and breath. He lamented and still came to trust the providence of God, not as he at first hoped, but in another truly saving way. May his memory be for a blessing.

WORKS CITED

Brueggemann, Walter. "The Psalms and the Life of Faith." In *The Psalms and the Life of Faith*, edited by Patrick D. Miller, 3–32. Minneapolis: Fortress Press, 1980.

Kekes, John. *Moral Wisdom and Good Lives*. Ithaca and London: Cornell University Press, 1995.

PART III
RECLAIMING
THE PUBLIC VOICE
OF LAMENT

Chapter 10

When Feeling Like a Motherless Child

Peter J. Paris

For African peoples everywhere the experience of lamentation is as ancient as their days of existence. Deep in the primeval forests of Africa, centuries before the dawn of modernity, Africans faced on a daily basis life's many threats, including the ubiquity of death. Most important, they understood both the attacks on life and death itself as spiritual matters caused by evil spirits, often exercising their powers through human agents.

From the days of antiquity up to the present time, African peoples have always viewed life's threats and even death itself as caused by the moral and spiritual failure perpetrated either by the afflicted one(s) or by some other member of the community. Further, they believed that sickness or death marked a breach in the cosmic order that necessitated repair in order to restore the cosmic balance. Most important, they believed that the restoration of communal harmony and well-being could be effected only by the exercise of specific rituals prescribed by a priest and faithfully practiced by the community. Invariably the rituals included prayers, music, song, and dance offered in the spirit of humility and trust.[1]

The dawn of modernity in the Western world stimulated the rapid growth of the Atlantic slave trade with West Africa. No other event in world history has been more horrendous than the commercialization of African peoples who were bought and sold as commodities for three and a half centuries. Suffice it to say that the breadth and depth of their suffering was unspeakable. They had been abducted from the communal life of their respective villages, forced to walk in chains to the coastal regions, where they were warehoused in dungeons while waiting to be packed like sardines in the hulls of the ships that transported them through the so-called "middle passage" to their destination in this foreign land of misery. Those who survived the ordeal were sold on the auction block to the highest bidders, who, in turn, treated them like livestock (mere chattel) with no recognized moral claims whatsoever. Additionally, the eventual abolition of slavery after a bitter Civil War was followed by another century of acute racial segregation and discrimination throughout the nation.

Now all African cosmologies share the understanding that individual persons are integrally related to their respective communities. That is to say, that which threatens the life of any individual member of the community also threatens the life of the whole community. Thus the community assumes responsibility in helping individuals bear their misfortunes as well as helping them celebrate their good fortunes. In short, there are no persons without a community. Accordingly, John S. Mbiti rightly concludes:

> Whatever happens to the individual happens to the whole group, and whatever happens to the whole group happens to the individual. The individual can only say: 'I am, because we are; and since we are, therefore I am'. This is a cardinal point in the understanding of the African view of man.[2]

The common experience of slavery both demonstrated the need and fostered the development of a community that included all the captives regardless of ethnic identity or geographical place of origin. Consequently, enslaved Africans from many diverse tribal groups gradually formed a community of belonging that transcended the narrow confines of tribal boundaries and loyalties. That nascent racial community manifested the spirit of resistance to the heteronomy that had defined them as subhumans incapable of either moral or spiritual development.

Thus African peoples in this nation endured for many generations countless forms of suffering with no sure means of escape, because even in those areas where the trade in human bodies had been outlawed, so-called "free or freed Negroes" constantly fell victim to the bounty hunters who could kidnap them and take them to a slaveholding state and sell them as chattel with impunity. Countless families were bereft of their members through this insidious practice, which was protected by the fugitive slave laws of the day.

Few can imagine the pain and suffering of a people who were afflicted and abused in every conceivable way. Abducted from a continent where their dignity had been ascribed in accordance with their family's status and forcibly brought to a land where they were afforded no dignity whatsoever, their loneliness was dreadful. In fact, that dread was expressed nowhere more aptly than in the words, "Sometimes I Feel Like a Motherless Child, a Long Ways from Home." The familial imagery of *mother* and *home* are altogether appropriate when speaking about the African experience because the family constituted then and now the paramount social reality. In fact, none would dispute that the family is a necessary condition for the development of personhood. Thus, to "feel like a motherless child" is virtually unimaginable to African peoples, because every woman in the village functions as mother to all the children. In fact, every older woman is actually called "mother" by everyone, and similarly every older man is called "father." Thus, no place is safer and more secure for African children than the African village. For an African to "feel like a motherless child" symbolizes the experience of radical alienation that destroys both persons and the communities to which they belong.

It is important to note, however, that the song, "Sometimes I Feel Like a Motherless Child, a Long Ways from Home," concludes its lament with words that depict the singer's hope for escape from the misery of loneliness to *heaven*, where all forms of estrangement and alienation are ended and people are reunited in eternal community with God and all the saints. Thus the final words, "Sometimes I'm almost gone, Way up to the heavenly land," depict that hopeful finale.

Sociologists and others have long bestowed a pejorative interpretation to the imagery of *heaven* in black religion. That is to say, they have often viewed the enslaved African's focus on heaven as a pathological escape from the realities of history in favor of what they viewed as wishful thinking about a transhistorical solution. In other words, they viewed such a focus on heaven as an escapist pursuit of compensation after death. The category of escapism implied either nonengagement in activities aimed at social change or accommodating themselves to the status quo.

But, contrary to such interpretations, the revisionist scholarship in African American religious studies during the past three decades has looked at the metaphor heaven differently. Rather than seeing it as escapist or accommodating, they have viewed it as a principle of social criticism well camouflaged in the prominent Christian language of the day. Most important, this revised interpretation claims that the African slaves discerned the symbol heaven as an implicit criticism of everything in the society that maintained slavery and racial oppression. Thus, far from being an otherworldly haven of relief, the symbol heaven represented for them and their heirs a societal norm symbolizing the parenthood of God and the kinship of all peoples. Such a perspective implied that those who denied that understanding of God would not inherit the eternal rewards God has promised all who remain faithful to God's mission for our common humanity, as revealed in the life and ministry of Jesus Christ.

Thus, the experience of lamentation among African peoples in general and African Americans in particular included elements of grief, protest, and hope fully integrated in the personal, familial, and communal rituals of response. The combined effect of such rituals strengthens all concerned: the relevant persons, immediate and extended families, and the wider community. In times of death, all of the above find ways to participate in the event before, during, and afterwards. Traditionally, they have participated in material ways of providing food and drink for the families, lodging for out-of-town mourners, and monies to help defray the cost of burials as well as memorial anniversaries in later years. Since funerals are such major community events among African peoples, the material assistance of others is a necessary requirement. For example, mutual benefit societies were formed very early in the African American churches to help with funeral expenses, and this continues to be one of the primary ministries in black churches everywhere. In addition to other services, it is not unusual for black churches to provide a full meal for the extended family members and their friends following the funeral service.

Now the title of this essay, "When Feeling Like a Motherless Child," implies a relationship between music and song, on the one hand, and the experience of African lament, on the other hand. Unlike the Israelites in the Babylonian captivity, who we are told hung up their harps on the willow trees because they were unable to sing in a foreign land, the enslaved Africans sang their way through their misery. Building on the rhythm and idiom of their African songs, they created new songs that would address their suffering. Those songs became their basic means for preserving hope in what seemed to be a hopeless situation. Their survival as persons and as a community depended greatly on the creative impulse that produced the *spirituals*.

Inspired by the teachings, worship, songs, and dances that they had brought with them from across the ocean, these enslaved peoples proved not to be a tabula rasa but, instead, the bearers of a rich storehouse of moral practices, religious traditions, and spiritual sensitivities. After living out of that storehouse of practical and theological wisdom for several generations, they slowly embraced Christianity both critically and constructively: an embrace that marked the beginning of a new reformation in this land.

After discerning that the religion of their captors contained within it major contradictions to what these enslaved Africans discovered to be the authentic teachings of Jesus Christ, they sought to build a community that would practice a nonracist Christianity. When they began interpreting the mission of Christ in the light of Moses, who had liberated his people from slavery, Africans soon came to see Jesus as a liberator of oppressed peoples. And that discovery made all the difference in how they would relate themselves to Christianity thereafter. With the support of the biblical pericope in Luke 4:16–20, where Jesus identified his mission with that of Israel as declared in Isaiah 61, their revised understanding of Christianity constituted a radical criticism of the Christianity of their slaveholders. In time, this new understanding gradually helped them produce a syncretism[3] of their African spirituality and this newly discovered view of the Scriptures as a basis for an alternative Christianity.

In due time, the enslaved Africans developed a tradition of concealed worship (known in the literature as the "invisible church"). In those hidden forest groves they built a repository of over six thousand songs that have long endured as America's most distinctive contribution to Christian devotion, namely, the spirituals, long known as the Negro Spirituals. Those songs were true folk songs because they have neither specific authors nor actual places of origin. Clearly they were created by and for worshipping communities of Christians whose collective pain and suffering were addressed by the biblical themes of faith, justice, and hope that comprise a large portion of their subject matter. Most important, this new form of Christianity initiated by African slaves represented an alternative to slave-holding Christianity, because it proclaimed a theology and anthropology that were thoroughly nonracist.

Enslaved Africans not only differed from the Israelites by singing and composing new songs in a foreign land, they also differed from them by singing about the goodness of God in the midst of all their sufferings. That kept hope alive for them and prevented them from despairing. Had they blamed God for their condition or distrusted God's goodness towards them, they would have surely despaired. But they never did. Fortunately, it was contrary to their nature as Africans either to doubt or to mistrust their ancestral God. Distrusting God would have implied distrusting their ancestors who shared eternity with God. Distrusting their ancestors would have implied distrusting their own identity as moral and spiritual beings, since their ancestors constituted their primary mentors in all matters pertaining to life and death.

Having experienced the intensity of evil as embodied in their captors, and knowing the many and varied weaknesses that attend vulnerable victims of oppressive conditions, African slaves soon discerned that they could not fully trust anyone except for a few family members. Thus they could put their trust only in the one whom they believed would never let them down: one whose power, love, justice, and mercy were eternally trustworthy. The joy of a personal and communal relationship with such a reliable source of strength was the greatest possible comfort. That experience of trusting in God and in Jesus, whom they fully equated with God, inspired them to celebrate God as the eternal friend of oppressed peoples, allied with them in both their suffering and their deliverance. Thus, the form of their celebration has always been vibrant, emotional, and festive. As in their native Africa, prayer, music, song, and dance comprised the principle means for expressing their praise and making their petitions and supplications. In brief, their trust in God motivated them to praise God in music, song, testimony, and prayer. Doing so in the company of others eventually led to secret gatherings where they created a sacred space that marked the beginning of the black church. In those contexts African slaves received the moral and spiritual strength needed to face the life-and-death struggles of daily life in courageous and hopeful ways.

Thus, the spiritual creativity of enslaved Africans in America was generated by an unquestioned faith in God and an abiding hope that suffering would not last always. Their faith and hope comprised the message of those immortal songs that testify to the transcendent dimension of a suffering people whose spirits manifested victory even in the midst of their suffering. In those songs, Africans expressed their sorrows, protestations, and hopes. Clearly, their singing and praise were not escapist flights into otherworldliness. Rather, they constituted conversations with God where they spoke directly about their pain and suffering in plaintive tones and sad rhythms. Invariably, their songs and prayers arose out of actual situations of pain and suffering. An early collector heard a slave tell how the songs originated:

> I'll tell you, it's dis way. My master call me up and order me a short peck of corn and a hundred lashes. My friends see it, and is sorry for me. When dey come to de praise-meeting dat night dey sing about it. Some's very good singers and know how; and dey work it in—work it in, you know, till they get it right, and dat's de way.[4]

As stated earlier, the spirituals are genuine folk songs, in spite of the fact that gifted persons of musical genius probably played leading roles in their formation. The ideas, symbols, idioms, images came from the people themselves, who often changed the lines, brought the songs up to date by adapting them to fit changing situations, and transmitted them from one generation to another.

An important part of the genius concerning these songs is what the historian and poet James Weldon Johnson said of them, namely, that "the capacity to feel these songs while singing them is more important than any amount of mere artistic technique."[5] The spirituals need to be sung by those who can feel them, and that in turn causes their listeners to feel them as well. Both singer and hearer need to feel the sorrow and the hope that is blended with the sorrow. That fact has been evidenced over and over again from one generation to another. For example, in the adaptations of many spirituals to fit the demands of the recent civil rights movement, observers (including jailors) were often deeply moved when they heard students singing those songs while being threatened by angry mobs and carried off to jail by hostile police.[6] No clearer evidence of the unity of protest and hope can be seen than in those old spirituals that were adapted for use as protest songs in the civil rights movement. This was not unusual, since those songs had always been sung not in the churches alone but virtually everywhere, including at work and for entertainment.

While many of the spirituals speak of immanent trouble and tribulation, of hard trials and the loneliness of being a long way from home, they spoke mostly of freedom. Such songs are filled with double meanings that conjoined their own desires for freedom with biblical stories of deliverance. For example:

> Didn't my Lord deliver Daniel, deliver Daniel, deliver Daniel,
> And why not every man?

Although the spirituals are replete with the Africans' awareness of their bitter plight, they were not nihilistic. Rather, they were hopeful and expressed their deep trust in the historical Jesus who had suffered and died triumphantly.

> Nobody knows the trouble I've seen,
> Nobody knows like Jesus;
> Nobody knows the trouble I've seen,
> Glory, Hallelujah.

The themes about which the spirituals speak are legion, even as the spirituals themselves are countless in number. They cover a broad expanse of the human spirit; their imagery is rich beyond belief; their symbols are filled with experiential meaning pointing always beyond the immediate circumstances of life to a final victory in the divine resolution where all will be made whole in both body and soul. Thus the soloist declares:

> There is a balm in Gilead
> To make the wounded whole.
> There is a balm in Gilead
> To heal the sin-sick soul.

These songs of faith and hope presuppose God's abiding presence throughout the ups and downs of life's experiences. Similar songs expressed the deep sorrow that African slaves felt for the suffering of Jesus, and especially their identification with his pain, which like theirs was unwarranted. Yet in similar tones they rejoiced in his victory over the grave. Thus, in tones of great reverence, they composed one of the enduring Easter hymns of the ages:

> 1. Were you there when they crucified my Lord?
> Were you there when they crucified my Lord?
> Oh, sometimes it causes me to tremble, tremble, tremble.
> Were you there when they crucified my Lord?
>
> 2. Were you there when they hanged him on a tree?
> 3. Were you there when the sun refused to shine?
> 4. Were you there when they pierced him in his side?
> 5. Were you there when they laid him in the tomb?
> 6. Were you there when he rose up from the grave?

As stated earlier, the experiences of bondage and oppression constitute the paramount reality of African American history. Accordingly, African Americans have been continuously in quest for freedom and justice. As a matter of act, the exodus event lies at the center of the religious strivings of our foreparents, and hence no other song has greater meaning for African Americans than "Go Down, Moses." Note that the command to liberate the people is given by God.

> Go down, Moses,
> 'Way down in Egypt's land,
> Tell Ole Pharaoh,
> To let my people go.
>
> When Israel was in Egypt's land,
> Let my people go,
> Oppressed so hard they could not stand,
> Let my people go.

Thus spoke the Lord, bold Moses said,
Let my people go,
If not I'll smite your firstborn dead,
Let my people go.

Though the spirituals spoke about the particularity of suffering, struggle, and striving, they also addressed the universal experience of mortality as seen in the tragic nature of human life. Inevitable struggles of good and evil, pain and suffering, death and dying, comprise the warp and woof of human life: a truth that was verified continually by the daily experiences of enslaved Africans in America, a truth that they did not deny but confronted boldly with hope for a better day.

African American Christians continue to sing the songs of our foreparents: those old songs of suffering and sorrow, of hopes and dreams, of faith and trust— songs that restore strength by helping suffering peoples cope with turmoil with a triumphant spirit. Clearly the singing itself is a sign of the victory, because one can sing in the midst of sorrow only when one's faith in ultimate victory is firm.

Some years ago I attended a wake for a twenty-five-year-old daughter of one of my students, Prathia Hall, who had been one of the founders of the Student Non-violent Coordinating Committee (SNCC) and was an extraordinary preacher. In the midst of her grief, Prathia got up from her seat and stood by her daughter's open casket and sang an African American song of faith and hope. I have long since forgotten what the song was, but the feeling she communicated through her singing embraced both her grief and the substance of her faith in the resurrected Christ to whom she was certain her daughter had returned. There in that place, in the company of family and friends, she boldly confronted the reality of her daughter's untimely death with the power of her faith, which alone enabled her to overcome her grief and to continue her life. All the mourners present had experienced similar times of sorrow when the comfort of the Christian faith vividly addressed them through the testimony of song, usually performed by a soloist whose power of singing unites all the mourners into the intensity of the feeling. Often in the African American Christian tradition, special soloists are called upon at such times because their ability to unify sorrow and faith is well known. Also, families usually try to identify the favorite song of the deceased to be performed at that time. Thus the singing unites the deceased and the mourners in the triumph of the faith.

Sometimes the art of dance serves a similar purpose. In 1997 I attended the funeral for a man in Ghana who was twenty-three years old. Under the broad expansive branches of massive trees in a village compound, the casket was placed, and the family and friends gathered in a circle around it for the last rites. Soon, a thin elderly woman came forth, obviously stricken with grief. Her entire body seemed to be nearly broken by the weight of her sorrow. Throughout the service, she quietly and gracefully danced around the casket while reaching out her arms and hands in gentle gestures as she tried to embrace the casket. I have never before or since witnessed such mournful beauty. The entire liturgy and all of the participants seemed to be drawn into the aura of that grieving woman's physical movements as her faith confronted the cold presence of death with sadness and love.

Throughout that service my attention was drawn to the fact that I could not see any young people present, and I wondered why. Towards the end, however, just before the benediction, my eyes caught the sight of many young people who had formed a virtual circle around the mourners at the back of the assembly. Immediately following the benediction they stridently came forward in extremely casual dress (unusual for a formal African event) and displaying a hostile spirit. They encircled the casket and suddenly picked it up onto their shoulders and literally ran out of the circle carrying the casket very recklessly down the road to the graveyard. The rest of the mourners joined the procession to the graveyard. As we walked a distance of approximately one half mile, the young people with the casket were seemingly playing with it in such a dangerous way that I feared they would drop it. They would toss it rather high in the air, catch it, and then charge forward with it, while singing songs protesting the death of their peer. I was told later that sometimes the youth even insult old people in the procession, saying that they should have died rather than their peer. Finally, arriving at the grave site, they dropped the casket in the grave, departed very abruptly and angrily, and formed a circle a good distance away singing and dancing among themselves. I am told that they choose not to remain in the graveyard because they do not believe it to be a place where young people should be.

I was impressed with this ritual of rage that is legitimated by the community and given a space of appearance in the funeral ritual. This incident took place among the Akan people of Ghana, and I do not know whether or not it exists elsewhere. Its therapeutic value appeared to be obvious, and its realism was altogether in keeping with African practices of sorrow, protest, and hope.

It is not unusual, however, to see a different but related form of protest occurring at African American funerals. Funeral directors, ushers, nurses units, and others are especially alert to such outbursts in order to ensure that no one is hurt, including the protesting mourner. In such situations some mourners are permitted to scream out with sorrow. In doing so, they often ask God to exchange themselves for the loved one's life, or they might even try to throw themselves into the grave. Often these outbursts are prompted by the emotion of the songs and the music.

Traditionally, the casket was left open throughout the funeral service and one last viewing was permitted at the end of the service just before the casket was closed for its removal from the church. Though that practice does continue in some places today, the present practice tends to be that of closing the casket in the presence of the family just before the service begins. At this point the funeral director often permits the family to do a last viewing, and that can be a very emotional period. Yet it is important to note that in both cases, all such protests are permitted within a controlling framework.

Thus, both in Africa and in the African diaspora, African peoples have always turned to music and song as the primary means for overcoming suffering and grief. It is a curious fact that one often gets over mourning by allowing oneself to mourn. The experience of hearing a sad song relevant to the occasion not only shows one how to be sad, but it also shows one how to overcome the sadness. The singing about sadness helps one overcome the loneliness of suffering. Consequently, enslaved Africans composed and sang countless songs celebrating God's liberating presence in the midst of suffering, for the purpose of strengthening a people to keep hope alive when it is threatened by terrible circumstances in life. The songs that have enduring value in such situations are those that tell the truth by critiquing their situation in light of a transcendent theological principle. African slaves equated that principle with God, the resurrected Jesus, and heaven. All three symbols constituted principles of criticism on the conditions of history that enable injustices to endure.

Ironically, America's unique contribution to the world has been the gift of music and song composed by enslaved Africans during their long struggle to sustain their humanity by resisting bondage of the mind, body, and soul. In their struggle, these people bequeathed to America and the world a beautiful enduring legacy of prayer, praise, and hope in the form of music and song.[7]

NOTES

1. For a good description of the importance of ritual in healing the cosmic order, see Malidoma Patrice Some's *The Healing Wisdom of Africa: Finding Life Purpose through Nature, Ritual, and Community* (New York: Penguin Putnam, 1999), chap. 1.
2. John S. Mbiti, *African Religions and Philosophy* (Oxford: Heinemann International, 1990), 106.
3. For a full discussion of this process, see the author's book *The Spirituality of African Peoples: The Search for a Common Moral Discourse* (Minneapolis: Fortress Press, 1995).
4. L. Hughes and A. Bontemps, *Book of Negro Folklore* (New York: Dodd, Mead and Co., 1958), 280.
5. James Weldon Johnson and J. Rosamond Johnson, *The Books of American Negro Spirituals* (New York: Da Capo Press, 1989), 29.
6. For a full-scale analysis of how the spirituals were adapted to fit the needs of the twentieth-century civil rights movement, see Jon Michael Spencer, *Protest and Praise: Sacred Music of Black Religion* (Minneapolis: Fortress Press, 1990), 83ff.
7. By no means has the legacy of the spirituals remained static. Rather, it has evolved into numerous musical forms such as blues, jazz, rhythm and blues, bebop, hip-hop, gospel, and rap.

Chapter 11

Woes of Captive Women: From Lament to Defiance in Times of War

Luis N. Rivera-Pagán

> Woe, woe is me!
> What words, or cries, or lamentations can I utter?
> Ah me! for the sorrows of my closing years!
> for slavery too cruel to brook or bear! . . .
>
> Where is any god or power divine to succour me? . . .
>
> Life on earth has no more charm for me . . .
> Queen of sorrows.
> —Euripides, *Hecuba*

To the women of Afghanistan and Iraq, that we may hear the lamentations of their hearts . . .

The image does not vanish from either my mind or my heart. A house destroyed in Iraq by coalition forces battling resistance insurgents. "Collateral damage" is the sanitized and cynical term coined for this kind of tragic mistake. A family decimated, some members killed, others wounded, the survivors walking in shock, as lifeless specters. An old Iraqi woman, the matriarch of the family, stands in the middle of what used to be her house and raises her gaunt face and wrinkled hands to the sky. Her countenance is an expression of immense affliction. Is she praying, crying to her God, cursing, or just wailing her profound distress? Is it an act of lamentation, of defiance, or both? We do not know and will probably never know.

Her photographic depiction, alas, will never fade away from my memory. It has become another portrait of the sorrows and pains inflicted by war upon the souls and bodies of women.[1] The image of that suffering, praying, cursing, lamenting, defiant Iraqi woman is the Ariadne's thread of this essay, its guiding leitmotiv even through what for some readers might be its labyrinthine incursions into classical Hellenic literature. It belongs to the tradition of Francisco Goya's powerful and horrifying etchings *The Disasters of War*.

SIMONE WEIL AND THE TRAGIC EPIC OF WAR

"The true hero, the real subject, the core of the *Iliad*, is might."[2] Thus begins Simone Weil's "The *Iliad*, Poem of Might," her splendid meditation on the most eminent Hellenic poetic text. It is a magnificent tour de force. The delicate and sensitive Weil, a prematurely withered genius, contemplates the sorrows and horrors of war, the cruelties and violence committed in the name of so many proclaimed ideals, in the altar of so many deceptively sacralized words. Weil pays tribute in a beautiful way to the awful immensity of the griefs and pains, the dashed hopes and illusions, caused by the violence of war.

Yet also evident is the immense admiration that Weil feels reading the *Iliad*. She relishes in the aesthetic grace of Homeric Greek (the learned Weil read the *Iliad* in its original language): "Nothing of all that the peoples of Europe have produced is worth the first poem to have appeared among them."[3] And, most of all, she deeply admires the courage of Patroclus, Hector, or Achilles when their turn to confront fate and death comes. There can be no doubt about the preference of this woman, of Jewish ancestry, for Homer over Moses, for the *Iliad* over Genesis, for the Greek language and culture over the Hebrew language and culture (also over the Roman culture and language).

Affliction is the unavoidable consequence of all human wars, cursed by the caprice and malice of the gods and by the human proclivity towards violence and force.[4] The human soul is overwhelmed by the rage and affliction of Achilles, saddened by the death of his dearest friend, Patroclus; impressed by the courage of Hector, beaten and mercilessly killed by Achilles; and, according to Weil, awed also by the agony of Jesus, when the hour of his arrest, torment, and execution is near.[5] "Unless protected by an armour of lies, man cannot endure might without suffering a blow in the depth of his soul."[6] Not many writers would join in the same story Achilles and Jesus!

War, according to Weil's elegant essay, is always very near, too near indeed, to the human heart. No other human endeavor compares to war in its ability to achieve the terrifying process of converting a human being into a *thing*, a non-person. By transforming living bodies into corpses, spiritual life into mere matter, and by inspiring overwhelming cruelty and violence in hearts where on many previous occasions tenderness and mercy have reigned, war becomes the most dehumanizing of all human enterprises. It spreads affliction across all social and intimate borders. It poisons the human heart and dissolves compassion. In the reign of violence, of the immense destruction and affliction unleashed by human bellicosity, "there is no room for either justice or prudence."[7]

The transformation of victim and victimizer from human beings into things is painfully shown in Achilles' refusal to heed the supplications of Hector and Priam. Hector has killed Patroclus and must therefore die in the hands of Achilles. No tears of a father, a wife, or a son will protect the brave Trojan prince from his fateful destiny.[8] And Achilles knows very well that he also, the killer of Hector, must die young, victim of a violent rage similar to his, away from the loving care of mother or lover. Affliction, courage, destruction, and death: these are the consequences of war. And the choice of war, that most lethal of all human enterprises, seems to elude personal liberty and ethical deliberation. War seems to be an unavoidable dimension of human destiny, so fated and cursed by the gods. *Thanatos* triumphs over *eros* or *agape*, this seems a reasonable way of reading the *Iliad*.

The *Iliad* is therefore, according to Weil, more than a magnificent and beautiful epic poem. It also discloses the tragic mystery of human violence, the ways in which human beings ceaselessly mutate into instruments of death and devastation. Fate and tragedy rule tyrannically over human affairs. Good and evil human beings are both crushed by the same violence that periodically demonically possesses human history. The discovery of this fateful truth is the great achievement of classic Greece, poetically narrated first by Homer's epic, then by Attic tragedy, and finally by the Gospels ("the last and most marvelous expression of Greek genius, as the *Iliad* is its first expression"[9]).

Weil's essay is doubtless an expression of her love for the classic Greek culture,[10] but it is more than that. It is also a deeply sensitive, eloquent, and serene meditation on the manners in which war destroys human culture and, even more important, human compassion. It was published in December 1939 and January 1940 in the French journal *Cahiers du Sud* at a crucial moment in which Europe was beginning its engulfment in the most savage war that history has ever experienced. It is both a warning against any kind of romantic beautification of war, by means of the ideological manipulations of solemn words—fatherland, race, nation, God, religion, liberty—and a convocation to epic and stoic confrontation of the merciless fate, death, and destruction entailed by war.

Her essay is a warning and convocation she knows very well will not be heeded. For, according to Weil, the modern state is a Leviathan poised to oppress and devour by means of the constant mobilization and preparation for war. Thus it achieves its goal of "the total effacement of the individual before the state bureaucracy."[11] If Weil admires the dignified and courageous ethos of the tragic Homeric heroes, she has nothing but contempt for modern technological warfare and for the states that wage it (whatever their ideological pigmentations). It is a "most atrocious" activity, "the most radical form of oppression," for soldiers, in modern warfare, "do not expose themselves to death, they are sent to slaughter." It transforms the relationship between state and citizens into "despotism and enslavement" and "calculated murder."[12]

No epic poem like the *Iliad* could be composed in honor of the modern system of devastation. For "modern war is absolutely different from everything designated by that name under earlier regimes."[13] It creates immense miseries devoid of any human integrity. There are no more tragic heroic warriors like Agamemnon, Hector, Patroclus, or Achilles, but expendable pawns used to slaughter and be slaughtered. No supplications are refused, for no supplications are heard. Painful lamentations are uttered, but they are immediately drowned by the cascade of chauvinistic propaganda, with its loquacious public convincers, and by the cynical conversion of military destruction into electronic spectacle.

This radical rejection of modern technological warfare leads Weil into an agonizing dilemma: what to do regarding the fascist and Nazi menace? Before the German invasion first of Poland and then of France, Weil assumes a firm position against war, for "weapons yielded by a sovereign state apparatus can bring no one liberty."[14] In case war erupts, she counsels revolt against the military machine of one's own state.

It is a desperate and forlorn situation; she knows it well. "But the helplessness one feels . . . cannot exempt one from remaining faithful to oneself." Thus she proclaims resistance not against the possible invading enemy, but against the state and military apparatus "that calls itself our defender and makes us slaves."[15] She will discover the fragility of that position, when the Nazi and fascist armies begin to spread devastation all over Europe, as never before since the Thirty Years' War (1618–1648). Then the immense lamentations uttered by so many distressed and downtrodden human beings will provoke a deep sorrow in Weil's sensitive soul that will escort her into the shadows of her own death. Death was sometimes the ultimate consolation for a delicate spirit unable to cope with the tensions of an epoch so aptly called the Age of Extremes.[16] As befits a lover of the *Iliad* and the Greek tragedies, she faced death with the fortitude of an epic heroine. Fortunately, she also left us an amazing literary heritage[17] that can provide a perspective to meditate upon our own times, an age when

> Things fall apart . . . and everywhere
> The ceremony of innocence is drowned.[18]

EURIPIDES AND THE WOES OF THE TROJAN WOMEN

When one revisits Weil's "The *Iliad*, Poem of Might" in the context of today's theoretical debates, one is struck by the glaring absence of a feminist gaze. The essay deals splendidly with the tragic and dignified manner in which Patroclus, Achilles, Hector, Agamemnon, and Priam confront fate and death, to be finally crushed by

the violence unleashed by war. A man, a male hero, stands in the center of her meditation on the *Iliad*, as well as in her allusions to the Attic tragedies of Aeschylus
and Sophocles, and to the Jesus of the Gospels. One could even perceive a certain
seduction in Weil's contemplation of the Homeric heroes, a paradoxical fascination with the courageous dignity with which these warriors assume their tragic destiny and curse. But what about the Trojan women? Curiously, this very sensitive
and perceptive woman and writer, Simone Weil, silences them. A writer that would
never heed Aristotle's apothegm—"Woman, silence is the grace of woman"[19]—
ends up by silencing the female victims of the *Iliad*'s courageous heroes.[20]

Weil clearly understands the awful consequences of the destruction of a city,
be it Troy, Warsaw, or Paris. And yet, as she follows the *Iliad*'s concern with Patroclus, Achilles, Hector, Agamemnon, and Priam, something important is missed:
the agonies and sorrows of Iphigenia, Hecuba, Andromache, Cassandra, Polyxena, and Helen, the female protagonists of the Trojan conflict. It is an epic poem
of war and force; therefore, Weil seems to be saying, men, not women, should
always take the center stage. She seems to overlook that the city is the place where
women not only give birth to human existence, but also confer meaning and
coherence to the life they have procreated. The destruction of a city entails therefore not only the death of the warriors, but also the enduring misery and distress
of captive women. Thus the anonymous author of the biblical Lamentations
poignantly feminizes the devastated city of Jerusalem:

> How lonely sits the city
> that once was full of people!
> How like a widow she has become,
> she that was great among the nations!
> She that was a princess among the provinces
> has become a vassal.

> She weeps bitterly in the night,
> with tears on her cheeks;
> among all her lovers
> she has no one to comfort her;
> all her friends have dealt treacherously with her,
> they have become her enemies.[21]

The curse of war, violence, and blood as unavoidable human destiny seems to
be the tragic enigma so beautifully displayed in the earliest Hellenic epic poem.
Weil indicates the diverse instances in which that iron law of human destruction
could have been disavowed. If only Agamemnon, Achilles, Odysseus, or Hector
would have been more moderate in his words or actions. . . . And yet the warriors seem unable to free themselves from the bloody fascination with Ares,
the merciless god of war. The curse of war proceeds unimpeded on its path of
death and devastation. Yes, indeed, but what about the affliction suffered by the
mothers, wives, daughters, lovers, or sisters of the heroic warriors? What about
the agonizing sorrow felt by the female nourishers of human existence when

struck by the pathos of the destruction of that life? What about the misery visited upon those women who have never wielded a sword or spear and have never curtailed prematurely the life of another fellow human being?

Weil shares the preference of many of her contemporaries for the "classic" style of Aeschylus's and Sophocles' tragedies over Euripides' more secular and profane outlook. Yet it was Euripides who never forgot that the Trojan War began not only with the abduction of Helen, a matter to which he devoted one play, but also with the sacrifice of Iphigenia, the unfortunate young daughter of Agamemnon and Clytemnestra.[22] The wars of men seem to require, at their beginning or at their conclusion, the sacrifice of a young maiden—be it that of Iphigenia, so that the war against Troy may proceed; that of Polyxena, the young daughter of Priam and Hecuba, sacrificed by Neoptolemus at Achilles' tomb, so that the ships of the victorious Greeks may depart for home;[23] or that of the nameless daughter of Jephthah, so that the vow between her father, the male commander of the Hebrew forces, and Yahweh, the Lord of hosts, may be fulfilled.[24] These stories seem to question Freud's thesis that the source of human religiosity is the sacrifice, by the band of sons and brothers, of the mythical primeval father,[25] and suggest that one should rather look into the sacrifice of a virginal daughter of the patriarch as the matrix of ritual practices of expiation and atonement. Men make war; the gods lust for the blood and flesh of young virgins.

It is also Euripides who in one of his more popular tragedies gives careful attention to the female lamentations in the midst of the Trojan War. He knows well that after the noisy devastation of war ceases, another clamor resounds, "the endless cries of captured women, assigned as slaves to various Greeks."[26] In *The Women of Troy* the plight of Hecuba, Andromache, and Cassandra is voiced. Not the brave and epic heroism of men of war, but the sorrows of the women who suffer its sinister consequences constitute the focus of this splendid drama.

As F. W. Dobbs-Allsopp has emphasized in another literary context, the poetic expression of profound existential grief is able to provide at least coherence and meaning, if not comfort or solace, to that grief.[27] For, as the Chorus sings, in *The Women of Troy*,

> In times of sorrow it is a comfort to lament,
> To shed tears, and find music that will voice our grief.[28]

Yes, indeed. But, alas, the poetic dirge also aggravates and deepens the afflictions. It reawakens the experienced nightmares.[29] Hecuba, Priam's widow and Hector's mother, former queen of Troy, now allotted to be a slave of Odysseus, the Greek general most disdained by the Trojan aristocracy as a tricky deceiver, a master of lies and weaver of fatal wiles, takes the lead by uttering a profoundly sad and heartrending expression of grief:

> I mourn for my dead world, my burning town,
> My sons, my husband, gone, all gone! . . .
> Now shrunk to nothing, sunk in mean oblivion!

How must I deal with grief? . . .
For those whom Fate has cursed
Music itself sings but one note—
Unending miseries, torment and wrong![30]

Andromache, widow of Hector, will have to contemplate the assassination of her only child, Astyanax, and suffer the lordship of Neoptolemus, the son of Achilles. She is forced to serve the murderer of her child, who is also the son of the warrior who killed her loved husband.

To be dead is . . . better far than living on wretchedness.
The dead feel nothing; evil then can cause no pain.
But one who falls from happiness to unhappiness
Wanders bewildered in a strange and hostile world.[31]

Andromache's body belongs now to the will of a hated man, who will dispose of it according to his whims and desires. For the rest of life, she will be a slave in a foreign land and a hostile house, devoid of any shred of hope of liberty or domestic happiness. During the days she will be subject to exhausting toil; during the nights she will dread her master's lust.

So I shall live a slave
In the house of the very man who struck my husband dead.
If I put from me my dear Hector's memory . . .
I prove a traitor to the dead; but if I hate
This man, I shall be hateful to my own master.[32]

Both Hecuba and Andromache are burdened not only by the extreme misery to which they have fallen, but also by the absence of any meaningful hope for redemption. Any remembrance of past joys, in the alleys and gardens of lovely Troy, can only aggravate their present predicament. Any consideration of forthcoming events, as slaves ("a shadow of death—a slave!"[33]) in Ithaca, Athens, Sparta, or Argos, can only deepen their sufferings. There is no mental space for hope, for the imagination of a joyful and meaningful future.

Andromache laments the absolute impossibility of dreaming her liberation from abject servitude.

For me there is not even
The common refuge, hope. I cannot cheat myself
With sweet delusions of some future happiness[34]

In another Euripides drama, Polyxena, a young daughter of Priam and Hecuba, expresses analogous hopelessness. Odysseus has informed her of the tragic decision by the Greek army: that the maiden be sacrificed at Achilles' tomb, to honor the brave Achaean warrior. Polyxena rejects her mother's pleas and refuses to supplicate clemency. She prefers to die rather than live as a slave.

Why should I prolong my days? . . .
Was I nursed . . . a maiden marked amid her fellows,
equal to a goddess, save for death alone,
but now a slave!
That name first makes me long for death . . .
No, never! Here I close my eyes upon the light
free as yet, and dedicate myself to Hades. . . .
For I see naught within my reach to make me hope
or expect with any confidence
that I am ever again to be happy.[35]

Those heartfelt woes, however, have to be expressed with utmost discretion, for as slaves they have lost the liberty to express openly their affliction or indignation. Their submission has to be complete, leaving no room even for their own inner selves. After hearing the horrifying news about the sentence of death decreed for her only child, Andromache is warned by the Greek messenger to accept her tragic fate in silence and submission.

This too: don't call down
Curses upon the Greeks. . . .
If you are quiet . . .
You'll find the Achaeans more considerate to yourself.[36]

CASSANDRA: FROM LAMENT TO DEFIANCE

The pain is thus mercilessly multiple: the death of loved ones, the bondage of slavery, the extinction of hope, the masquerade of submission, and the silencing of lamentation and protest. Slavery, submission, hopelessness, simulation, silence: that is the cruel destiny of the captive Trojan women.

There is one exception: Cassandra. A beautiful Trojan princess, a consecrated virgin to the altar of Apollo, Cassandra has been sacrilegiously chosen by Agamemnon as his slave and concubine, a toy for his lust and pleasure. Hecuba, her mother, is in pain for the fate of her daughter, compelled to serve the most implacable enemy of her city and people. Cassandra, however, fearlessly sings her disdain for the triumphant Achaeans, and intones a hymn in honor of the dead Trojan warriors.

How different for the men of Troy, whose glory it was
To die defending their own country! Those who fell
Were carried back by comrades to their homes, prepared
For burial by hands they loved, and laid to rest
In the land that bore them . . . joys denied
To the invaders.[37]

When her mother laments her lot ("A slave taken in war, a plunder of a conquering Greek"[38]), Cassandra, endowed by Apollo with prophetic powers, celebrates, not her submission, but the future catastrophe and tragedy of the house of Agamemnon, the cursed lineage of Atreus. Cassandra's cries of woe mutate into resistance and defiance, vociferously singing and celebrating the assassination of Agamemnon, the oldest son of Atreus, by the hands of his own wife, an event that will transform his military victory into defeat and tragedy.

> Agamemnon,
> This famous king, shall find me a more fatal bride
> Than Helen. I shall kill him and destroy his house
> In vengeance for my brothers' and my father's death. . . .
> My bridal-bed promises death to my worst enemy. . . .
>
> At the porch of death my bridegroom waits for me.
> Great chief of the Hellenes, fleeting shadow of magnificence,
> Your accursed life shall sink in darkness to an accursed grave. . . .
>
> I will come triumphant to the house of Death,
> When I have brought to ruin the sons of Atreus, who destroyed us.[39]

She is the only captive Trojan woman who is able to metamorphose her misery and slavery into defiance and resistance. Like her sister Polyxena, Cassandra willingly accepts her premature and violent death as unavoidable destiny; but in a unique way she is also able to deny her captors any honor and rejoices in the tragic reversal of destiny that awaits the Argive royal house. She calls forth the inner strength, unconquerable pathos, rejecting the iron logic of war by assuming and accepting in her own self the death and sacrifice entailed by that logic. Cassandra is graced by a fortitude and bravery sometimes unperceived by readers who, like Simone Weil, are fascinated by the seductive and poetic heroism of the *Iliad*.

Thus Euripides, in a very different way from Aristophanes' delicious comedy *Lysistrata*,[40] not only gives voice to women's sufferings and lamentations as ominous consequences of war, but also foregrounds, in the character of Cassandra,[41] female defiance and resistance to violence and destruction. Thus, early in the origins of our cultural and historical awareness, in the creative period between Homer and Euripides, the vast dramatic canvas of war and affliction, violence and defiance, military oppression and obstinate resistance is magnificently displayed. We can admire the courage of the ill-fated Hector and Achilles, yet share as well the afflictions of Hecuba and Andromache, marvel at the dignity of Polyxena's choice of death rather than slavery, and rejoice in the resistance and defiance of Cassandra under the sinister shadows of war and death.

GRIEVING BETWEEN BURKAS AND BOMBS

"The whole *Iliad* is overshadowed by the greatest of griefs that can come among men; the destruction of a city."[42] Thus Simone Weil summarizes the tragic drama of the most famous Hellenic epic poem. In the beginning there was war. Yes, indeed, and throughout the entire human history cities have been destroyed, and lamentations have been uttered to express the profound afflictions entailed by such catastrophes. The pathos of war has too frequently defeated the ethos of peace. The biblical lament over the devastated Jerusalem echoes the agonies of the dwellers of many other destroyed cities:

> Jerusalem remembers,
>   in the days of her affliction and wandering
> . . . .
> When her people fell into the hand of the foe
> . . . .
> My eyes flow with rivers of tears
>   because of the destruction of my people.[43]

Of all the afflictions narrated by the anonymous Hebrew poet, the most heartrending are the descriptions of the agony of the women survivors of the catastrophe, who face the horrifying temptation of maternal cannibalism.

> Should women eat their offspring,
>   the children they have borne?
> . . . .
> The hands of compassionate women
>   have boiled their own children;
> they became their food
>   in the destruction of my people.[44]

During the last century the strategic understanding of war as a conflict between nations, not only between armies, coupled with the awesome development in military technology, has made cities a choice target of attack and destruction. Picasso's *Guernica* is the artistic symbol, as Hiroshima is the painful living incarnation, of the transmogrification of the city, in times of war, from a place of human fulfillment into a Dantean metaphor of hell. Guernica, Dresden, Hiroshima, Groznyy, Sarajevo, Kabul, and Baghdad, among many other cities, have witnessed stories of affliction similar to the woes uttered in the biblical Lamentations or in Euripides' *Women of Troy*.

Women's lament in the wake of war and their resistance against the perennial proclivity to make force the arbiter of human conflicts have emerged from the margins of history and are now at the core of the early twenty-first century labors to forge a more humane and less violent world.[45] In many different languages and cultural contexts, the sad and defiant cries to God of contemporary Hecubas, Andromechas, and Cassandras have been vociferously expressed, in lamentation and protest for the ominous divine silence and absence, enacting once more the dramatic biblical voice of grief,

> I am one who has seen affliction
>   under the rod of God's wrath.
> . . . .

> Though I call and cry for help,
>   he shuts out my prayer.
>   . . . .
>   —does the Lord not see it?[46]

Classical Greek literature springs from aristocratic sources. Homer's *Iliad* and Euripides' plays are stories of the fateful and tragic endeavors of noble and aristocratic protagonists. Achilles, Hector, and Agamemnon are neither peasants nor laborers. They are of royal ancestry. Hecuba, Andromache, Polyxena, and Cassandra lament their drastic reversal of fortune, from royal comfort to misery and servitude. Aristocracy matters here. As the chorus of one of Euripides' dramas affirms:

> Oh! To have never been born,
> or sprung from noble sires,
> the heir to mansions richly stored . . .
> there is honour and glory for them
> when they are proclaimed scions
> of illustrious lines.[47]

A more popular, more inclusive, and less aristocratic consideration of violence and afflictions is indispensable today in our analysis of the woes of women enmeshed in war. If we truly strive to understand intellectually and share emotionally the sufferings and travails of so many women in ill-fated places like Afghanistan and Iraq, plagued by the violence of native tyrants and foreign invaders, their lives and liberties threatened by burkas and bombs, we must extend the horizon of our outlook to include and highlight those devoid of noble lineage and wealth. In desperation and defiance, today's women voice their bitter lament as does the female chorus in T. S. Eliot's *Murder in the Cathedral*:

> We know of oppression and torture,
> We know of extortion and violence,
> Destitution, disease, . . .
> The child without milk in summer, . . .
> Our sins made heavier upon us.
> We have seen the young man mutilated,
> The torn girl trembling by the mill-stream.
> And meanwhile we have gone on living . . .
> Picking together the pieces . . .
> For sleeping, and eating and drinking and laughter[48]

An international humanitarian worker has thus assessed the new situation of women in "liberated" Afghanistan: "During the Taliban era if a woman went to market and showed an inch of flesh she would have been flogged; now she's raped."[49] Emerging from the margins of political or social power, in times of preventive and preemptive wars declared by mighty nations against weaker adversaries, the women of conflict-torn places like Afghanistan and Iraq cry to God and to their fellow human beings for compassion and solidarity, for the recognition and restoration of their wounded and battered humanity. Their plight, endurance, and hope cry out to us in the powerful and painful texts of the Egyptian writer Nawal El Saadawi. In her novels and feminist treatises, El Saadawi has given eloquent voice to the struggles of women in Middle East Islamic societies to shape their own destiny between the burkas and the bombs, to free themselves from the dominion of priests and warriors who in the name of God or war try to possess and control female existence.[50]

"No one listens to us and no one treats us as human beings," is their bitter and defiant lamentation.[51] It is our sacred duty and ethical responsibility to hear in contrition and commitment their clamors for justice and solidarity.[52]

NOTES

1. On the portraits of the violence and sorrows of war, see Susan Sontag, *Regarding the Pain of Others* (New York: Farrar, Straus & Giroux, 2003).
2. Simone Weil, "The *Iliad*, Poem of Might," in *The Simone Weil Reader*, ed. George A. Panichas (New York: David McKay Co., 1977), 153. The original reads: "Le vrai héros, le vrai sujet, le centre de l'*Iliade*, c'est la force" (Simone Weil, "L'*Iliade* ou le poème de la force," in *Oeuvres complètes* [Paris: Gallimard, 1989], tome 2:3, 227).
3. "The *Iliad*, Poem of Might," 183.
4. See her essay "The Love of God and Affliction," in *The Simone Weil Reader*, 439–68.
5. "The *Iliad*, Poem of Might," 180: "The accounts of the Passion show that a divine spirit united to the flesh is altered by affliction, trembles before suffering and death, feels himself, at the moment of deepest agony, separated from men and from God."
6. Ibid., 182.
7. Ibid., 163.
8. Weil's translation and reading of Achilles' rejection of Priam's supplication has been disputed. See Christopher Benfey, "A Tale of Two Iliads," *New York Review of Books*, September 25, 2003, 82. Yet Benfey's critique does not affect the core of Weil's argument, namely, that the raging violence of war impedes Achilles from heeding the supplication of a father, Priam, anguished by the fate of his son, Hector.
9. "The *Iliad*, Poem of Might," 180.
10. Weil's writings display her love for the Hellenic culture, as well as her peculiar disdain for the Hebrew and Roman roots of Western civilization.
11. "Reflections on War," in Simone Weil, *Formative Writings, 1929–1941*, ed. and trans. Dorothy Tuck McFarland and Wilhelmina Van Ness (Amherst: University of Massachusetts Press, 1987), 246.
12. Ibid., 242, 246.
13. Ibid., 241.
14. Ibid., 242.
15. Ibid., 248.
16. Eric Hobsbawm, *Age of Extremes: The Short Twentieth Century, 1914–1991* (London: Michael Joseph, 1994).
17. Robert Coles, *Simone Weil: A Modern Pilgrimage* (Woodstock, VT: Skylight Paths, 2001).

18. William Butler Yeats, "The Second Coming" (1919/1920), in *The New Oxford Book of English Verse, 1250–1950*, chosen and edited by Helen Gardner (Oxford: Oxford University Press, 1972), 820.

19. Aristotle, *The Politics*, Bk. I, 1260a 30. Aristotle is quoting Sophocles, *Ajax*, 293.

20. For a different perspective, see Sylvie Courtine-Denamy, *Three Women in Dark Times: Edith Stein, Hannah Arendt, Simone Weil* (Ithaca, NY: Cornell University Press, 2000).

21. Lamentations 1:1–2. With the exception of Job, Weil tends to disregard with contempt the Hebrew sacred Scriptures.

22. Cf. Euripides, *Iphigenia in Tauris* and *Iphigenia in Aulis*.

23. See Euripides, *Hecuba*, in *The Complete Greek Drama*, ed. Whitney J. Oates and Eugene O'Neill Jr. (New York: Random House, 1938), vol. 1, 818–19. This eloquent text, dealing with the sacrifice of Polyxena, might have resonances of earlier sacrifices of maidens to propitiate the gods or expiate transgressions of sacred laws.

24. Judges 11:29–40. Yahweh did not provide a substitute for Jephthah's unfortunate daughter. A comparison with the story of Abraham and Isaac might suggest that gender distinction makes quite a difference in the way the God of Israel deals with the cultic rite of human sacrifice.

25. See Sigmund Freud, *Totem and Taboo* (1913) and *Moses and Monotheism* (1939).

26. Euripides, *The Women of Troy*, in *The Bacchae and Other Plays* (London: Penguin, 1973), 90.

27. F. W. Dobbs-Allsopp, *Lamentations* (Louisville, KY: John Knox Press, 2002).

28. *The Women of Troy*, 110.

29. Cf. Ariel Dorfman, *Death and the Maiden* (New York: Penguin Books, 1992).

30. *The Women of Troy*, 93.

31. Ibid., 111.

32. Ibid., 112.

33. Ibid., 96.

34. Ibid., 112.

35. *Hecuba*, 814.

36. *The Women of Troy*, 114.

37. Ibid., 103.

38. Ibid., 102.

39. Ibid., 102–5.

40. Aristophanes, *Lysistrata*, in *The Complete Greek Drama*, vol. 2, 803–60. This is the literary source of that famous antiwar slogan: "Make love, not war!"

41. Similar resistance and defiance are also expressed by Andromache's fierce confrontation with Menelaus, in the play that bears as title the name of the unfortunate Trojan widow, forced to be the slave and concubine of Neoptolemus, her husband's slayer. Euripides, *Andromache*, in *The Complete Greek Drama*, vol. 1, 843–78.

42. "The *Iliad*, Poem of Might," 178.

43. Lamentations 1:7; 3:48.

44. Lamentations 2:20; 4:10.

45. See Julie Mostov, "'Our Women'/'Their Women': Symbolic Boundaries, Territorial Markers, and Violence in the Balkans," in *Peace and Change*, vol. 20, no. 4 (1995): 515–29, and Elise Boulding, "Feminist Inventions in the Art of Peacemaking: A Century Overview," ibid., 408–38.

46. Lamentations 3:1, 8, 36.

47. *Andromache*, 865.

48. *Murder in the Cathedral*, in Thomas Stearns Eliot, *The Complete Poems and Plays, 1909–1950* (New York: Harcourt, Brace & Co., 1958), 195.

49. Amnesty International, *Afghanistan. "No one listens to us and no one treats us as human beings": Justice Denied to Women*, AI Index: ASA 11/023/2003 (October 6, 2003), 18.
50. See, for example, her novel *The Fall of the Imam* (London: Saqi Books, 2002) and her literary self-portrait *Walking through Fire: A Life of Nawal El Saadawi* (London and New York: Zed Books, 2003).
51. Amnesty International, *Afghanistan*, 25.
52. For a female perspective on war and peace, see Elise Boulding, *Cultures of Peace: The Hidden Side of History* (Syracuse, NY: Syracuse University Press, 2000), and Anaida Pascual Morán, *Acción civil noviolenta: fuerza de espíritu, fuerza de paz* (Río Piedras, PR: Publicaciones Puertorriqueñas, 2003).

Chapter 12

4 *Ezra*'s Lament:
The Anatomy of Grief

Richard K. Fenn

A lament is a heartfelt complaint against time. We may address our complaints to God, whose heart seems incredibly hardened against our own suffering, like a mother who seems indifferent to the agony of an infant and is inexplicably taking her own time to respond. The purpose of the lament is to soften the heart of God and thus to shorten the time of our own distress. If the lament succeeds, however, it is our heart that will be softened, to the point that we can imagine and embrace the suffering of others who have long been far beyond the range of our own knowledge, experience, and compassion. A lament that works its way into our souls will enable us to wait for our own relief until the suffering of everyone else is also being relieved. If the lament fails, we will continue to ask for a reserved seat among those who rejoice while others still weep and lament their own misfortune.

One complaint against time is that it is going too slowly, and that God's own way of doing things is unnecessarily and unfairly lengthening the days of our sorrow. If you can, imagine that you are an infant again, lying in a crib, in serious distress. You may be hungry or sore, but your discomfort is far more than physical. You see signs of your parents, can hear their voices and footsteps, but they seem utterly indifferent and unresponsive to your cries. They seem to be operating in another world, beyond the reach of your pleas. Although you cannot wait much longer, they seem to be taking their own sweet time. "How long and when will these things be?"[1]

If you ever have been in severe pain of the body or soul, you will understand immediately why Ezra wanted to know how much longer it would take for relief to come. You may have wondered if you were already at least halfway to the end of your suffering. If so, you could go on, because there would be less time to be spent in agony ahead of you than already lay behind you. Time would be on your side. That is just why Ezra asks the angel, "If I have found favor in your sight, and if it is possible, and if I am worthy, show me this also: whether more time is to come than has passed, or whether for us the greater part has gone by. For I know what has gone by, but I do not know what is to come."[2]

Ezra does not know what is to become of him, because he cannot imagine himself holding out much longer. He asks the angel about the end times, when all suffering will be finished and even the dungeons of hell will release their prisoners: "Do you think that I shall live until those days?"[3] Certainly he is in hell now and longs for release, and he wonders how much more, how much *longer*, he can endure. Certainly, he is in danger of dying, spiritually and perhaps also physically. At the every least, he is running out of time because something in him is dying. It may be an old dream that is dying, an old belief in his importance to the world; we will get into that shortly. It may be a view of the future, a kind of hope that has kept him going until now, but that at last seems virtually hopeless. He cannot go on much longer because the future that has been drawing him on has already perished. What may be dying is his infantile self, whose departure will make way for an adult willing and able to experience life on its terms rather than his own. It may be his own soul that is dying, consumed from within by a rage that has no outlet. In order to keep his anger from destroying himself, Ezra may be in a hurry for the end of the world to come; certainly he would find some comfort, even vindication, in seeing others in similar torment. All these possibilities will come to mind as we listen further to Ezra's lament. In so doing, we may be better able, not only to understand our own complaints against time, but also to listen with greater depth and compassion to the often-untold agony of others.

Of all the reasons for Ezra to be in a hurry, the most obvious is to find release for his anger, and he has plenty about which to be angry. If the book was indeed written about thirty years after the destruction of Jerusalem in the first century CE, the prophet has lost everything on which he could have pinned a faith that had always been immersed in history itself.[4] Ezra says that he wanted to ask God "why Israel had been given over to the gentiles as a reproach; why the people whom you loved has been given over to godless tribes, and the Law of our fathers has been made of no effect and the written covenants no longer exist: and why we pass from the world like locusts, and our life is like a mist, and we are not worthy to obtain mercy."[5] Let there be no mistake about the anger here. He goes on to ask God "why those who opposed your promises have trodden down on those who believe your covenants. If you really hate your people, they should be punished at your own hands."[6] The hatred, of course, is Ezra's own: a long-standing hatred toward those who have humiliated and destroyed Israel. Thus he has God say that "when the humiliation of Zion is complete . . . friends shall make war on friends like enemies, and the earth and those who inhabit shall be terrified, and the springs of the fountains shall stand still."[7] There will be no escape, no sanctuary, no safe place among friends, no place of refreshment and peace, but total devastation for those who have hated and humiliated Israel.

It is worth understanding the fierceness and scope of this anger, if only because we live in a world where such rage is widespread and close to home: not only in Sarajevo and Baghdad, but also in America after the bombing of the World Trade Center and the Pentagon. I add the Pentagon if only to remind us that a general of the U.S. military has declared the war in Iraq to be a war on Islam, and his statement has yet to be repudiated by the administration of the United States. Ever since the war of 1967, in which Israel destroyed the armies of Syria and Egypt, an apocalyptic fervor has gained momentum in Islam, fueled by humiliation and angry enough to send legions of Muslims into battle and suicidal attacks on defenseless civilians.

In this country the Christian Right, notably among Pat Robertson and his followers, have been eager for a showdown with all the enemies of the United States. Indeed, they see America as the lead nation in the world, entitled to Christian sovereignty without entangling alliances with international bodies like the U.N., and wholly entitled to preemptive strikes and to world conquest as America fulfills its destiny as the new Israel. Our anger has become more lethal to many, fueled as it is by an aggravated sense of our own national self-importance. Look in laments, then, for the fury that can go on a killing spree.

Not only does such grandiose rage endanger others, but it can also be turned against oneself. It is enough to make Ezra hate his own life. Because he cannot understand why Israel should be so devastated by its enemies, when it should have had the Lord on its side, he asks, "Why then was I born? Or why did not my mother's womb become my grave, that I might not see the travail of Jacob and the exhaustion of the people of Israel?"[8] If in Islam we see humiliation and fury against the enemy taking on suicidal forms, we must ask ourselves what forms of collective self-hatred may be the result of our passion for national vindication and for revenge after the destruction of the World Trade Center. Clearly to enrage our enemies and alienate our friends and allies is the path to national self-destruction.

More than a national self-examination is suggested by such a lament as Ezra's. The problem is in one's heart, at the very beginning, throughout our lives, and at the end. Ezra's God promises Ezra that he "will not grieve over the multitude of those who perish; for it is they who are now like a mist, and are similar to a flame and smoke—they are set on fire and burn hotly, and are extinguished."[9] "Will not grieve": The voice is God's, but the hardened heart belongs to the visionary himself, whose grief has turned to anger. Sorrow, anguish, a terrible sense of being lost in the world and headed for extinction, unbearable sadness over what has been lost and can never be brought back again: all these may well turn into anger. It is far easier to rage than to weep, to look forward to a day of vindication and revenge than to face a future deprived of the presence of those whom we long have loved and will never see again. Ezra knows this. He admitted early on that "out of my grief I have spoken; for every hour I suffer agonies of heart, while I strive to find out the way of the Most High and to search out part of his judgment."[10] If we will not grieve directly, however, but turn our grief into an attack of conscience, our anger will feed on our own souls.

Ezra is searching out the divine judgment in the hope of relief from his own torment, part of which is surely the sense that Israel is in some way being judged by these actions: condemned and humiliated. "For we and our fathers have passed our lives in ways that bring death."[11] To transmute grief into anger and to transform anger into a search for judgment, an attack of conscience, is to give one's anger a weapon that can be turned viciously against the soul. Shortly after Ezra has the Lord say that he looks forward to seeing the wicked consumed in the fires of his own divine anger and turning into nothing more than a mist, Ezra says that "it would have been better if the dust itself had not been born, so that the mind might not have been made from it. . . . For it is much better for them [the "beasts of the field" (*rkf*)] than with us, for they do not look for a judgment, nor do they know of any torment or salvation promised to them after death."[12]

It is no wonder that this lament looks forward to a day of final judgment and release from the torments of a conscience that has turned the experience of disaster into a fault-finding expedition focused on the self. Ezra asks the angel whether in the last day there will be any chance to pray and intercede for others, that they too might be saved in the final judgment and given rest and joy rather than eternal torment. The answer given is curt enough: "Therefore no one will then be able to have mercy on him who has been condemned in the judgment, or to harm him who is victorious."[13] It is an unsatisfying answer to Ezra, and perhaps also to some of you who read this: no chance for mercy, for forgiveness, and for reconciliation. Ezra clearly mourns the loss of those who have "lived wickedly" and asks "For what good is it to us, if an eternal age has been promised to us, but we have done deeds that bring death?"[14] He has been looking back on the days in which the prophets and kings of Israel prayed for people, and he has asked whether friends and relatives may not intercede for those who are dear to them. To imagine that the bonds of affection could be cut off once and for all is virtually unbearable. Still the answer comes back, "Therefore there shall not be grief at their damnation, so much as joy over those to whom salvation is assured."[15] The angel's answer splits the positive affections from the negative, separating love for the saved from any affection for the damned. Indeed the angel sanctifies a split in the psyche between love and an arrogant dismissal of the damned as beneath the dignity of one's own affections.

This split in the psyche shows up again as ambivalence toward time itself. Affection even for the dead does not die easily, because old and deep loves have a life of their own. This continuing but apparently hopeless affection puts those of us who grieve in a terrible dilemma. On the one hand, anger at having lost a world that we loved and that gave us life turns into an attack on our very souls for not having lived purely enough, for not having loved enough, and for not having fulfilled the promises that we made in our youth. When anger rushes to judgment, the end cannot come soon enough. Therefore one prays for the Lord to hasten the day of judgment. How much longer must we wait for vindication and the satisfaction of seeing others suffer in such torment that we now bear? On the other hand, our continuing affection for those who have died and who may not survive a day of final judgment leads us to beg for more, not less, time. Indeed Ezra has asked if there is not some way that those who love one another can intercede for each other, as if to buy some more time in which the souls of both the living and the dead can finish the work of purification. Certainly the living have long prayed for the dead, as though there were still some way for love to gain more time. The angel's answer suggests that such a purgatory is only for the living; it is in this life alone that the struggle for self-purification must be won or lost.

The split in the psyche between love and anger, grief and rage, causes a further division in Ezra's lament: a split between his feelings for Israel and for all humankind. "If then you suddenly and quickly destroy him who with so great labor was fashioned by your command, to what purpose was he made? And now I will speak out: About mankind you know best; but I will speak about your people, for whom I am grieved, and about your inheritance, for whom I lament, and about Israel, for whom I am sad, and about the seed of Jacob, for whom I am troubled. Therefore I will pray before you for myself and for them, for I see the failings of us who dwell in the land, and I have heard of the swiftness of the judgment that is to come. Therefore hear my voice, and understand my words, and I will speak before you."[16]

We are on holy ground here, when untold agony begins to find its voice. If there ever is a sacred moment, it is when a soul whose torment has been suppressed and silenced finally begins to speak. Such moments occur when rituals fail, and the dead lie unburied. Such moments occur when grief, long buried below the surface of consciousness, finally breaks through, perhaps years later, and tears flow at long last. These are moments that could bind humankind into one family.

However, the psyche split by grief divides the world into those whose death is to be mourned and those whose lives and deaths do not touch the heart at all, but are a matter of indifference. There is yet to be common grieving by white America over the deaths caused by midnight lynchings, yet to be grieving in America over the victims of "collateral damage" caused even by the smartest of bombs. Until our victims can hear the sound of America's laments over their losses, we will be left with the ghastly division that cuts across even Ezra's lament: the division of the world between humankind and Israel.

The split in the psyche between love and hate finally allows Ezra to claim an exemption for himself from the fate that awaits many other Israelites. Thus, deeper than his attachments to friends and relatives, more lasting even than his love for the people of God, is his sense that he should receive special consideration in the end. The very attack of conscience that has filled him with a sense of the sinfulness of himself and of the people of Israel is now turned into a basis for special pleading. The Most High says to Ezra, "But you have often compared yourself to the unrighteous. Never do so! But even in this respect you will be praiseworthy before the Most High, because you humble yourself, as is becoming for you, and have not deemed yourself to be among the righteous in order to receive the greatest glory."[17] A similar reassurance has long allowed the church, so long as it is contrite, to separate its fate from a world that it regards as secular.

If at heart one is convinced of his or her inherent uniqueness and superiority, that conviction will add an overtone even to the most poignant and heartfelt of confessions of sorrow and unworthiness. Clinicians sometimes use the word *narcissism* to describe this strange complex of feelings about oneself. As I have indicated here, Ezra combines enormous anger with self-hatred. His self-love and self-hatred are mixed; note his inner conviction that his self-loathing will seem meritorious to God. Scratch a narcissist, and you will find a masochist: someone whose attachment to people protracts his own suffering, even when his desires are hopeless. It is hard for Ezra to say no or good-bye, and he leaves that up to God, while in the meantime extending his own sadness for the souls of those whom he loves but will never see again, even in paradise.

The split in the psyche between self-love and a self-hatred that is redirected outward is very costly. Ask a Palestinian whose baby has been shot by a sniper taking target practice, or whose well has run dry because the Israeli settlements surrounding the village are digging deeper into the aquifer while prohibiting Palestinians from doing the same, or the family whose house has been bulldozed to the ground because one of the children had fought back. Ask an African American naval officer whose career began in the boiler room of a ship, where his fellow seamen overpowered him, greased his body, strapped him to pipes, and left him to cook. Ask an African American who heard tales from his grandmother of slaves being taken from their quarters at night to be lynched in the woods, and whose childhood nightmares have turned into fears that he will lose his home. Ask an African American whose experience of white America has been civil rather than brutal, but who knows that he or she will never be considered fully an equal by white Americans, let alone loved like a member of the family. Ask a woman who knows that men will never take her as seriously as they would a man, regardless of her achievements. These pay the price for the narcissism of a people or a gender who set themselves apart from the rest of "mankind."

For Ezra, what has been wounded is not only his own narcissism but Israel's. The sense of having been a privileged nation has long given Israel the sense that it would be immune from final prosecution. After all, they had been told that God regarded the other nations as "nothing, and that they are like spittle, and you have compared their abundance to a drop from the bucket. . . . But we your people, whom you have called your first-born, only begotten, zealous for you, and most dear, have been given into their hands. If the world has indeed been given for us, why do we not possess our world as an inheritance? How long will this be so?"[18]

Like the new Israel, the old Israel had long imagined itself to have a special relationship to God that would exempt it from the fate of other peoples and nations. "For what good is it to us, if an eternal age has been promised to us, but we have done deeds that bring death?"[19] Indeed, Israel had been the aggressor against neighboring peoples and had pushed for a greater Israel that would extend from the Jordan to the Mediterranean. They had converted other peoples, sometimes by force. One of their kings had even crucified those who opposed him, and rival brothers of the priestly class had brought disastrous civil war upon the nation in their contest for the office of chief priest. "For while we lived and committed iniquity we did not consider what we should suffer after death."[20]

So long as the church lays claim to one who is the only begotten, it has a reason to set itself apart from the rest of humankind. Those who have the Son have life; those who do not have the Son have death. This theological and psychological split in the way the church views its relation to the rest of the world resembles the old Israel's way of dividing the world up between those who will make the final cut and those who will not. Like Ezra, those who insist on distinguishing the church from the world see the world itself as a rival or the enemy. It is a rival for the time, money, attention, and loyalty that otherwise could go into the church. How many sermons have been preached echoing Ezra's lament that, whereas the people of God should be instructing the world, the world is indeed giving lessons to the church? The church, in the meantime, has learned only too well from the world. It has learned how to let policies and procedures take the place of compassion. It has learned how to compete with other organizations for time and talent, for money and loyalty, as if one could meet God best under the auspices of the church. It has forgotten that Jesus promised that he could raise children of Abraham from the very stones of the street, and that the Spirit has been doing so for centuries. It has forgotten that the Spirit blows where it will, and that those who insist on specifying the time and place of its arrival will miss the Spirit altogether.

This pernicious division of the world into the people of God and all others still informs the rhetoric of the United States as an evangelical nation, the new Israel on whose leadership depends the fate of the world itself. The Christian Right is still spoiling for a day of judgment in which the enemies of Israel will do their worst, Israel having already done its best to reclaim the entire possession of the West Bank and the Temple Mount. On that day, according to seers like Pat Robertson, there will be 144,000 Jews left, all of whom will become Christians who will evangelize the world for Christ. Leading the charge will be the United States, at last fully installed as the New Israel. When that day comes, it will be hard on all the people who are not the sons of Abraham: the Babylonians, as Robertson calls them, who include the followers of Islam, secular humanists, homosexuals, and others abhorrent to the visionaries of the Right. Their apocalyptic vision goes back a lot further than Ezra, but in *4 Ezra* we get some of the familiar strains that have found their way into the New Testament: longings for a day when "the Most High shall be revealed upon the seat of judgment, and compassion shall pass away, and patience will be withdrawn . . . and the furnace of Hell shall be disclosed, and opposite the Paradise of delight."[21]

As I have been suggesting, this longing for a division of the world reflects the splitting of the psyche under the impact of grief, relentless anger, and intolerable sadness. What is being split off from the psyche, of course, is the individual's own suffering, and it may be very acute—too much to bear, in fact. So it is pushed off into the psyche's equivalent of the furnace of hell. When Ezra imagines a day on which "the pit of torment shall appear," he is looking forward to a return of that part of the psyche that has been silenced and buried, where its groans cannot be heard and its anguish felt.[22] That part of the psyche, however, once it is split off, goes through a death agony. No wonder, then, that Ezra imagines the day of judgment as being one on which "the chambers shall give up the souls which have been committed to them."[23] The dead come back to life, and the buried suffering of the soul comes finally to light.

The split-off part of the soul that has suffered a lengthy death agony in this life, unable to take part in the pleasures of the rest of the psyche, finally reappears in the apocalyptic vision, but even there it is still separated from the part of the psyche that has been saved through penitence and purification. What is revealed in the end is the sadness and grief that have long been segregated in the psyche. Immediately after death, Ezra is told by the Most High, "as the spirit leaves the body to return again to him who gave it," those spirits who have failed the tests of devotion "shall immediately wander about in torments, ever grieving and sad, in seven ways."[24] It is too late for them to enjoy the pleasures of the saved, but it is not too late for them to see what those pleasures will be. They look, in torment, at the prospect of a bliss they will never achieve.

What returns, in this apocalyptic vision, is a tiny remnant of the psyche that has been separated from the grandiose psyche that feels itself to be the favorite of God and thus entitled not only to final vindication but also to the satisfactions of spiritual revenge. Having been long closed off in its own chambers, as Ezra puts it, this segregated part of the psyche is destined to sense its own impending death from spiritual isolation. Of course, it is easier for the visionary to imagine such a day occurring after the end of life: a preliminary day of judgment in which the soul sees its future punishments and the joys that it is going to miss. However, that split-off part of the soul is already dying and lives in dread of its end, resentful that it should have been condemned to spiritual isolation and a slow death in this life. What good is it, Ezra asks on behalf of the condemned soul, "that the faces of those who practiced self-control shall shine more than the stars, but our faces shall be blacker than darkness?"[25] Note the color of despair and rejection.

If the Christian community is to recover the lament as a way of engaging in the cure of souls, several steps will be necessary. Beneath the mask of anger and remorse, grief and sadness, may be deeper levels of sadness: the sadness of a part of the self that is slowly isolated and therefore dying, or sadness for the parts of the self that have been tied to a hopeless affection for the departed. However, defending the psyche from either type of sadness may be a chronic form of narcissism: a grandiose sense of entitlement that comes with infancy and stays when the world has not been satisfying enough on a regular basis. To move beyond dreams of glorious vindication and revenge to the small part of the soul whose agony has long remained segregated and untold, however, it will be necessary to listen carefully to the many ways in which such suffering can be hidden behind concern for poor souls or behind judgments on those souls, blackened by sin, who deserve to remain indefinitely or forever in a private hell of their own.

Of course, these are just the preliminary steps in pastoral care, and each of them may be hindered by the residues of magical thinking left over from infancy and by the powerful resistance that comes with pain, where the soul, like the body, can become relatively stiff and inarticulate with too much suffering. Memories and feelings alike may be buried in parts of the body and come to light, like the souls from their graves on the last day, only when summoned in dreams and fantasies as a prelude to painful recollection.

There is also a prophetic dimension to this care of the soul. The individual's projections of desire and remorse, of mourning and humiliation, onto another people has been a long story, beginning long before Ezra, and it continues today, of course, in the ways in which whites and African Americans imagine each other. Thus some communities and even the larger society conspire to make it easy to protect oneself from crushing memories, from the stings of humiliation, and from overwhelming passion, by coloring entire peoples with the hues of despair and rejection, as in the case of those whose faces are "blacker than darkness." The recovery of the grieving and anguished parts of the psyche enables the soul to empathize with others who have long seemed to be unfamiliar or even strange. The recovery of the soul might make others become less unfamiliar and enhance the capacity for empathy and friendship.

To overcome the tendency of the anguished soul to split itself—and the world—into two parts, one blessed and the other headed for condemnation and eternal torment, it will be necessary for the church to revise or eliminate some of its own doctrines. I have in mind especially the doctrines of the last days and the final judgment. Dear as they may be to believers of various persuasions, these beliefs have made it legitimate to imagine the world as split into two parts. The Christian Right would not find it so easy to divide the world between the sons of Abraham and those of Babylon, between true believers among Christians and Jews, on the one hand, and a world of Muslims and secular humanists on the other, if it were not for the honored place that the apocalyptic imagination still has in the canon and the Christian liturgy. So long as the mainline Protestant and Catholic churches postpone the recovery of the buried aspects of the psyche, with their long-standing grief and grievances, to a final day, such beliefs will continue to act like magnets that attract all the filings of self-hatred and despair and mold them into a weapon of mass—and mutual—destruction.

NOTES

1. *4 Ezra* 4:33; B. M. Metzger, "The Fourth Book of Ezra, A New Translation and Introduction," in *The Old Testament Pseudepigrapha*, vol. 1, *Apocalyptic Literature and Testaments*, edited by James H. Charlesworth (Garden City, NY: Doubleday & Co., 1983), 531.
2. *4 Ezra* 4:44–46, in Charlesworth, 531.
3. *4 Ezra* 4:51, in Charlesworth, 531.
4. "According to most scholars, the original Jewish document known today as 4 Ezra was composed about A.D. 100," in Metzger, "The Fourth Book of Ezra," Introduction, in Charlesworth, 520.
5. *4 Ezra* 4:23–24, in Charlesworth, 531.
6. *4 Ezra* 5:29–30, in Charlesworth, 533.
7. *4 Ezra* 6:20, 24, in Charlesworth, 533.
8. *4 Ezra* 5:35, in Charlesworth, 533.
9. *4 Ezra* 7:61, in Charlesworth, 539.
10. *4 Ezra* 5:34, in Charlesworth, 533.
11. *4 Ezra* 8:31, in Charlesworth, 543.
12. *4 Ezra* 7:63, 66, in Charlesworth, 539.
13. *4 Ezra* 7:45[115], in Charlesworth, 541.
14. *4 Ezra* 7:49[119], in Charlesworth, 541.
15. *4 Ezra* 7:61[131], in Charlesworth, 541.
16. *4 Ezra* 8:14–19, [131], in Charlesworth, 542.
17. *4 Ezra* 8:48–49, in Charlesworth, 544.
18. *4 Ezra* 6:56, 58–59, in Charlesworth, 536.
19. *4 Ezra* 7:49[119], in Charlesworth, 541.
20. *4 Ezra* 7:56[126], in Charlesworth, 541.
21. *4 Ezra* 7:33, 36, in Charlesworth, 538.
22. *4 Ezra* 7:36, in Charlesworth, 538.
23. *4 Ezra* 7:32, in Charlesworth, 538.
24. *4 Ezra* 7:78, 80, in Charlesworth, 539.
25. *4 Ezra* 7:55[125], in Charlesworth, 541.

Chapter 13

Breaking Point: A Sermon

Brian K. Blount

> *When he opened the fifth seal, I saw under the altar the souls of those who had been slaughtered for the word of God and for the testimony they had given; they cried out with a loud voice, "Sovereign Lord, holy and true, how long will it be before you judge and avenge our blood on the inhabitants of the earth?" They were each given a white robe and told to rest a little longer, until the number would be complete both of their fellow servants and of their brothers and sisters, who were soon to be killed as they themselves had been killed.*
>
> Revelation 6:9–11

Introduction

This sermon was preached in May 2002 at the Montreat Conference Center of the Presbyterian Church (USA) in Montreat, North Carolina. The theme for the conference was "Reclaiming the Text: Recovering the Language of Lament." I chose a text from the Apocalypse because apocalyptic language is intrinsically all about lament. It is the language of a people who feel themselves to be oppressed by powers so superior that no human effort seems capable of accomplishing effective resistance. Since the present cannot be changed, the apocalyptic writer looks to the future. This is not necessarily, however, a far-off future in some alternative, mythological reality. Apocalyptic hope can also be historical hope. Many apocalyptic writers believed that the future they envisioned was imminent and that it was about the transformation of this world. However, since human power was insufficient for the transformation so desperately sought, God, or God's duly appointed messianic agent, would move directly into the human scene to effect the necessary change. Humans could either wait passively for that moment to

145

come, or they could join in the struggle. Revelation, I believe, encourages the latter option. Its writer, John, believing that God is on the precipice of monumental historical action, calls his people to apocalyptic attention. He wants them to join in God's struggle with demonstrative acts of nonviolent resistance against the great power that afflicts them. Acknowledging the depth of their misery, he not only joins in their lament; he tries to turn that lament into transformative behavior. He sees a people at the breaking point and sees within this tragic reality a powerful opportunity. A people being broken have two viable and yet alternative responses. They can either take it, or they can take it upon themselves to fight back. Revelation, I believe, wants them to use their lament as a springboard for fighting back. That is why I believe the image of those lamenting souls under the altar in heaven has such a powerful motivational effect in John's work. John turns it from what could easily be read as a self-pitying call for blind vengeance into a cry for justice and a plea to the people of faith to keep witnessing for the God who will very soon bring that justice about.

————————

Back somewhere around January *22*, when I was almost drowning amidst a sea of paperwork, and choking on a flurry of *urgent* e-mail, I received this diplomatic one that was obviously a very gentle reminder intended to spur some slackers to action, while at the same time not getting them upset. I must say, it was *very* nicely done. Here was the crucial part: "I am e-mailing you regarding the text, title, and general theme of your two worship services for the upcoming Reclaiming the Text Conference: Recovering the Language of Lament. The deadline we established for this information to be submitted to our office was January *15th,* and we are in the process of reminding those who have not yet responded."

In case you haven't gotten the point, one of those who had not yet responded was me. Well, that official recognition of my tardiness initiated my own personal lament. I had all this stuff to do, all of which was due *immediately,* I had new classes starting, my responsibilities for my old classes weren't finished, I had a book manuscript to complete, I had students calling, I had people sending me manuscripts to read for another publication I was editing, I had lectures to fine-tune and other lectures to write. All of that was right there in front of me, that very minute, that very hour, that very day, the very next day, the very next week. And then here comes this e-mail from Montreat saying they needed a Scripture and a sermon title for this presentation here on May 27. That's four months, almost half a year away! I was thinking to myself after I finished reading that e-mail, "Those damn Presbyterians. I'll bet they won't let God bring the kingdom in unless we can have God's final revelation in hand at least two millennia ahead of time." Gee whiz, I grew up Baptist, and I figure half the preachers I knew weren't hitting their sermon stride until at least the Saturday afternoon the day before they were going to preach it. "Those damn Presbyterians." I was thinking, whether the topic fits the Scripture reading or not, I'm going to entitle my first sermon "Breaking Point," because I'm at mine.

You know I'm not altogether serious, because I am Presbyterian, I love being Presbyterian, and actually this whole anal retentive thing suits my own obsessive compulsive personality rather nicely. My mom and dad swore that they would have never just shown up on my college or seminary campus to surprise me, because if they hadn't gotten themselves on my schedule, I might have refused to see them. Everybody who knows me knows I don't like people messing up my schedule. You can imagine, then, how difficult this messy book of Revelation is for me and the rest of us orderly Presbyterians. John seems to *like* being messy. In fact, I wonder what John would have done if one of his churches had asked him for the title of his prophecy and a sample of his visions a half year before he'd finished having them. Probably he would have said something like, "Those damn Asia Minor churches!"

John knew, though, that for all his pain over imprisonment on the penal property of Patmos, it was *their* suffering that mattered most. His visions don't focus on *his* circumstance; his prophecy doesn't whine about *his* situation; his revelation is about *their* messy world and the danger *their* world was in. *That's* the presentation he gives us at 6:9–11. We get the picture of his seven churches. They are a branded community, tattooed with the mark of God, standing toe to toe with the public professions of lordship claimed by the Roman Empire, being socially ostracized and some times even physically butchered because of their witness to the *contrary* profession that Jesus Christ is Lord. In the Christian enclaves of Asia Minor, there was much to lament.

Rome's eastern provinces of Asia Minor were hotbeds of emperor worship. Rome tried to be reasonable about the situation. You know Rome; it was the kinder, gentler empire. Rome was tolerant. It declared that people could worship any gods they wanted to worship. All Rome asked in turn was that a people also recognize the divinity of Rome and its Caesar. This religious recognition demonstrated a simultaneous political loyalty. The Romans believed that people who worshipped Caesar as god would also acknowledge and thus obey Caesar as king. Rome didn't ask a lot of those Christians. All Rome wanted was a small portion of their liturgical life. When they were finished with that eight o'clock worship service of Rome, they could then have all the ten and eleven o'clock worship services of Jesus Christ that they wanted. Rome was tolerant. It was those Christians who were the intolerant ones. And those intolerant Christians wouldn't play along. They had to worship Jesus at eight o'clock, too. Eight o'clock, nine o'clock, ten o'clock, eleven o'clock, twelve o'clock—they wanted to worship Jesus all around the clock. They couldn't even spare a few minutes to recognize the reign of Rome. That's when Rome reached its breaking point and it set out to break the Christians.

John symbolized the horror of Rome's actions with his vision of a great red dragon. It was the dragon who made Rome believe it was lord of history. It was the dragon who set the Caesars about the task of enforcing that belief even to the death. It was the dragon who took hold of human weakness and misshaped it into sin and evil and then sat back in delight as that evil metastasized into military, political, social, and even religious cancer. It was the dragon who made it appear that history was totally, completely, irrevocably out of control—even God's control. In the Christian enclaves of Asia Minor, there was much to lament.

You know, when I first saw the theme for this conference, "The *Recovery* of Lament," I must admit that my first thought was, "Those damn middle-class, white Christians!" *Recover lament?! Recover lament?!* Don't they realize that there are people who live with lament the way most of us live with the air we breathe? Black folk. Native American folk. Hispanic folk. Women folk. Palestinian folk. Israeli folk. Afghani folk. But then I realized that the conference planners are right. For some reason most of us Christians don't see it. We are so impressed with the superior state of our own spiritual salvation and so mesmerized by the debilitating effects of our own emotional angst that we don't feel the sting of the social, medical, political, economic, religious, and military disruption all around us. Most of the people in our world live every day they are blessed enough to keep on living right there on the edge of existence, right at the dragon's demonic break point, *literally* running for their lives. *Every* moment we live, *every* breath we take, at *that* moment there are thousands upon thousands for whom lament is as natural and as regular as the beating of our hearts. Even the souls up in heaven feel it. Things are so bad *down here*, they're even crying out in lament *up there*. Here we stand and sit right beside it, and yet so far removed from it all that someone must call upon us, must conference us, to get us to lament.

There's just one thing I'm afraid of, though, when counseling folk to recover lament. I'm afraid they're going to confuse lamenting with whining. *There's no whining in Christianity! Real Christians don't whine!* I was a pastor long enough to know the difference between Christians whining for what they think they oughta have and downtrodden and oppressed people lamenting for what all of us know oughta be. You want to know the difference between a lament and a whine? Well, if you're a minister and your testimony is all about how mad you are because the people on your board or in your church won't do what you tell them to do, you're whining. If you're a Christian and you're crying out because the minister doesn't look at you the right way when you're walking out the church on Sunday morning, or doesn't pay enough attention to you on Monday afternoon, you're whining. If you're an institutional official of a church, seminary, presbytery, synod or whatever and you're singing the blues because the capital campaign didn't make its goal last year, when a huge proportion of the people on this earth can't scrape together enough pennies to feed their children, you're whining. If you're crying to the Lord because you've got to put a new roof on your $200,000 house when people are living in tin boxes, I'm sorry, but you're whining. If you stand up on your soapbox in the midst of global poverty, famine, and starvation and rail against the heavens about how high your property taxes are in your paved-road, somebody-picks-up-your-trash-every-Tuesday, police-protected, electricity-supplied, cable-and-satellite-networked, Internet-connected, municipally bonded existence, I don't care what tax bracket Uncle Sam has got you in, you, baby, are whining.

Revelation-like lament comes from people driven to the depths of social, economic, and political despair in a world without hope. Revelation-like lament cries out, "How long, Sovereign God? How long?" Revelation-like lament is the sound you hear at the human breaking point. And yet Revelation-like lament isn't a whine that cries out from surrender or defeat or fear. It is the call of one who believes in the truth that despite all you see God *is* in control.

Now I have to be honest. When I was in school, I started to get a little shaky on God when I prayed for an A and a B+ came back. That was enough to knock my universe out of joint. Not these slaughtered souls. They believe. And they're mad. Christians get angry. Souls slaughtered to the breaking point for testifying to and living out the transformative lordship of Jesus Christ? They get *mad*. They're ready for God to do something. And they're doing their part to help.

This is one of those texts that has proved increasingly embarrassing for contemporary Christians. There is no doubt that what John hears is a cry for vengeance. John uses the Greek word ἐκδικέω, which is a verb of revenge. There are many Christians who wonder why he doesn't demonstrate here the same kind of love that Jesus showed when he forgave his enemies, even as he hung on their cross. John, they say, breathes a most un-Christlike spirit. The whiny comments of commentator T. Francis Glasson are representative: "If only John the seer had found some way of maintaining the principle that love is the strongest power in the world, what a great work this would be!"[1]

But John has driven past whine to the point of lament. This is not really the language of private revenge; it's the language of public justice. Justice *must* be done; whatever cost justice requires must be paid. And that's where John's language comes in. For ἐκδικέω also has the sense of "getting someone justice." Here Allan Boesak's commentary is of assistance. Writing from the context of a black living in South African apartheid, he points out that people who do not know oppression and suffering react strangely to the language of the Bible, particularly this language of justice. He writes that "the oppressed do not see any dichotomy between God's love and God's justice."[2] I like how he goes on to talk about the matter.

> God takes up the cause of the poor and the oppressed precisely because in this world their voices are not heard—not even by those who call themselves Christians. God even has to take up the cause of the poor *against* "Christians." Christians who enjoy the fruits of injustice without a murmur, who remain silent as the defenceless are slaughtered, dare not become indignant when the suffering people of God echo the prayers of the psalms and pray for deliverance and judgment.[3]

This brings me to my final question about the theme of our conference. Are you sure you really *want* to recover lament? A lot of us might want to recover legalized whining, but are we sure we really want to recover lament? Because lament breeds fury at the oppressions and the people who caused them, and—in John's scenario at least—it drives those who lament to resist. Are you ready to recognize what lament recognizes and to do what lament demands, no matter the cost, to bring the change that lament envisions? John knows how hard this is. That's because John knows middle-class Christianity. He was writing to middle-class Christians. He's writing to people who have stuff to lose. That's why he tells them you must decide either to lament and do everything that lament requires, risk everything lament requires to risk, or you must decide to do nothing. Either be hot or be cold. You can't be both. Either accommodate yourself to the ways of Rome and the draconian things it does, or join the resistance of the Lamb.

I can almost see the vision with him. There on the decimated battlefield he calls Armageddon, the dragon's head slowly swivels in satisfaction as it scans all the terror it has wreaked upon the earth. Strewn out like toppled timber on the scorched earth lie the mangled bodies of the humans who would soon become those slaughtered souls crying out under the heavenly altar. The dragon is turning now, fire dripping from its inflamed nostrils, terror rumbling in the underbelly of its hate. And when it has finally wheeled around full circle, the span of its wings casting a shadow of death across the onetime valley of hope, it faces a Lamb, reeling, but still standing, as if slaughtered. Behind the Lamb stands yet another army of witnesses, us perhaps, an army whose lament has turned to fury, and whose posture is that of a people who just aren't gonna take it any more.

As Boesak puts it, "The martyrs are dead, but their witness is still alive."[4] If *their* witness lives in life *after* death, so should *our* witness live in life *before* death. We must, John believes, stand before the force of death that mocks and destroys so many in our world and, on the backside of our lamenting it, resist it.

As I see that dragon staring us down, waiting for its moment to pounce, I can't help but think of the great issues that face our church today, issues like the momentous one of slavery that once tore apart so many denominations of the church. I think how we stand before those issues, too often playing it safe, like the lukewarm believers whom John criticizes, gleefully harvesting sinners inside the church building while the world deteriorates outside it. You don't need lament in a world where everybody stays indoors and plays it safe. Because in that kind of world you don't want to let anybody you know risk their own safety in an attempt to go outside and bring safety to somebody else.

I remember one episode of a Star Trek movie where Captain Kirk and the crew of the famed USS Enterprise—I think the USS stands for United Starship—are being bombarded by a pirate ship they cannot see with weapons against which they have no defense. One of the captain's former crew, Sulu, now a captain himself, is commanding another ship that is coming to the rescue. But he is a long ways away and he has to *drive* the ship at well past its maximum tolerances if he has any prayer of getting to his friends in time. Feeling the vibrations in the ship, knowing the danger they are in, knowing that they may blow up their own ship in their haste to stop their enemies from blowing up the ship of their friends, one of Sulu's play-it-safe crewmen starts whining and calls out with a warning, "If you keep pushing her like this, she'll fly apart." Sulu's response is quick, angry, and to the point: "Well, fly her apart then!" This is no lukewarm stance. This is the stance of a character who believes in the strength and integrity of his ship and believes that its cause is either to render aid or to be rent asunder. There is no middle ground.

On our Christian ship, the USS Church—I sometimes fear the USS stands for U only Save Souls—we have many lukewarm, stay-in-the-house-of-worship, whiny, play-it-safe crew people whose self-appointed task it is to hold everything together. We worry about placating this group, giving in to that group. It's all on us! On the brilliance of our deal making. We're God's gift to the church. *We* are the ones responsible for holding God's church together, as if it's a fragile egg, and if we don't treat it just right, if we don't coddle it and sit on it just so, it'll break apart.

The time has come when we ought to lament a church like that. That's the kind of church that will stand by slavery in order to placate slave owners, stand by the abuse of women to hold the hand of abusive men, stand by homophobes who bar church doors to those they deem unholy in order to placate the loud voices of powerful church lobbies, stand by economic policies that choke the future from the lives of entire peoples in order to get a better interest rate, stand by church tradition that tramples the very people whom the church is charged to protect in order to keep traditional ways of doing church intact. Too many Christians don't trust that the house Jesus built will stand, unless we Christian crew people do all the politicking we can to protect it.

We need to be more like the fictional Captain Sulu. We need to trust God to take the church out into the conflict where God wants it to be, not back in the dry dock where our fear and manipulation want to mothball it. We need to have the courage to shout out to those who whine, "If we don't slow down, she'll fly apart," with the responding, furious lament, "Well, fly her apart then!" If *God* wants to hold her together, there's nothing *we* can do that will tear her apart. So *do* the radical, transformative witness that God calls us to do! Let God take care of the rest. If only the church could consistently muster the courage of that slaughtered Lamb's convictions. Be careful. Because recovering lament will push us to *that* breaking point and beyond.

Don't confuse the issue now! The fact that these souls rest in heaven does not mean that they rested while they were living here on earth. In fact, they are in heaven, as slaughtered souls, *precisely because* they acted in resistance here on earth. Ironically, this oppositional witness that has caused their deaths also participates in the transformation that it seeks. Even as the souls cry out for God to act, John's description of their situation leaves one with the impression that the efforts of their earthly compatriots continue the transformative effort they began. He implies in verse 11 that the souls in heaven have but a little while to wait for the justice they seek, just until the deaths of witnesses like themselves have come to a completion. Their deaths, in this way, contribute, then, to the coming of God's vindication and justice, God's reign. John, though, is not commending death. It is the witnessing that leads to the coming of God's reign. It is the witnessing that mixes with God's own efforts to accomplish the universal and abiding lordship of Jesus Christ. John makes this explicit at 12:11, where he says that *they* conquer by the blood of the Lamb *and* by the witness of their testimony. That's the great irony. The very testimony that caused their deaths, when it is continued by those who lament their deaths and follow their paths, will be the very same testimony that will bring defeat to the dragon and the powerful forces like Rome that the dragon manipulates. Our witness matters *that much!* *This* is the Revelation of Jesus Christ. *This* is the consequence of Revelation-like lament.

You might want to say that we could envision it this way. The intractable, great horrors facing us are like a great wall that separates us from each other and God. The dragon uses that wall to frighten us, and as a shield behind which it takes cover as it fires out against us. But every time someone witnesses with his or her life for the lordship of Jesus Christ by standing up for those pushed down, by speaking out for those silenced by impoverishment, by breaking laws that mutilate human living—every time that happens, that person creates a small, imperceptible, but still real crack in that wall. God cobbles those acts of witness, those acts of resistance together, until the time when they become a great fault line that one day quakes and brings the great wall of the dragon down and the eternal reign of God up. *That's* the Breaking Point we want. That's the one where the Reign of God, with our help, *breaks* in. And it all begins, oddly enough, with the crying out of those heavenly souls.

In the end, though, even though I know how much it can revitalize and reenergize our churches and our faith and transform our world, I'm *still* nervous about this whole lament-recovery enterprise. That's because I know how oddly people can respond even to a good thing. For some people, lament turns into a whine. I don't want those people recovering lament. For some people, lament turns into depression. Their friends and family don't want those people recovering lament. For some people, lament turns into existentialism. Anybody with any sense doesn't want those people recovering lament. For some people, lament means that since there's absolutely *no way* that you can save the struggling people *in* this world, you turn to saving their souls *from* the world. The man who died on the cross for those very same struggling people doesn't want those people recovering lament.

We need more people among our people of faith who will stop concentrating so myopically on saving souls and turn just a little bit of attention toward saving this planet. That's got to be what John is feeling. Exiled out there on that island for standing up for what he believes in, when he chastises five out of the seven churches to whom he writes, he must be thinking, "Those damn Christians! When will they *finish focusing* on their *famously folded* hands and *fight*?" We need people like those slaughtered souls. For them, for people like them, lament turns to anger, and the anger turns to resistance, because when these people reach the breaking point, they don't break down, they break back, and they break back hard. They don't fall down, they stand up. They don't whine, they whet their appetite for struggle and nonviolent resistance. They don't give in, they give everything they have.

When *some* people lament, they stand up with a Gandhi against the greatest empire on earth. When *some* people lament, though enslaved on mighty Southern plantations backed up by centuries of tradition and military power, they gather for outlaw worship in the woods at night after they've worked their bodies to the breaking point in the fields all day. When *some* people lament, they stand before their own church leaders, who are hooked on the past way of doing and being church the way some people are hooked on drugs, and say, "Go ahead, keep fighting for the past, go ahead, keep fighting for the belief that a thing is good today *simply and only* because it was good in the *first century*, and one day you may find yourselves fighting against a *twenty-first century*, living God." When *some* people lament, they stand before the greatest of powers, the fire-breathing dragons, the terrorizing empires, the despoilers of communities, and, like slaughtered souls, like a slaughtered lamb on a dragon-infested battlefield, they go out *beyond* their altars, and their spacious sanctuaries, and their multiroom education wings, and their inviting recreation centers, and cry out *in their world*, "We've had all we're gonna take; we're not taking any more. We're at *God's* breaking point!"

That's what happens when you recapture lament. So, let me ask you one more time, "Do you really, really want to recover it?!"

NOTES

1. Allan A. Boesak, *Comfort and Protest: The Apocalypse from a South African Perspective* (Philadelphia: The Westminster Press, 1987).
2. Boesak, 72.
3. Ibid., 72–73.
4. Ibid., 68.

CONCLUSION

Chapter 14

Till God Speaks Light: Devotional Reflections on Lamentation with Verse

Charles L. Bartow

There is a madness in lamentation, a soulful fury born of ineffable grief. Job's wife's cry is an instance: "Curse God, and die" (Job 2:9). The woman did not wish her husband dead. She wished him out of his suffering and out from under what seemed at best God's indifference. Her cry was a cry of agony and rage, spoken to Job, but aimed at heaven's heart. So too the psalmist's lament:

> O that you would kill the wicked, O God,
>   and that the bloodthirsty would depart from me—
> those who speak of you maliciously,
>   and lift themselves up against you for evil!
> Do I not hate those who hate you, O LORD?
>   And do I not loathe those who rise up against you?
> I hate them with perfect hatred;
>   I count them my enemies.
>
> (Ps. 139:19–22)

There is a perfect hatred that casts out even love, except as it is holy, that will not be reconciled with "the last enemy" (1 Cor. 15:26), for instance, but seeks its demise. Such hatred waits, silent if it must be silent, defiant, unyielding, engorged

157

with grief, yet ardent in hope. Something like it came over me in the dead of winter, late in the afternoon, five years ago. I was sipping port. I was remembering my deceased mother's losses: a sister who died at nine, a mother who died while my mother was a teenager, a father who fell to his death from a water tower right about the time my mother was married, another sister who died in her forties from a transfusion of tainted blood, a brother who died at forty-seven from a sudden heart attack. Then my father died at age sixty-three. My mother was not yet out of her fifties. While doing this remembering and sipping my port, incongruously, I was reading Helen Vendler's magisterial commentary on Shakespeare's sonnets.[1] However, I turned not to the Shakespearian but to the Petrarchan form of the sonnet when I wrote:

SONNET ON GRIEF
February 28, 1998

> I think I'd rather curse my God and die
> Than bear the empty silence grief imparts
> To those who cannot grieve, whose grieving starts
> No flow of thought, no feeling deep or high,
> No fretting for what might have been, no sigh,
> No discontent, no working of the arts
> Of grief, no poetry of rage, no darts
> Of perfect hate. So venture this: To try
> The silence with a silence dreadful, still,
> A still-life gesture, vacant, dumb and cold,
> Indifferent, vast and deep as silent night,
> More quiet, more reserved, more stark, more chill
> Than death. I'd grieve grief with a silence bold,
> A curse on empty night till God speaks light.

Grief as an instance of lamentation is universal, just as "the last enemy" is an enemy in waiting for us all. Yet grief is always personal too, almost private, your grief and mine, sometimes ours. But grief is not eternal, even if it is true, as some assert, that the Eternal knows our grief and shares it. Perhaps, with Auden, we can follow to "the bottom of the night"[2] because we have someone to follow who has not been held by the night, but who has gone through it, cradle to cross to glory, the Son to the Father in the Spirit. So the apostle can say: "For in hope we were saved. Now hope that is seen is not hope. For who hopes for what is seen? But if we hope for what we do not see, we wait for it with patience" (Rom. 8:24–25). That text—improbably and therefore, doubtless, providentially—came to mind on the occasion of my composition of the following poem at the time of death of my youngest brother-in-law, aged fifty-eight. In the poem I make use of a seldom used adjective, *prow*, meaning valiant or gallant or brave, from the Old French *prou*. Its noun form, prowess, meaning skill or strength, especially in battle, is more common.

CANCER VIGIL
A Sonnet in Memory of John Wesley Goetschius
d. January 2, 2001

There is no room for hosts of angels now
To wage their holy war on Satan's horde,
For now the cosmic course of death is toward
The finite body which does not allow
Infinity in burning form a prow,
Seraphic flight against the dreaded lord.
Here darkened, microscopic paths afford
Frail molecules of care the chance to plough
Through fevered cells a chastened hope of life
. Beyond the sting of death, and nothing more.
All grander measures are of no avail.
Heroic interventions prolong strife.
For cancers of this type there's no known cure.
Death wins, yet in the winning still shall fail.

I continued in personal grief and lamentation when my friend of thirty-six years and my colleague in the teaching of speech communication in ministry, G. Robert Jacks, died suddenly and unexpectedly June 5, 2002. He was, in his life and work, a lover of children and children's stories, of children's art and poetry, of children's prayers, the very things many children themselves believe they have grown out of when they become adult. Mistaking childlikeness for childishness, they come to loathe what they formerly loved. In that loathing they may fail to see what, for example, the prophet saw as the vanguard of the peaceable kingdom—"a little child shall lead them" (Isa. 11:6)—and what Jesus saw when he said, "Truly I tell you, whoever does not receive the kingdom of God as a little child will never enter it" (Mark 10:15). So grief may descend upon us human beings as judgment, the mercy of God giving back in anguish what was forsaken with alacrity.

WHEN I GREW UP
A Sonnet in Memory of G. Robert Jacks
d. June 5, 2002

When I grew up I lost the worlds of cloud
My summer daydreams conjured in the sky.
No time to waste, I up and let them die
And turned to face the world the facts allowed,
The world of purposes and plans that crowd
Our days with "have to do," for we must ply
Those trades that make the world go round and shy
Away from dream-filled hours. Yet though I vowed
To work and dream no more, lost worlds came back
When late spring clouds rained grief into my toil.

> Now all my purposes and plans were spent.
> The facts gave way to sums no math could track.
> My grown-up world was left to age and spoil,
> And wasted daydreams saw their heavens rent.

Lamentation and grief are not synonymous, but they are inseparable, as suffering is inseparable from life and love. The heart grieves because it can be broken. Is there a heart worth having that cannot be broken? The soul cries out for God, "for the living God" (Ps. 42:2), because God, who once seemed so near, now seems long ago and far away:

> These things I remember
>   as I pour out my soul:
> how I went with the throng,
>   and led them in procession to the house of God,
> with glad shouts and songs of thanksgiving,
>   a multitude keeping festival.
>   (Ps. 42:4)

Further, there is no way for people bereft of the divine presence to inch their way toward it until at last they can lay hold of it. Bound in time, we cannot grasp eternity, nor by adding one to one do we stand any chance of measuring the infinite. The movement must be all the other way, eternity encompassing time, infinity taking the measure of the finite, "the accounting beyond the account";[3] then this above all: "God of God, Light of Light, Very God of Very God" lifting the burden of human God-bereftness as a weight of glory. Lamentation and grief imply the gospel. In fact they are signs of its truth taking hold of a life under duress. The cry of lamentation is the sound of a human heart breaking, breaking for want of God, and for love of God, and for love of what God loves.

Lamentation, then, is never merely a soul's self-centering. Instead, it is a soul's getting caught up in grief over what grieves God. The scope of lamentation is cosmic:

> For the creation waits with eager longing for the revealing of the children of God; for the creation was subjected to futility, not of its own will but by the will of the one who subjected it, in hope that the creation itself will be set free from its bondage to decay and will obtain the freedom of the glory of the children of God. (Rom. 8:19–21)

Nature groans in travail, awaiting the "revealing of the children of God" because its own rescue from futility is bound up in the rescue of human life from God-bereftness. There is no rescue of human life apart from the earth from which human life was made. There is only the rescue of human life with the earth, with all of creation, the rescue of inhabitants, that is to say, with—and not without—their habitation. Therefore what is cause for lament in human life may be cause for lament in the life of the world of nature that is humanity's home. The gospel implicit in lamentation, which gospel is our only sure hope in "the bottom of the night," thus gives us, with all else, "tongues in trees, books in the running brooks," and "sermons in stone."[4] Instance: We may find disclosed in the legend of the dogwood—namely that the cross of Christ was hewn of dogwood—and in an actual dogwood tree's demise something of our own very human predicament and what makes it truly precarious, that is, full of prayers. Here the hope of self-possessed immortality—"what vanity believes"—is contradicted. What hope is left is resurrection hope, the hope of the Eternal's victory over the temporal, with the presence of God vouchsafed through what appears to be the absence and silence of God, as faltering memory is quickened to anamnesis. I composed this sonnet June 22, 1999. It is intended as a sonnet for Good Friday.

THE DOGWOOD STAYS

> The dead dogwood shone in the steady sun,
> In ebony and red it shone, no leaves,
> No blossoms hinting life within. What grieves
> The human heart: An inner life undone,
> A soul's dark night grown long from having won
> Its final round with reasoned hope—fine sieves
> To strain from thought what vanity believes—
> The soulless bark sustains. But lest we shun
> With careless disregard a holy sign,
> That other tree of death that shines in rays
> Eternal as the sun, its ebony
> Stained red with life's blood strained through veins divine
> And so lose hope entire, the dogwood stays
> Encroaching dark with brightened memory.

Lamentation, I have been trying to show, is not faith eclipsed by grief, doubt, confusion, and despair. Lamentation is faith expressed as hope in God in the depths of despair, in the midst of acknowledged doubt, where confusion—including not least of all confusion about God—abounds but does not overwhelm, and where despair, precisely through the crying out to God of the God-bereft soul, is kept at bay. Lamentation is agonistic, not pusillanimous. It is a windhover, that is, a kestrel or sparrow hawk, hovering head-on into the gale. In lamentation the faithful soul rages "against the dying of the light"[5] in expectation of being heard by that Power "Which makes the darkness and the light, and dwells not in the light alone."[6]

Lamentation arises simultaneously from the human predicament before God and from God's self-disclosure, which is always veiled, always signaled by something other than itself. Thus we may find joy hidden in the heart of sorrow, disappointment, and grief, as our funeral liturgies remind us. Humanity, after all, can be blinded by excess of light, and unmediated glory would not thrill, but devastate us.

So too unguarded truth, especially about oneself, would doubtless seem unbearable. Lovers would never treat their beloved so ruthlessly as to speak to them unguarded truth. The light shines in the darkness, but does not obliterate the darkness or those who are in the darkness. The Word becomes flesh and lives among us "full of grace and truth" (John 1:14), the purest, most loving light in the midst of the darkness. But the darkness does not overcome it (John 1:5). It is all quite unimaginable. Who could have—would have—dreamed it up? Yet it is given to human imagination precisely as that which is beyond imagination that we may speak of it, and speak to it in prayer, including especially prayers of lamentation. It is not for nothing that Christ entered the deepest darkness and took upon his lips the faithful lament of the God-bereft soul: "My God, my God, why have you forsaken me?" (Ps. 22:1; Matt. 27:46; Mark 15:34). It is for us that he did so, making our lamentation—all lamentation—and the cause of lamentation his own. The scene was as of a macabre dance at the Place of the Skull, that is, Golgotha.

All this came home to me in a terrible instant with the terrorist bombing of Pan American Flight 103 that crashed December 21, 1988, in Lockerbie, Scotland. Among those killed—all on board were killed—was a young woman of college age named Gretchen Dater. In the summers of her early childhood she had been a playmate of my middle daughter, Paula Sue. Gretchen's parents grew up with my wife, Paula. The Daters, in fact, were friends of the Goetschius family across many generations. The atrocity at Lockerbie played havoc with traditional Christmastide sentiments. Yet, at a deeper level than sentiments can run, it seemed not to compromise the truth of the gospel but to afford opportunity to come to terms with that truth. Light shone through the darkness of the season, so much so that the darkness, while deep, was not all and was not godless. The sonnet that follows was composed December 26, 1988, and revised August 31, 1998. The intent of the revisions was to strengthen the note of lamentation.

SONNET IN REMEMBRANCE
OF PAN AMERICAN FLIGHT 103

Flight 103 went off the radar screen,
A silent signal of swift, certain doom
For those aboard her and for others, gloom
To overwhelm the season calm, serene
In which she fell. The happy Christmas green,
The festive, red poinsettias in full bloom,
The fire-warmed cheer that filled the living room
All failed. Yet, from out this grief-stricken scene,
The scattered bones of innocents, the cries
Of mourning, rage draws voice, and claims its chance
To hear the Christmas requiem, fleshed Word
Divine now crashed to earth with tears, and sighs
Too deep for words, that mournful prayers might dance
Before their God, and there, by grace, be heard.

If lamentation, as I have attempted to show, is not faithless, but faithful speech, it also must be acknowledged that lamentation is not nice, polite, fastidious, scrupulous. Persons engaged in lamentation are not seeking general approval of their state of mind. Much less are they seeking to render or receive moral adjuration. For example, it would take something approaching temerity for somebody above the storm of violence in Iraq—or, in days just past, in Liberia, the Sudan, or Indonesia, or endlessly, it would appear, in Israel or Palestine—to speak in condemnation of the mother who cries out to God in wrath against those responsible for the death of her children. So also the not so nice, perhaps even virulent, speech of the biblical psalmists of old should not be condemned as if we ourselves could not possibly imagine ourselves complaining to God so boldly. Already we have heard the bitter words of Psalm 139:

> Do I not hate those who hate you, O LORD?
>   And do I not loathe those who rise up against you?
> I hate them with perfect hatred;
>   I count them my enemies.
>
> (Ps. 139:21–22)

This lament is from the mouth of someone anxious for his life. He is seeking from God deliverance from the "bloodthirsty" (v. 19), his would-be murderers, who already, in his hearing, have spoken "maliciously" (v. 20) even about God. Is the psalmist to be pilloried for being at once enraged and full of terror? Or is he to be pitied for the gravity of his circumstance? Is it the duty of the church to condemn his thought, or, rather, to hear and give voice to his cry, and, in doing that, to claim some measure of solidarity with those endangered perhaps by the weapons deployed abroad to protect our national and commercial interests and our lives? Could it be that hearing and speaking the biblical laments—and not editing them so as to render them less disturbing—has something to do with loving one's enemies and not hating them, however much the language of hatred may appear in the biblical laments themselves?

The matter is made more urgent yet in Psalm 137:

> Remember, O LORD, against the Edomites
>   the day of Jerusalem's fall,
> how they said, "Tear it down! Tear it down!
>   Down to its foundations!"
> O daughter Babylon, you devastator!
>   Happy shall they be who pay you back
>   what you have done to us!
> Happy shall they be who take your little ones
>   and dash them against the rock!
>
> (Ps. 137:7–9)

The Edomites, Israel's neighbors and ancestral relatives, joined league with Babylon to destroy Jerusalem, kill its children, and send remnants of its population off to exile. Endlessly I have heard complaints about the savagery of this lament, but seldom have I heard any outcry against the savagery—not of words, but of deeds—of Edom and Babylon. Strange what wanting too much to be nice can bring about: solidarity with the tyrant and the oppressor, and condemnation of the tyrannized and the oppressed. Better, I should think, to have it the other way around: to bear with ancient Israel—and with others in our own times—in their distress, tears and fury. Better to hear and voice the complaint of the abused, neglected, and angry than to become deaf to their cries and mute concerning their plight. Better also to brave the storm in our own inner being in the face of atrocities committed against us than to attempt to deceive God about how we actually feel. There may be those who would say: "Oh! I could never think or say such a thing! Too horrible!" But others—Paul the apostle for one—apparently regard themselves as capable not only of feeling, thinking, and saying the horrible, but of actually doing it (Rom. 7:15). Honest lamentation then, however bitter, may flow from a heart set right with God through frank acknowledgment and confession of its condition.

When the September 11, 2001, suicide bombing of the World Trade Center towers in New York City occurred—in conjunction with additional terrorist events, similar in nature if not in magnitude—it was not difficult to imagine mothers crying out to God in anger over the loss of their children, and their children's children, and the children of friends, neighbors, and relatives. It was my own mother who taught me to pray, at bedtime, every night, in the near dark that filled my early childhood dreams with eerie phantoms. For months the lines "Last night my mother came to me in dreams / To tuck me in and help me say my prayers" played in my mind, the beginning of a tribute to my mother's diligence in prayer. But I had no idea where to go with the lines, what to make of them. Then came the events of 9/11, as we have come to call it, and the following sonnet, through hours of labor, began to emerge. *Bassamat al-farah*, which may be translated "the smile of joy," refers to the smile known to appear on the lips of suicide bombers as they crash into their targets. The smile indicates the bombers' belief that their death is a martyr's death and a guarantee of their entrance into paradise. *Bassamat al-farah* was completed October 15, 2001, and was published in *Theology Today* in January of 2002.[7]

BASSAMAT AL-FARAH
(The Smile of Joy)

Last night my mother came to me in dreams
To tuck me in and help me say my prayers,
As long ago she used to climb the stairs
To where I'd lie awake, in dread of schemes
Drawn up by attic demons who, with screams
Of terror, hauled young children to their lairs
And turned them into demons with no cares—
No souls for caring. Mother's prayers cast beams

Of searing light against the nightmare dark
And still they do, as I attempt to pray
My rage at careless demons in the sky,
Bassamat al-farah etched cold and stark
Upon their lips, who crash in flame and flay
Grown children's souls for whom fierce mothers cry.

Lamentation is going on all about us always. Truth to tell, however, for the most part we are unaware of it, do not hear it, and only now and then give voice to it, either individually or corporately as a church at worship. It is not that we are indifferent and could care less. It is, instead, that we find ourselves, as it were, insulated from the lamentation ongoing in the world about us. Perhaps this is actually best for us. Perhaps it is best for others as well, particularly those for whom we are in a measure responsible. It would not be to the good for us to become sated with grief, immobilized by it, and unable to do what we are called upon to do in the daily round. We must live and work, be and do, not just to "get ahead," but to meet our obligations. We are in prayer always, for the Spirit intercedes for us always "with sighs too deep for words" (Rom. 8:26). But we are not always praying. "Pray without ceasing" (1 Thess. 5:17) is not a command to give up the daily round. It is, instead, a command to take up the daily round prayerfully and with thanksgiving. There is a time to offer lamentation. On the other hand, there also is a time—and it is most of the time—to measure up to our duties, however much the outcries of the God-bereft may be claimant. According to Jesus, God's commandments rightly are summarized thus:

> You shall love the Lord your God with all your heart, and with all your soul, and with all your strength, and with all your mind; and your neighbor as yourself. (Luke 10:27; cf. Deut. 6:5)

In other words, love is something we do, and lamentation is part of the love we do; but it is not the whole of it.

Yet there are those times when we might half wish the whole world could stop and take note of what troubles us—as, for example, when we mourn, in advance of death, the failing too soon of a life well lived, and when we marvel at an imminent death bravely faced, not without fear, but in spite of fear. The passing crowd will not, cannot grant our half wish. No one's lamentation is that claimant. All the same, our frustration with this incontrovertible fact of human existence itself can be offered as lament; and the world of nature, the habitat for our humanity, can be enlisted to aid us in our lamentation.

This is what is attempted in the poem that follows. It is not a sonnet. It is rather an impressionistic piece of verse, a succession of images asserting nothing directly, but leaving much to be inferred. "White noise" refers to that frequency and intensity of sound that is at once both inaudible and deafening. The Jericho Turnpike, besides having by its very name a certain resonance with Jesus' parable (Luke 10:30–37), is a strip of highway on Long Island running east to west and west to east. I have never traveled it, but have heard of it and imagined myself driving it.

HEADING WEST ON THE JERICHO TURNPIKE
January 25, 2003, 5:05 p.m.
For Dana Charry

Down the slope
    of a winter wood
        wind-cleared thicket
            dead leaves scattered

The sun roiled
    at the horizon
        a howling brilliance
            soon to flame out

White noise
    to the deaf ear
        of turnpike traffic
            eager for Jericho.

If I could "utter all myself into the air," said Elizabeth Barrett Browning, "my flesh would perish there, / Before that dread apocalypse of soul."[8] So, we may suppose, if we could hear all lamentation and enter it in solidarity with those who must wait in the night till God speaks light, our flesh too would perish. The human condition is such that it cannot bear all grief, all sorrow, all rage, all fear of death and of death-dealing, all the disquiet of the human intellect concerning God and the nature and destiny of the human spirit, all dread of principalities and powers beyond human ken. We are daunted. We in fact must turn from such a terrible prospect, or die. The limit of lamentation, its *telos*, thus is not set among us women and men. Instead, it is set with God himself who alone, in the perfection of the love that he is as Father, Son, and Holy Spirit, "bears all things, believes all things, hopes all things, endures all things" (1 Cor. 13:7). All things we bear, believe, hope, and endure, we bear, believe, hope, and endure according to God's capacity, not our own. In God the laments to which we cannot attend are heard. For those laments, he is both ear and answer. And when human speech fails altogether—and even the music of the spheres ceases—the Word that was in the beginning with God and was God (John 1:1) resounds with the meeting of human flesh, human habitation, and Holy Spirit. Our hope in lamentation—as in all prayer, as in all things—is there in that Word who is for us light in the darkness. So Elizabeth Barrett Browning, in her sonnet "Substitution" (1844), can turn toward that Word and pray and offer lamentation, painfully, faithfully, hopefully for us all.

SUBSTITUTION

When some beloved voice that was to you
Both sound and sweetness, faileth suddenly,
And silence, against which you dare not cry,
Aches round you like a strong disease and new—
What hope? what help? what music will undo
That silence to your sense? Not friendship's sigh,
Not reason's subtle count; not melody
Of viols, nor of pipes that Faunus blew;
Not songs of poets, nor of nightingales
Whose hearts leap upward through the cypress-trees
To the clear moon; nor yet the spheric laws
Self-chanted, nor the angels' sweet 'All hails,'
Met in the smile of God: nay, none of these.
Speak THOU, availing Christ!—and fill this pause.[9]

NOTES

1. Helen Vendler, *The Art of Shakespeare's Sonnets* (Cambridge, MA: Harvard University Press, 1997).
2. W. H. Auden, "In Memory of W. B. Yeats (d. Jan. 1939)" III, in *Collected Poems*, ed. Edward Mendelson (New York: Random House, 1976), 198.
3. A. R. Ammons, "Corson's Inlet," in *Collected Poems: 1951–1971* (New York: W. W. Norton & Co., 1972), 148.
4. William Shakespeare, *As You Like It*, 2.1.16–17, in *Shakespeare: The Complete Works*, ed. G. B. Harrison (New York: Harcourt, Brace & Co., 1952), 784.
5. Dylan Thomas, "Do Not Go Gentle into That Good Night," in *The Collected Poems of Dylan Thomas* (New York: New Directions Publishers, 1957), 128.
6. Alfred, Lord Tennyson, "In Memoriam," XCVI, in *The Poetical Works of Alfred, Lord Tennyson* (New York: Thomas Y. Crowell & Co., 1900), 511.
7. *Theology Today*, vol. 58, no. 4 (January 2002): 567.
8. Elizabeth Barrett Browning, "The Soul's Expression," in *The Complete Poetical Works of Elizabeth Barrett Browning*, ed. Horace E. Scudder (Boston: Houghton Mifflin & Co., 1900), 98.
9. Browning, 99.